# THE YOUNG HITLER
# I KNEW

# THE YOUNG HITLER
# I KNEW

## The Memoirs of Hitler's
## Childhood Friend

### August Kubizek

*Introduction by*
Ian Kershaw

*Translated by*
Geoffrey Brooks

FRONTLINE BOOKS

A Greenhill Book

## A Greenhill Book

This edition published in 2011 by Frontline Books,
an imprint of Pen & Sword Books Limited,
47 Church Street, Barnsley, S. Yorkshire, S70 2AS
www.frontline-books.com

and

Published and distributed in the United States of America and Canada
by Arcade Publishing, 307 West 36th Street, 11th Floor, New York, NY 10018

Arcade Publishing books may be purchased in bulk at special discounts for sales
promotion, corporate gifts, fund-raising, or educational purposes. Special editions can also be
created to specifications. For details, contact the Special Sales Department, Arcade Publishing,
307 West 36th Street, 11th Floor, New York, NY 10018 or info@skyhorsepublishing.com.

Arcade Publishing® is a registered trademark of Skyhorse Publishing, Inc. ®,
a Delaware corporation. Visit our website at www.arcadepub.com.

Frontline edition ISBN 978-1-84832-607-1
Arcade edition ISBN 978-1-61145-058-3

PUBLISHING HISTORY
First published in 1953 by Leopold Stocker Verlag as *Adolf Hitler Mein Jugendfreund*.
An abridged English language version entitled *Young Hitler* was published in 1954 by Allan
Wingate Publishers Ltd. Greenhill Books released a hardback edition with a new introduction by
Ian Kershaw in 2006.

A CIP data record for this title is available from the British Library.

Library of Congress Cataloging-in-Publication Data
Kubizek, August.

[Adolf Hitler, mein Jugendfreund. English]

The young Hitler I knew : the definitive inside look at the artist who became a monster / by
August Kubizek ; introduction by Ian Kershaw.
p. cm.
Includes index.
ISBN 978-1-61145-058-3 (pbk. : alk. paper)
1. Hitler, Adolf, 1889-1945--Childhood and youth. 2. Hitler, Adolf, 1889-1945--Friends and
associates. 3. Kubizek, August. 4. Friendship--Case studies. 5. Art students--Austria--
Biography. 6. Heads of state--Germany--Biography. I. Title.

DD247.H5K813 2011
943.086092--dc22
[B]

2011004538

Printed in Great Britain by MPG Books Limited

# Contents

# Illustrations

# Introduction

For a vital phase during the early years of his life, his late teenage years in Linz and Vienna, when we otherwise have tantalisingly little to go on, Hitler had a personal – and exclusive – friend, who later composed a striking account of the four years of their close companionship. This friend was August Kubizek. His account is unique in that it stands alone in offering insights into Hitler's character and mentality for the four years between 1904 and 1908. It is unique, too, in that it is the only description from any period of Hitler's life provided by an undoubted personal friend – even if that friendship was both relatively brief and almost certainly one-sided.* For, like everyone else who came into contact with Hitler, Kubizek would soon learn that friends, like others, would be dropped as soon as they had served their purpose.

For every study of Hitler's early years, including the first parts of my own biography, Kubizek's story has proved an indispensable source. His recollections of his time together with Hitler, first published in 1953, are now in their sixth edition. An English translation, with an introduction by H. R. Trevor-Roper, later Lord Dacre, was published in 1954 and later reprinted, and has had to serve for those without access to the German original until the present. Yet this earlier English-language version was neither a complete nor an altogether satisfactory translation of Kubizek's German text. Numerous passages, in fact some entire chapters, were omitted. This new translation remedies these deficiencies and omissions. For the first time, it makes the entire text of Kubizek's recollections of his friendship with Hitler available to an English readership. This is greatly to be welcomed.

August Kubizek was born in Linz in 1888. After leaving school he served

---

* Kubizek later claimed that he had 'had only one friend in his life: Adolf'. – Letter to Franz Jetzinger, 24 June 1949, Oberösterreichisches Landesarchiv, Linz, NL Jetzinger, 64/19.

as an apprentice in his father's small upholstery workshop. But he was musically talented, and this offered him an exit-route from the upholstery trade. While the Academy of Fine Arts in Vienna was rejecting his friend Hitler, Kubizek was gaining entry to the Vienna Conservatoire to study music. He subsequently obtained a position as second conductor in the municipal theatre at Marburg on the Drau, and was just married when war broke out in 1914. He served in the Austrian Army for the duration of the war, suffering a serious lung infection in 1915 from which he never fully recovered. After the war he became town clerk of Eferding, near Linz, where his duties included organising the small community's musical events. And there he remained, a quiet, retiring family man, helping to bring up his three sons, and conscientiously involved in the local cultural life.

In the meantime, his erstwhile friend had become famous. Kubizek sent a note of congratulation when Hitler became Reich Chancellor in January 1933, and later received a personal reply. Hitler even suggested that Kubizek might pay him a visit one day. Nothing came of this for five years. But shortly after the *Anschluss*, Kubizek made his way to Hitler's hotel in Linz, and was allowed in to see his former friend for the first time since their ways had parted in 1908. Hitler greeted him warmly – though now used the formal 'Sie' mode of address not the more intimate 'Du' (which he had still used in his note to Kubizek five years earlier). Invitations followed to the Bayreuth Festival in 1939 and again in 1940, when, with Hitler at the height of his power, he and Kubizek met for the last time.

Kubizek had by then gained recognition among leading Nazis as a 'friend of the Führer' as a young man, and was known to have memorabilia from that time. He had already in 1938 been approached and agreed to write his recollections for the Party archive. His insights were said to be 'staggering', revealing 'the inconceivable greatness of the Führer in his youth'.* By 1942, after Kubizek had joined the Nazi Party and become a local functionary (mainly in charge of propaganda and cultural matters in Eferding), he had received a direct commission from the Party leadership to write about his early friendship with the 'Führer'. Kubizek had certainly made a start by 1943, and was given a better-paid position by the Party to help him to complete his task. But he made slow progress. When the Third Reich fell, he was interned for sixteen months by the Americans. But he had hidden his draft 'memoirs' and memorabilia in a cavity of a wall in his house

---

* Institut für Zeitgeschichte, Munich, MA-731, NSDAP-Hauptarchiv, 'Notizen für Kartei: Bericht über meinen Besuch bei Herrn Kutbitschek [*sic*] in Eferding'.

in Eferding. These became the basis of the book, *Adolf Hitler – Mein Jugendfreund*, published in 1953, and an immediate sensation. Kubizek died three years later, now widely known as a first-hand witness to Hitler's early, formative years.

But how valuable is Kubizek's book as a source for Hitler's life in Linz and Vienna? The core of the book, we should recall, began life as a manuscript commissioned by the Nazi Party. A copy of the second part of this original text survives today.* The fifty typescript pages, dealing with the Vienna period, are far shorter than the corresponding sections of the book. A great deal, therefore, has been added to the original account – itself composed over thirty years after the events it describes.† Glowing adulation of Hitler is abundantly evident in the typescript, whereas the book is inevitably more guarded, even though an unmistakable current of admiration remains. And the style of the original is prosaic, compared with the far more fluent, even literary style of the book. Episodes recounted briefly and without literary graces in the original text are far more extensively and elegantly described in the published work.‡ Kubizek admitted that writing the original manuscript had not come easily to him. 'Writing for me is a cross to bear. It doesn't suit me', he conceded in 1949.§ There must, therefore, be some suspicion that the embellished 'memoirs' which appear in the book are the result of help from a 'ghost-writer'. In fact, Kubizek acknowledged in June 1949 that his text required a complete reworking. Producing a more 'effective' version meant that the completion of his work 'belonged in the hands of a writer (*Dichter*)', he wrote. He even contemplated publication as a stage play.¶ The Austrian publishing house denied that it had provided any assistance. But either Kubizek suddenly discovered the art of writing, or he had help from a person or persons unknown.

Kubizek's recollections need to be read critically and treated with great care for other reasons. The young Hitler, for example, is frequently and

* In the Oberösterreichisches Landesarchiv, NL Jetzinger 63.
† At the end of his typescript, Kubizek admits that much else had happened but with the passage of time now escaped his memory. NL Jetzinger 63, p. 48.
‡ In his letters, he recalled incidents and episodes, prompted by Jetzinger's questions, that did not figure in his typescript. He also indicated that he was in the process of rewriting some passages after discussion with Jetzinger since he recognised that they were incorrect as drafted. NL Jetzinger, 64/18, 19 June 1949.
§ NL Jetzinger, 64/18, letter to Jetzinger, 19 June 1949.
¶ NL Jetzinger, 64/14, letter to Jetzinger, 3 June 1949; 64/18, 19 June 1949.

extensively cited verbatim in Kubizek's published text (though seldom in the original manuscript). Kubizek is far from alone among those who later wrote of their experiences of Hitler in putting words directly into his mouth years after the events described. But it is self-evidently impossible that he could have remembered exactly what Hitler said over four decades later. The direct quotations have, therefore, to be seen as a literary device of Kubizek (or his ghost-writer) rather than precise expressions of the young Hitler. This does not in itself discredit their veracity as statements of Hitler's views. But, obviously, they ought not to be taken at face value as quotations.

Beyond this, some of Kubizek's recollections have more than an air of fabrication about them. His story of Hitler denouncing to the police a kaftan-clad Jew was probably an embellishment of a well-known episode in *Mein Kampf* (on which Kubizek drew quite extensively in his book). The description of a visit together with his friend to a synagogue sounds equally dubious. The claim that Hitler joined the Anti-Semitic League in 1908, and registered Kubizek for membership at the same time, is plainly wrong. No such organisation existed in Austria at the time. Kubizek's passages on Hitler's anti-semitism, in fact, deserve generally to be treated with scepticism. They are clearly designed to distance himself from his former friend's radical views (which he, almost certainly wrongly and in contrast to Hitler himself, dated back to the influence of home and school in Linz), though his own anti-semitism had not been concealed in the manuscript version.

Another story described by Kubizek, and repeated in countless books on Hitler, also seems elaborated to the point of near fantasy. This is the lengthy episode of the nocturnal climb up the Freinberg, a mountain just outside Linz, following a visit to a performance of Wagner's *Rienzi*, an early work about a Roman tribune of the people who was eventually cast down by his one-time followers. Kubizek has Hitler, in near ecstasy, elucidating the meaning of what they had seen in almost mystical terms. After the war Kubizek remained insistent that the story was true.* The evening evidently left its mark on him, and he reminded Hitler of it when they met at Bayreuth in 1939. Kubizek concludes his chapter on the 'vision' by telling how Hitler recounted the episode to his hostess, Winifred Wagner, ending: 'in that hour it began'. But this was Hitler showing off his 'prophetic qualities' to an important admirer, Frau Wagner. Whatever happened on the

---

* NL Jetzinger 64/18, letter to Jetzinger, 19 June 1949; 64/20, 28 June 1949.

Freinberg that night that so impressed the impressionable Kubizek, nothing 'began' then.

A further episode, that of Stefanie, a young woman in Linz who, Kubizek claims, was Hitler's first love, has a distinctly improbable ring to it. There can be little doubt that Kubizek greatly embellishes what was at most a passing juvenile infatuation. But the story has at least one point of interest. Franz Jetzinger, a librarian in Linz who himself was working on Hitler's early life, was able to track Stefanie down. She did exist (though she knew nothing of Hitler's supposed passion for her at the time). In his letters to Jetzinger, Kubizek refers to her surname before she married – Isak.* It was plainly Jewish-sounding. She was, in fact, not Jewish – though neither Hitler nor Kubizek could have known that. The irony that Hitler's one and only boyhood 'flame' might have been Jewish at least suggests that Kubizek's emphasis upon his friend's pronounced anti-semitism already in Linz is incorrect.

Despite these, and other, undoubted weaknesses, limitations, and distortions – even outright inventions – which underline the need for great caution in using Kubizek, his account of his experiences with Hitler cannot be dismissed – as it was by the more scholarly, but jaundiced, early historian of Hitler's youth, Franz Jetzinger – as a mere 'work of fable'. Jetzinger was originally on good terms with Kubizek (who showed him his typescript and memorabilia of his time with Hitler). But he became an implacable critic once Kubizek's book appeared. His own book on Hitler's youth, which appeared three years later, is replete with attacks on Kubizek.† Jetzinger was certainly able to expose Kubizek's memory as fallible. Kubizek admitted that his original typescript contained errors, which he put down to the constant interruptions through Party work at the time. He insisted, however, that he was telling the truth, and not making things up.‡

Jetzinger's scholarship is, in fact, not invariably superior to Kubizek's vivid pen-picture of the young Hitler, and contains some weaknesses of its own, both factual and interpretative. Kubizek's description of a distraught Hitler at his mother's deathbed in December 1907 was, for instance, rejected by Jetzinger, who, largely on the basis of the oral testimony of an

---

* He calls her 'Isaak' (NL Jetzinger 64/20, letter to Jetzinger, 20 June 1949). Her family name (in its correct spelling) only came to light, however, in Anton Joachimsthaler, *Hitlers Liste. Ein Dokument persönlicher Beziehungen*, Munich, 2003, pp. 46–52.
† Franz Jetzinger, *Hitlers Jugend. Phantasien, Lügen und die Wahrheit*, Vienna, 1956.
‡ NL Jetzinger 64/18, letter to Jetzinger, 19 June 1949.

old lady he himself described as 'senile', preferred the image of a heartless son turning up only once his mother was dead. Jetzinger's interpretation was for long preferred by most historians. But Kubizek's version, though not without factual errors, nevertheless has the backing of two crucial witnesses: Hitler's sister, Paula, and his mother's Jewish physician, Dr Eduard Bloch. On this important point, Kubizek's account is preferable to Jetzinger's interpretation. Kubizek is here an important source.

In another instance, as the detailed research of the Austrian historian Brigitte Hamann has shown, Kubizek proves a reliable source despite Jetzinger's sustained attempt to discredit him.* This is the question of his financial standing during his time in Vienna. Where Kubizek portrays Hitler as hard-up, Jetzinger claims that inherited money left him well-off. Certainly Hitler was not poverty-stricken until his money ran out, after contact with Kubizek had been broken off. But the picture of a modest, even downright frugal lifestyle painted by Kubizek was accurate, whereas Jetzinger's calculations had exaggerated the funds allegedly at Hitler's disposal (again something taken up in a number of secondary works). Once more, Kubizek proves an important source and corrective.

Above all, for all its manifold flaws, Kubizek's book rings true in the portrait of Hitler's personality and mentality. In particular, the lengthy parts of the book which tell of Hitler's views on history, art, architecture, and music (where Kubizek was especially at home) illustrate facets of his character which become only too familiar in later years. The docile, impressionable, compliant Kubizek, a few months older than his friend but with a pronounced inferiority complex, was a perfect receptacle for the domineering, opinionated, know-all young Hitler. He listened. Hitler talked – and talked, and talked. The dogmatic opinions – and outright prejudices – on art and music are similar to those we come across in the later Hitler. The precise words Hitler used can only be Kubizek's invention but the sentiments are surely genuine. And since it is certain that Hitler and Kubizek did spend a great deal of time in each other's company for close to four years, in Linz then in Vienna, and since they were both passionately interested in music and art, it can be presumed that these topics figured prominently in their conversations and made a lasting impact (even if not a precise one) on Kubizek's memory.

Like so many 'memoirs' and recollections of those who knew Hitler at

* Brigitte Hamann, *Hitler's Vienna. A Dictator's Apprenticeship*, Oxford & New York, 1999, pp. 58–9.

first hand, Kubizek's account is faulty and inaccurate in many respects. Medieval historians are used to working with flawed and inaccurate sources which can nevertheless provide important insights. Kubizek's book has to be used in a similar way – recognising its deficiencies, but acknowledging the intrinsic value of the portrait of the young Hitler which it provides.

*Ian Kershaw*

# THE YOUNG
# HITLER I KNEW

# Original Publisher's Foreword

In 1951 our attention was drawn to a civil servant of sixty-two years of age employed by the municipal council at Eferding in Upper Austria. We were told that August Kubizek had been a musical conductor and spent four years of his youth as a soul-mate of Adolf Hitler.

We realised that Kubizek's story was of the greatest importance for the historical record of the German dictator, because Kubizek had been Hitler's only friend in his teens and must have influenced Hitler's development to a large degree. The human personality begins to take shape at that stage and it is there that the historian must begin his research if he proposes to lay the groundwork for a biography of Hitler as politician and statesman. For these reasons we asked August Kubizek it he would write his recollections of those years as well as memory allowed. We knew that Kubizek could be relied upon. He was an idealist who, after re-establishing contact with Hitler in 1938, politely but firmly turned down the German leader's every suggestion that he leave the Austrian civil service and accept a leading position in Reich music. When Hitler's star had begun to wane in 1942, however, Kubizek, although inwardly opposed to National Socialism, joined the NSDAP in an act of solidarity towards the friend of his youth.

It was with considerable reflection and self-examination that Kubizek set about his task as author. His book was published for the first time in 1953 and caused great excitement. It was translated into English, French and Spanish, while extracts appeared in the world's press and were much referred to subsequently by historians.

By the time of his death on 23 October 1956, Kubizek's account had received international recognition. The allegation made in many publications that 'guidelines' for a memoir of this kind had been agreed as early as 1938 between Kubizek and 'the main NSDAP archive' is false. The Leopold Stocker publishing house knows of no such agreement, and

Kubizek's widow wrote to assure us that her husband had never visited the NSDAP archive at Munich.

There is, in any case, nothing to suggest that he had drafted his memoirs pre-war. From our knowledge of him, moreover, we believe that Kubizek was not the kind of author who was suited to writing material 'within guidelines', and on page 294 of the German language first edition he emphasised that his memoir had been 'neither influenced nor commissioned' by anybody.

*Leopold Stocker Verlag*
Graz,
June 1966

# Author's Introduction

## My Decision and Justification

My decision to commit to paper my reminiscences of the Adolf Hitler I knew in our late childhood did not come easy, for the danger of being misunderstood is great. But the sixteen months I spent in US detention as a 57-year-old ruined my health, and so I must employ usefully whatever time is left to me.

Between 1904 and 1908 I was the single and exclusive friend of Adolf Hitler, first in Linz and then in Vienna, where we shared a room together. Of these formative years of Hitler, in which his personality began to take shape, little is known, and much of what is known is incorrect. In *Mein Kampf* it suited his purposes to gloss over the period with a few fleeting references, and so it may be that my own observations may serve to fortify the image which the passage of time leaves us of Adolf Hitler, from whatever standpoint one happens to look at it.

I have been at pains neither to add anything untrue, nor leave out any-thing for political reasons: I want to be able to say: this was exactly how it happened. It would have been wrong, for example, to attribute to Hitler thoughts and ideas which were typically his of the later period, and I have taken great care to avoid this pitfall and set out my narrative as if this same Adolf Hitler, with whom I shared such a close friendship, were somebody with whom I had lost contact for ever after 1908, or who had fallen in the Great War.

I am mindful of the difficulty in recalling accurately ideas and events which occurred more than forty years ago, but my friendship with Adolf Hitler bore from the outset the stamp of the unusual, and details of the relationship are more firmly impregnated on the memory than would normally be the case. Furthermore I was indebted to Adolf Hitler for his having convinced my father that, by virtue of the special musical talents which nature had bestowed upon me, I belonged in the Vienna Conservatoire rather than a furniture workshop. This decisive change in my life, engineered by Adolf Hitler against the determined resistance of my family, gave our friendship greater substance in my eyes. Additionally, thank God, I have an excellent memory linked to my fine acoustic sense. In writing my book, I have been able to call upon letters, postcards and sketches I received from my friend, and my own brief notes, which I set down some considerable time ago.

*August Kubizek*
Eferding,
August 1953

# Chapter 1

# First Meeting

I was born in Linz on 3 August 1888. Before his marriage my father had been an upholsterer's assistant to a furniture manufacturer in Linz. He used to have his midday meal in a little café and it was there that he met my mother, who was working as a waitress. They fell in love, and were married in July 1887.

At first the young couple lived in the house of my mother's parents. My father's wages were low, the work was hard, and my mother had to give up her job when she was expecting me. Thus I was born in rather miserable circumstances. One year later my sister Maria was born, but died at a tender age. The following year, Therese appeared; she died at the age of four. My third sister, Karoline, fell desperately ill, lingered on for some years, and died when she was eight. My mother's grief was boundless. Throughout her life she suffered from the fear of losing me too; for I was the only one left to her of her four children. Consequently all my mother's love was concentrated upon me.

There was a noteworthy parallel between the destinies of the Kubizek and Hitler households, and the two mothers shared much suffering in common. Hitler's mother had lost three children, Gustav, Ida and Otto. Adolf was an only child for a considerable time. When Hitler was five, brother Edmund came along, but died in his sixth year. The only other survivor was sister Paula, born in 1896. Although Adolf and I rarely mentioned our deceased brothers and sisters, nevertheless we felt like the survivors of an endangered lineage which brought with it a special responsibility.

Without realising it, Adolf referred to me occasionally as 'Gustav' instead of August – even a letter he sent me has this forename on the envelope. It had been the name of his first brother who died. Possibly it was a sort of mix-up with the diminutive 'Gustl' for August, or perhaps he wanted to please his mother by bestowing the name on a person such as myself who was received into the Hitler family like a son.

Meanwhile my father had set up on his own and had opened an upholsterer's business at No. 9 Klammstrasse. The old Baernreitherhaus, heavy and ungainly, which still stands there unaltered, became the home of my childhood and youth. The narrow, sombre Klammstrasse looked rather poor in comparison with its continuation, the broad and airy promenade, with its lawns and trees.

Our unhealthy housing conditions had certainly contributed to the early death of my sisters. In the Baernreitherhaus things were different. On the ground floor there was the workshop and, on the first floor, our apartment which consisted of two rooms and a kitchen. But now my father was never free from money troubles. Business was bad. More than once he contemplated closing down the business and again taking a job with the furniture makers. Yet each time he managed to overcome his difficulties at the last moment.

I started school, a very unpleasant experience. My mother wept over the bad reports I brought home. Her sorrow was the only thing that could persuade me to work harder. Whereas for my father there was no question but that in due course I should take over his business – why else did he slave from morning to night? – it was my mother's desire that I should study in spite of my bad reports; first I should have four years at the grammar school, then perhaps go to teachers' training college. But I would not hear of it. I was glad that my father put his foot down and, when I was ten, sent me to the council school. In this way, my father thought, my future was finally decided.

For a long time, however, there had been another influence in my life for which I would have sold my soul: music. This love was given full expression when, at Christmas 1897 when nine years old, I was given a violin as a present. I remember distinctly every detail of that Christmas and, when today in my old age I think back, my conscious life seems to have started with that event. The eldest son of our neighbour was a young pupil-teacher and he gave me violin lessons. I learned fast and well.

When my first violin teacher took a job in the country I entered the lower grade of the Linz School of Music, but I did not like it there very much, perhaps because I was much more advanced than the other pupils. After the holidays I once more had private lessons, this time with an old sergeant-major of the Austro-Hungarian Army Music Corps, who straight-away made clear to me that I knew nothing and then began to teach me the elements of violin playing 'in the military fashion'. It was real barrack-square drill with old Kopetzky. Sometimes when I got fed up with his rough sergeant-major manners he consoled me with the assurance that, with more progress, I should certainly be taken as an apprentice-musician by the Army: in his opinion the peak of a musician's glory. I gave up my study with Kopetzky and entered the intermediate class of the School of Music where I was taught by Professor Heinrich Dessauer, a gifted, efficient and sensitive teacher. At the same time I studied the trumpet, trombone and musical theory, and played in the students' orchestra.

I was already toying with the idea of making music my life's work when hard reality made itself felt. I had hardly left the council school when I had to join my father's business as an apprentice. Formerly, when there was a shortage of labour, I had had to lend a hand in the workshop and so was familiar with the work.

It is a repulsive job to re-upholster old furniture by unravelling and remaking the stuffing. The work goes on in clouds of dust in which the poor apprentice is smothered. What rubbishy old mattresses were brought to our workshop! All the illnesses that had been overcome – and some of them not overcome – left their mark on these old beds. No wonder that upholsterers do not live long. But soon I also learned the more pleasant aspects of my work: personal taste and a feeling for art are necessary in it, and it is not too far removed from interior decorating. One would visit well-to-do homes, one saw and heard a lot and, above all, in winter there was little or nothing to do. And this leisure, naturally, I devoted to music. When I had successfully passed my journeyman's test, my father wanted me to take on jobs in other workshops. I saw his point, but for me the essential thing was not to improve my craftsmanship, but to advance my musical studies. Thus, I chose to stay on in my father's workshop, since I could dispose of my time with more freedom there than under another master.

'There are generally too many violins in an orchestra, but never enough violas.' To this day, I am grateful to Professor Dessauer for having applied this maxim and turned me into a good viola player. Musical life in Linz in those days was on a remarkably high level; August Göllerich was the director of the Music Society. Being a disciple of Liszt and a collaborator of Richard Wagner at Bayreuth, Göllerich was the very man to be the musical leader of Linz, so much maligned as a 'peasant's town'. Every year the Music Society gave three symphony concerts and one special concert, when usually a choral work was performed, with orchestra. My mother, in spite of her humble origin, loved music, and hardly ever missed one of these performances. While still a small boy, I was taken to concerts. My mother explained everything to me and, as I came to master several instruments, my appreciation of these concerts grew. My highest aim in life was to play in the orchestra, either on the viola or the trumpet.

But for the time being it was still a matter of remaking dusty old mattresses and papering walls. In those years my father suffered much from the usual occupational diseases of an upholsterer. When persistent lung trouble once kept him in bed for six months, I had to run the workshop alone. Thus the two things existed side by side in my young life: work, which made calls on my strength and even on my lungs, and music, which was my whole love. I should never have thought that there could be a connection between the two. And yet there was. One of my father's customers was a member of the provincial government, which also controlled the theatre. One day there came to us for repair the cushions of a set of rococo furniture. When the work was done my father sent me to deliver them to the theatre. The stage manager directed me to the stage, where I was to replace the cushions in their frames. A rehearsal was in progress. I do not know which piece was being rehearsed, but it was certainly an opera. But what I remember still is the enchantment which came over me as I stood there on the stage, in the midst of the singers. I was transformed as though now, for the first time, I had discovered myself. Theatre! What a world! A man stood there, magnificently attired. He seemed to me like a creature from another planet. He sang so gloriously that I could not imagine this man could ever speak in the ordinary way. The orchestra responded to his mighty voice. Here I was on more familiar ground, but in this moment everything that music had hitherto meant to me seemed to be trifling. Only in conjunction with the stage did music seem to reach a higher, more solemn plane, the highest imaginable.

But there I stood, a miserable little upholsterer, and fitted the cushions back into their place in the rococo suite. What a lamentable job! What a wretched existence! Theatre, that was the world that I had searched for. Play and reality became confused in my excited mind. That awkward fellow with ruffled hair, apron and rolled-up shirt-sleeves who stood in the wings and fumbled with his cushions as though to justify his presence – was he really only a poor upholsterer? A poor, despised simpleton, pushed from pillar to post and treated by the customer as if he were a step-ladder, placed here, placed there according to the moment's need and then, its usefulness over, put aside? It would have been absolutely natural if that little upholsterer, tools in hand, had stepped forward to the footlights and, at a sign from the conductor, had sung his part to prove to the audience in the stalls, nay to an attentive world, that in reality he was not that pale, lanky fellow from the upholsterer's shop in the Klammstrasse, but that his place was really on the stage in the theatre.

Ever since that moment I have remained under the spell of the theatre. Washing down the walls in a customer's house, slapping on the paste, affixing the undercoat of newspaper and then pasting on the wallpaper, I was all the time dreaming of roaring applause in the theatre, seeing myself as conductor in front of an orchestra. Such dreaming did not really help my work, and at times it would happen that the pieces of wallpaper were sadly out of position. But, once back in the workshop, my sick father soon made me realise what responsibilities faced me.

Thus I vacillated between dream and reality. At home nobody had any inkling of my state of mind, for rather than utter a word about my secret ambitions, I would have bitten off my tongue. Even from my mother I hid my hopes and plans, but she perhaps guessed what was occupying my thoughts. But should I have added to her many worries? Thus there was no one to whom I could unburden myself. I felt terribly lonely, like an outcast, as lonely as only a young man can be to whom is revealed, for the first time, life's beauty and its danger.

The theatre gave me new courage. I did not miss a single opera performance. However tired I was after my work, nothing could keep me from the theatre. Naturally, with the small wages that my father paid me, I could only afford a ticket for the standing area. Therefore I used to go regularly into the so-called 'promenade', from where one had the best view; and, moreover, I found, no other place had better acoustics. Just above the promenade was the royal box supported by two wooden columns. These columns were very popular with the habitués of the promenade as they were the only places where one could prop oneself up with an undisturbed view of the stage. For if you leaned against the walls, these very columns were always in your field of vision. I was happy to be able to rest my weary back against the smooth pillars, after having spent a hard day on the top of a step-ladder! Of course, you had to be there early to be sure to get that place.

Often it is the trivial things which make a lasting impression on one's memory. I can still see myself rushing into the theatre, undecided whether to choose the left or right-hand pillar. Often, however, one of the two columns, the right-hand one, was already taken; somebody was even more enthusiastic than I was.

Half-annoyed, half-surprised, I glanced at my rival. He was a remarkably pale, skinny youth, about my own age, who was following the performance with glistening eyes. I surmised that he came from a better-class home, for he was always dressed with meticulous care and was very reserved.

We took note of each other without exchanging a word. But during the interval of a performance some time later we started talking as, apparently, neither of us approved of the casting of one of the parts. We discussed it together and rejoiced in our common adverse criticism. I marvelled at the quick, sure grasp of the other. In this he was undoubtedly my superior. On the other hand, when it came to talking of purely musical matters, I felt my own superiority. I cannot give the exact date of this first meeting, but I am sure it was around All Saints' Day, in 1904.

This went on for some time – he revealing nothing of his own affairs, nor did I think it necessary to talk about myself – but we occupied ourselves intensely with whatever performance there happened to be and sensed that we both had the same enthusiasm for the theatre.

Once, after the performance, I accompanied him home, to No. 31 Humboldtstrasse. When we took leave of each other he gave me his name: Adolf Hitler.

# Chapter 2

# Growth of a Friendship

From now on we saw each other at every operatic performance and also met outside the theatre, and on most evenings we would go for a stroll together along the Landstrasse.

Whilst Linz, in the last decade, has become a modern industrial city and attracted people from all parts of the Danube region, it was then only a country town. In the suburbs there were still the substantial fortress-like farmhouses, and tenement houses were springing up in the surrounding fields where cattle were still grazing. In the little taverns the people sat drinking the local wine; everywhere you could hear the broad country dialect. There was only horse-drawn traffic in the town and the carriers took care to see that Linz remained 'in the country'. The townspeople, though largely themselves of peasant origin and often closely related to the country folk, tended to draw away from the latter the more intimately they were connected with them. Almost all the influential families of the town knew each other; the business world, the civil servants and the military determined the tone of society. Everybody who was anybody took his evening stroll along the main street of the town, which leads from the railway station to the bridge over the Danube and is called significantly Landstrasse. As Linz had no university, the young people in every walk of life were all the more eager to imitate the habits of university students. Social life on the Landstrasse could almost compete with that of Vienna's Ringstrasse; at least the Linzers thought so.

Patience did not seem to me to be one of Adolf's outstanding characteristics; whenever I was late for an appointment, he came at once to the workshop to fetch me, no matter whether I was repairing an old, black, horsehair sofa or an old-fashioned wing chair, or anything else. My work was to him nothing but a tiresome hindrance to our personal relationship. Impatiently he would twirl the small black cane which he always carried. I was surprised that he had so much spare time and asked innocently whether he had a job.

'Of course not', was his gruff reply. This answer, which I thought very peculiar, he elaborated at some length. He did not consider that any particular work, a 'bread-and-butter job' as he called it, was necessary for him.

Such an opinion I had never heard from anybody before. It contradicted every principle which had so far governed my life. At first I saw in this talk nothing more than youthful bragging, although Adolf's bearing and his serious and assured manner of speaking did not strike me at all as that of a braggart. In any case, I was very surprised at his opinions but refrained from asking, for the time being at least, any further questions, because he seemed to be very sensitive about questions that did not suit him; that much I had already discovered. So it was more reasonable to talk about *Lohengrin*, the opera which enchanted us more than any other, than about our personal affairs.

Perhaps he was the son of rich parents, I thought, perhaps he had just come into a fortune and could afford to live without a 'bread-and-butter' job – in his mouth that expression sounded full of contempt. By no means did I imagine he was work-shy, for there was not even a grain of the superficial, carefree idler in him. When we passed by the Café Baumgartner he would get wildly worked up about the young men who were exhibiting themselves at marble-topped tables behind the big window panes and wasting their time in idle gossip, without apparently realising how much this indignation was contradicted by his own way of life. Perhaps some of those who were sitting 'in the shop window' already had a good job and a secure income.

Perhaps this Adolf is a student? This had been my first impression. The black ebony cane, topped by an elegant ivory shoe, was essentially a student's attribute. On the other hand it seemed strange that he had chosen as his friend just a simple upholsterer, who was always afraid that people would smell the glue with which he had been working during the day. If Adolf were a student he had to be at school somewhere. Suddenly I brought the conversation round to school.

'School?' This was the first outburst of temper that I had experienced with him. He did not wish to hear anything about school. School was no longer his concern, he said. He hated the teachers and did not even greet them any more, and he also hated his schoolmates whom, he said, the school was only turning into idlers. No, I was not allowed to mention school. I told him how little success I had had at school myself. 'Why no success?' he wanted to know. He did not like it at all that I had done so badly at school in spite of all the contempt he expressed for schooling. I was confused by this contradiction. But this much I could gather from our conversation, that he must have been at school until recently, probably a grammar school or perhaps a technical school, and that this presumably had ended in disaster. Otherwise this complete rejection would hardly have been possible. For the rest, he presented me with ever-recurring contradictions and riddles. Sometimes he seemed to me almost sinister. One day when we were taking a walk on the Freinberg he suddenly stopped, produced from his pocket a little black notebook – I can still see it before me and could describe it minutely – and read me a poem he had written.

I do not remember the poem itself any longer; to be precise, I can no longer distinguish it from the other poems which Adolf read to me in later days. But I do remember distinctly how much it impressed me that my friend wrote poetry and carried his poems around with him in the same way that I carried my tools. When Adolf later showed me his drawings and designs which he had sketched – somewhat confused and confusing designs which were really beyond me – when he told me that he had much more and better work in his room and was determined to devote his whole life to art, then it dawned on me what kind of person my friend really was. He belonged to that particular species of people of which I had dreamed myself in my more expansive moments: an artist, who despised the mere bread-and-butter job and devoted himself to poetry, to drawing, painting and to going to the theatre. This impressed me enormously. I was thrilled by the grandeur which I saw here. My ideas of an artist were then still very hazy – probably as hazy as were Hitler's. But that made it all the more alluring.

Adolf spoke but rarely of his family. He used to say that it was advisable not to mix too much with grown-ups, as these people with peculiar ideas would only divert one from one's own plans. For instance, his guardian, a peasant in Leonding called Mayrhofer, had got it into his head that he, Adolf, should learn a craft. His brother-in-law was also of this opinion.

I could only conclude that Adolf's relations with his family must have been rather peculiar. Apparently among all the grown-ups he accepted only one person, his mother. And yet he was only sixteen years old, nine months younger than I.

However much his ideas differed from bourgeois conceptions it did not worry me at all – on the contrary! It was this very fact, that he was out of the ordinary, that attracted me even more. To devote his life to the arts was, in my opinion, the greatest resolution that a young man could take; for secretly I too played with the idea of exchanging the dusty and noisy upholsterer's workshop for the pure and lofty fields of art, to give my life to music. For young people it is by no means insignificant in what surroundings their friendship first begins. It seemed to me a symbol that our friendship had been born in the theatre, in the midst of brilliant scenes and to the mighty sound of great music. In a certain sense our friendship itself existed in this happy atmosphere.

Moreover my own position was not dissimilar to Adolf's. School lay behind me and could give me nothing more. In spite of my love and devotion to my parents, grown-ups did not mean very much to me. And, above all, in spite of the many problems that beset me there was nobody in whom I could confide.

Nevertheless, it was at first a difficult friendship because our characters were utterly different. Whilst I was a quiet, somewhat dreamy youth, very sensitive and adaptable and therefore always willing to yield, so to speak a 'musical character', Adolf was exceedingly violent and highly strung. Quite trivial things, such as a few thoughtless words, could produce in him outbursts of temper which I thought were quite out of proportion to the significance of the matter. But, probably, I misunderstood Adolf in this respect. Perhaps the difference between us was that he took things seriously which seemed to me quite unimportant. Yes, this was one of his typical traits; everything aroused his interest and disturbed him – to nothing was he indifferent.

But in spite of all the difficulties arising out of our varying temperaments, our friendship itself was never in serious danger. Nor did we, as so many other youngsters, grow cool and indifferent with time. On the contrary! In everyday matters we took great care not to clash. It seems strange, but he who could stick so obstinately to his point of view, could also be so considerate that sometimes he made me feel quite ashamed. So, as time went on we got more and more used to each other.

Soon I came to understand that our friendship endured largely for the reason that I was a patient listener. But I was not dissatisfied with this passive role, for it made me realise how much my friend needed me. He, too, was completely alone. His father had been dead for two years. However much he loved his mother, she could not help him with his problems. I remember how he used to give me long lectures about things that did not interest me at all, as for example the excise duty levied at the Danube bridge, or a collection in the streets for a charity lottery. He just had to talk and needed someone who would listen to him. I was often startled when he would make a speech to me, accompanied by vivid gestures, for my benefit alone. He was never worried by the fact that I was the sole audience. But a young man who, like my friend, was passionately interested in everything he saw and experienced had to find an outlet for his tempestuous feelings. The tension he felt was relieved by holding forth on these things. These speeches, usually delivered somewhere in the open, under trees on the Freinberg, in the Danube woods, seemed to be like a volcano erupting. It was as though something strange, other-worldly, was bursting out of him. Such rapture I had only witnessed so far in the theatre, when an actor had to express some violent emotions, and at first, confronted by such eruptions, I could only stand gaping and passive, forgetting to applaud. But soon I realised that this was not play-acting. No, this was not acting, not exaggeration, this was really felt, and I saw that he was in deadly earnest. Again and again I was filled with astonishment at how fluently he expressed himself, how vividly he managed to convey his feelings, how easily the words flowed from his mouth when he was completely carried away by his own emotions. It was not what he said that impressed me at first, but how he said it. This to me was something new and magnificent. I had never imagined that a man could produce such an effect with mere words. All he wanted from me, however, was one thing – agreement. I soon came to realise this. Nor was it hard for me to agree with him because I had never given any thought to the many problems which he raised.

Nevertheless, it would be wrong to assume that our friendship confined itself to this unilateral relationship only. This would have been too cheap for Adolf and too little for me. The important thing was that we were complementary to each other. In him, everything brought forth a strong reaction and forced him to take a stand, for his emotional outbursts were only a sign of his passionate interest in everything. I, on the other hand, being of a contemplative nature, accepted unreservedly all his arguments on things that interested him and yielded to them, always excepting musical matters.

Of course, I must admit that Adolf's claims on me were boundless and took up all my spare time. As he himself did not have to keep to a regular timetable I had to be at his beck and call. He demanded everything from me, but was also prepared to do everything for me. In fact I had no alternative. My friendship with him did not leave me any time for cultivating other friends; nor did I feel the need of them. Adolf was as much to me as a dozen other ordinary friends. Only one thing might have separated us – if we had both fallen in love with the same girl; this would have been serious. As I was seventeen at the time this might well have happened. But it was precisely in this respect that fate had a special solution in store for us. Such a unique solution – I describe it later in the chapter called 'Stefanie' – that, rather than upsetting our friendship, served to deepen it.

I knew that he, too, had no other friend besides me. I remember in this connection a quite trivial detail. We were strolling along the Landstrasse when it happened. A young man, about our age, came around the corner, a plump, rather dandified young gentleman. He recognised Adolf as a former classmate, stopped, and grinning all over his face, called out 'Hallo, Hitler!' He took him familiarly by the arm and asked him quite sincerely how he was getting on. I expected Adolf to respond in the same friendly manner, as he always set great store by correct and courteous behaviour. But my friend went red with rage. I knew from former experience that this change of expression boded ill. 'What the devil is that to do with you?' he threw at him excitedly, and pushed him sharply away. Then he took my arm and went with me on his way without bothering about the young man whose flushed and baffled face I can still see before me. 'All future civil servants,' said Adolf, still furious, 'and with this lot I had to sit in the same class.' It was a long time before he calmed down.

Another experience sticks out in my memory. My venerated violin-teacher, Heinrich Dessauer, had died. Adolf went to the funeral with me, which rather surprised me as he did not know Professor Dessauer at all. When I expressed my surprise he said, 'I can't bear it that you should mix with other young people and talk to them.'

There was no end to the things, even trivial ones, that could upset him. But he lost his temper most of all when it was suggested that he should become a civil servant. Whenever he heard the term 'civil servant', even without any connection with his own career, he fell into a rage. I discovered that these outbursts of fury were, in a certain sense, still quarrels with his long-dead father, whose greatest desire it had been to turn him into a civil servant. They were, so to speak, a 'posthumous defence'.

It was an essential part of our friendship at that time, that my opinion of civil servants should be as low as his. Knowing his violent rejection of a career in the civil service, I could now appreciate that he preferred the friendship of a simple upholsterer to that of one of those spoilt darlings who were assured of patronage by their good connections and knew in advance the exact course their life would follow. Hitler was just the opposite. With him everything was uncertain. There was another positive factor which made me seem, in Adolf's eyes, predestined to be his friend; like him I considered art to be the greatest thing in a man's life. Of course, in those days, we were not able to express this sentiment in such high-faluting words. But in practice we conformed to this principle, because in my life music had long since become the decisive factor – I worked in the workshop only to make my living. For my friend art was even more. His intense way of absorbing, scrutinising, rejecting, his terrific seriousness, his ever-active mind needed a counterpoise. And only art could provide this.

Thus I fulfilled all the requirements he would look for in a friend: I had nothing in common with his former classmate; I had nothing to do with the civil service; and I lived entirely for art. In addition I knew a lot about music. The similarity of our inclinations welded us closely together as did the dissimilarity of our temperaments.

I leave it to others to judge whether people who, like Adolf, find their way with a sleep-walker's sureness, pick up at random the companion they need for that particular part of their path, or whether fate chooses for them. All I can say is that from our first meeting in the theatre up to his decline into misery in Vienna I was that companion for Adolf Hitler.

# Chapter 3

# Portrait of the Young Hitler

I have no photograph of Adolf taken during the years of our friendship – probably there are none of him from this period. The absence of photos from that epoch is by no means odd. At the turn of the century there were no cameras which one could carry comfortably, and even if there had been we could not have afforded one. If you wanted a portrait done, you went to a studio. This was also expensive and needed a lot of thought before indulging. As far as I remember, my friend never expressed the need to be photographed. He was never vain, not even when Stefanie entered his life. I suppose there are no more than five photos of Adolf Hitler taken during his formative years.

The earliest known photograph is that of the baby Adolf a few months old in 1889. It shows the characteristic proportions of nose – cheeks – mouth, the light, piercing eyes and the fringe. What strikes one most about this portrait is the boy's great likeness to his mother. I noticed it at once on first meeting Frau Hitler. On the other hand, his sister Paula resembled their father. I never knew him and so I rely on what Frau Hitler told me.

The photos from Hitler's schooldays are all of the whole class – there are no portraits; despite the lapse of time between them, we see the same alien face in both as if nothing had changed it. For me, they reflect the essential characteristic of his personality, that 'I remain unchanged' look. There is a sketch of his profile from schooldays at Steyr when he was sixteen; the artist, Sturmlechner, called it *'nach der Natur'* – 'true to life'. He was an amateur, of course, but nevertheless I consider it to be a pretty good likeness.

Adolf was of middle height and slender, at that time already taller than his mother. His physique was far from sturdy, rather too thin for its height, and he was not at all strong. His health, in fact, was rather poor, which he was the first to regret. He had to take special care of himself during the foggy and damp winters which prevailed in Linz. He was ill from time to time during that period and coughed a lot. In short, he had weak lungs.

His nose was quite straight and well-proportioned, but in no way remarkable. His forehead was high and receded a little. I was always sorry that even in those days he had the habit of combing his hair straight down to his brow. Yet this traditional forehead – nose – mouth description seems rather ridiculous to me. For in this countenance the eyes were so outstanding that that one did not notice anything else. Never in my life have I seen any other person whose appearance – how shall I put it – was so completely dominated by the eyes. They were the light eyes of his mother, but her somewhat staring, penetrating gaze was even more marked in the son and had even more force and expressiveness. It was uncanny how these eyes could change their expression, especially when Adolf was speaking. To me his sonorous voice meant much less than the expression of his eyes. In fact, Adolf spoke with his eyes, and even when his lips were silent one knew what he wanted to say. After he first came to our house and I introduced him to my mother, she said to me in the evening, 'What eyes your friend has!' And I remember quite distinctly that there was more fear than admiration in her words. If I am asked where one could perceive, in his youth, this man's exceptional qualities, I can only answer 'in the eyes'.

Naturally, his extraordinary eloquence, too, was striking. But I was then too inexperienced to attach to it any special significance for the future. I, for one, was certain that Hitler one day would be a great artist, a poet I thought at first, then a great painter, until later, in Vienna, he convinced me that his real talent was in the field of architecture. But for these artistic ambitions his eloquence was of no use, rather a hindrance. Nevertheless, I always liked to listen to him. His language was very refined. He disliked dialect, in particular Viennese, the soft melodiousness of which was utterly repulsive to him. To be sure, Hitler did not speak Austrian-German in the true sense. Rather, in his diction, especially in the rhythm of his speech, there was something Bavarian. Perhaps this was due to the fact that, from his third to his sixth year, the real formative years for speech, he lived in Passau, where his father was then a customs official.

There is no doubt that my friend Adolf had shown a gift for oratory from his earliest youth. And he knew it. He liked to talk, and talked without pause. Sometimes when he soared too high in his fantasies I could not help suspecting that all this was nothing but an exercise in oratory. But then again I thought otherwise. Did I not take everything for gospel that he said? Sometimes Adolf would try out his powers of oratory on me or on others. It always stuck in my memory how, when not yet eighteen, he convinced my father that he should release me from his workshop and send me to Vienna to the Conservatoire. In view of the awkward and unforthcoming nature of my father this was a considerable achievement. From the moment I had this proof of his talent – for me so decisive – I considered that there was nothing that Hitler could not achieve by a convincing speech.

He was in the habit of emphasising his words by measured and studied gestures. Now and then, when he was speaking on one of his favourite subjects, such as the bridge over the Danube, the rebuilding of the museum or even the subterranean railway station which he had planned for Linz, I would interrupt him and ask him how he imagined he would ever carry out these projects – we were only impoverished devils. Then he would throw at me a strange and hostile glance as though he had not understood my question at all. I never got an answer; at the most he would shut me up with a wave of his hand. Later I got used to it and ceased to find it ridiculous that the sixteen- or seventeen-year-old boy should develop gigantic projects and expound them to me down to the last detail. If I had listened only to his words the whole thing would have appeared to be either idle fantasy or sheer lunacy, but the eyes convinced me that he was in deadly earnest.

Adolf set great store by good manners and correct behaviour. He observed with painstaking punctiliousness the rules of social conduct, however little he thought of society itself. He always emphasised the position of his father, who as a customs official ranked more or less with a captain in the army. Hearing him speak of his father, one would never have imagined how violently he disliked the idea of being a civil servant. Nevertheless, there was in his bearing something very precise. He would never forget to send regards to my people, and every postcard bore greetings to my 'esteemed parents'.

When we lodged together in Vienna, I discovered that every evening he would put his trousers carefully under the mattress so that the next morning he could rejoice in a faultless crease. Adolf realised the value of a good appearance and, in spite of his lack of vanity, knew how to make the best of himself. He made excellent use of his undoubted histrionic talents, which he cleverly combined with his gift for oratory. I used to ask myself why Adolf, in spite of all these pronounced capabilities, did not get on better in Vienna; only later did I realise that professional success was not at all his ambition. People who knew him in Vienna could not understand the contradiction between his well-groomed appearance, his educated speech and his self-assured bearing on the one hand, and the starveling existence that he led on the other, and judged him either haughty or pretentious. He was neither. He just did not fit into any bourgeois order.

Adolf had brought starvation to a fine art, though he ate very well when occasion offered. To be sure, in Vienna he generally lacked the money for food. But even if he had it, he would prefer to starve and spend it on a theatre seat. He had no comprehension of enjoyment of life as others knew it. He did not smoke, he did not drink, and in Vienna, for instance, he lived for days on milk and bread only.

With his contempt for everything pertaining to the body, sport, which was then coming into fashion, meant nothing to him. I read somewhere of how audaciously the young Hitler had swum across the Danube. I do not recollect anything of the sort; the most swimming we did was an occasional dip in the Rodel stream. He showed some interest in the bicycle club, mainly because they ran an ice-rink in the winter. And this, only because the girl he adored used to practise skating there.

Walking was the only exercise that really appealed to Adolf. He walked always and everywhere and even in my workshop and in my room he would stride up and down. I recall him always on the go. He could walk for hours without getting tired. We used to explore the surroundings of Linz in all directions. His love of nature was pronounced, but in a very personal way. Unlike other subjects, nature never attracted him as a matter for study; I hardly ever remember seeing him with a book on the subject. Here was the limit of his thirst for knowledge. At school he had once been very keen on botany and had cultivated a little herb garden, but it was simply a schoolboy's fancy and nothing more. Details did not interest him, but only nature as a whole. He referred to it as 'the outdoors'. This expression sounded as familiar on his lips as the word 'home'. And in fact he did feel at home with nature. As early as the first years of our friendship I discovered his peculiar preference for nocturnal rambles, or even for staying overnight in some unfamiliar district.

Being in the outdoors had an extraordinary effect on him. He was then quite a different person from what he was in town. Certain sides of his character revealed themselves nowhere else. He was never so collected and concentrated as when walking along the quiet paths in the beech-woods of the Mühlviertel, or at night when we took a quick walk on the Freinberg. To the rhythm of his steps his thoughts would flow more smoothly and to better purpose than elsewhere. For a long time I could not understand one peculiar contradiction in him. When the sun shone brightly in the streets and a fresh, revivifying wind brought the smell of the woods into the town, an irresistible force drove him out of the narrow, stuffy streets into the woods and fields. But hardly had we reached the open country, than he would assure me that it would be impossible for him to live in the country again. It would be terrible for him to have to live in a village. For all his love of nature, he was always glad when we got back to the town.

As I grew to know him better, I also came to understand this apparent contradiction. He needed the town, the variety and abundance of its impressions, experiences and events; he felt there that he had his share in everything, that there was nothing in which his interest was not engaged. He needed people with their contrasting interests, their ambitions, intentions, plans and desires. Only in this problem-laden atmosphere did he feel at home. From this point of view the village was altogether too simple, too insignificant, too unimportant, and did not provide enough scope for his limitless need to take an interest in everything. Besides, for him, a town was interesting in itself as an agglomeration of houses and buildings. It was understandable that he should want to live only in a town.

On the other hand, he needed an effective counterweight to the town, which always troubled and excited him and made constant demands on his interests and talents. He found this in nature, which even he could not try to change and improve because its eternal laws are beyond the reach of the human will. Here he could once more find his own self, since here he was not obliged, as he was in town, eternally to be taking sides.

My friend had a special way of making nature serve him. He used to seek out a lonely spot outside the town, which he could visit again and again. Every bush and every tree was familiar to him. There was nothing to disturb his contemplative mood. Nature surrounded him like the walls of a quiet, friendly room in which he could cultivate undisturbed his passionate plans and ideas.

For some time, on fine days, he used to frequent a bench on the Turmleitenweg where he established a kind of open-air study. There he would read his books, sketch and paint in water-colours. Here were born his first poems. Another spot, which later became a favourite, was even more lonely and secluded. We would sit on a high, overhanging rock looking down on the Danube. The sight of the gently flowing river always moved Adolf. How often did my friend tell me of his plans up there! Sometimes he would be overcome by his feelings and give free rein to his imagination. I remember his once describing to me so vividly Krimhild's journey to the country of the Huns that I imagined I could see the mighty ships of the kings of Burgundy drifting down the river.

Quite different were our far-ranging excursions. Not much preparation was necessary – a strong walking stick was the only requisite. With his everyday clothes Adolf would wear a coloured shirt and, as a sign of his intention to undertake a long trip, would sport, instead of the usual tie, a silk cord with two tassels hanging down. We would not take any food with us, but somewhere would manage to find a bit of dry bread and a glass of milk. What wonderful, carefree times those were!

We despised railways and coaches and went everywhere on foot. Whenever we combined our Sunday trip with an outing for my parents, which for us had the advantage that my father treated us to a good meal in a country inn, we started out early enough to meet them at our destination, to which they had come by train. My father was particularly fond of a little village called Walding, which attracted us because nearby was the Rodel stream in which we liked to bathe on warm summer days.

A little incident stands out in my memory. Adolf and I had left the inn for a bathe. We were both fairly good swimmers, but my mother, nevertheless, was nervous. She followed us and stood on a protruding rock to watch us. The rock sloped down to the water and was covered with moss. My poor mother, while she was anxiously watching us, slipped on the smooth moss and slid into the water. I was too far away to help her at once, but Adolf immediately jumped in after her and dragged her out. He always remained attached to my parents. As late as 1944, on my mother's 80th birthday, he sent her a food parcel.

Adolf was particularly fond of the Mühlviertel. From the Pöstlingberg we would walk across the Holzpoldl and the Elendsimmerl to Gramastetten or wander through the woods round the Lichtenhag ruins. Adolf measured the walls, though not much of them remained, and entered the measurements in his sketchbook, which he always carried with him. Then with a few strokes he sketched the original castle, drew in the moat and the drawbridge and he adorned the walls with fanciful pinnacles and turrets. He exclaimed there once to my surprise, 'This is the ideal setting to my sonnet!' But when I wanted to know more about it he said, 'I must first see what I make of it.' And on our way home he confessed that he was going to try and extend the material into a play.

We would go to St Georgen on the Gusen to find out what relics of that famous battle in the Peasants' War still remained. When we were unsuccessful Adolf had a strange idea. He was convinced that the people who lived there would have some faint memory of that great battle. The following day he went again alone, after a vain attempt to get my father to give me the day off. He spent two days and nights there, but I do not remember with what result.

For the sole reason that Adolf wanted, for a change, to see his beloved Linz from the east, I had to make with him the unattractive climb up the Pfennigberg, in which the Linzers, as he complained, did not show enough interest. I also liked the view of the city, but least of all from this side. Nevertheless, Adolf remained for hours in this uninviting spot, sketching.

On the other hand, St Florian became for me, too, a place of pilgrimage, for here, where Anton Bruckner had worked and hallowed the surroundings by his memory, we imagined that we actually met 'God's musician' and heard his inspired improvisations on the great organ in the magnificent church. Then we would stand in front of the simple gravestone let into the floor beneath the choir, where the great master had been buried ten years earlier. The wonderful monastery had aroused my friend to the heights of enthusiasm. He had stood in front of the glorious staircase for an hour or more – at any rate much too long for me. And how much did he admire the splendour of the library! But the deepest impression was made on him by the contrast between the over-decorated apartments of the monastery and Bruckner's simple room. When he saw its humble furniture, he was strengthened in his belief that on this earth genius almost always goes hand in hand with poverty.

Such visits were revealing to me, for Adolf was by nature very reserved. There was always a certain element in his personality into which he would allow nobody to penetrate. He had his inscrutable secrets, and in many respects always remained a riddle to me. But there was one key that opened the door to much that would have remained hidden: his enthusiasm for beauty. All that separated us when we stood in front of such a magnificent work of art as the monastery of St Florian. Then, fired by enthusiasm, Adolf would lower all his defences and I felt to the full the joy of our friendship.

I have often been asked, and even by Rudolf Hess, who once invited me to visit him in Linz, whether Adolf, when I knew him, had any sense of humour. One feels the lack of it, people of his entourage said. After all, he was an Austrian and should have had his share of the famous Austrian sense of humour. Certainly one's impression of Hitler, especially after a short and superficial acquaintance, was that of a deeply serious man. This enormous seriousness seemed to overshadow everything else. It was the same when he was young. He approached any problem with which he was concerned with a deadly earnestness which ill suited his sixteen or seventeen years. He was capable of loving and admiring, hating and despising, all with the greatest seriousness. But one thing he could not do was pass over something with a smile. Even with a subject in which he did not take a personal interest, such as sport, this was nevertheless, as a phenomenon of modern times, just as important to him as any other. He never came to the end of his problems. His profound earnestness never ceased to attack new problems, and if he did not find any in the present, he would brood at home for hours over his books and burrow into the problems of the past. This extraordinary earnestness was his most striking quality. Many other qualities which are characteristic of youth were lacking in him: a carefree letting go of himself, living only for the day, the happy attitude of 'what is to be, will be'. Even 'going off the rails', in the coarse exuberance of youth, was alien to him. His idea, strange to say, was that these were things that did not become a young man. And because of this, humour was confined to the most intimate sphere as if it were something taboo. His humour was usually aimed at people in his immediate circle, in other words a sphere in which problems no longer existed for him. For this reason his grim and sour humour was often mixed with irony, but always an irony with friendly intent. Thus, he saw me once at a concert where I was playing the trumpet. He got enormous amusement out of imitating me and insisted that with my blown-out cheeks I looked like one of Rubens's angels.

I cannot conclude this chapter without mentioning one of Hitler's qualities which, I freely admit, seems paradoxical to talk about now. Hitler was full of deep understanding and sympathy. He took a most touching interest in me. Without my telling him, he knew exactly how I felt. How often this helped me in difficult times. He always knew what I needed and what I wanted. However intensely he was occupied with himself he would always have time for the affairs of those people in whom he was interested. It was not by chance that he was the one who persuaded my father to let me study music and thereby influenced my life in a decisive way. Rather, this was the outcome of his general attitude of sharing in all the things that were of concern to me. Sometimes I had a feeling that he was living my life as well as his own.

Thus I have drawn the portrait of the young Hitler as well as I can from memory. But for the question, then unknown and unexpressed which hung above our friendship, I have not to this day found any answer: 'What did God want from this person?'

## Chapter 4

# Portrait of His Mother

When I first met her, Klara Hitler was already forty-five years old and a widow of two years' standing. She looked then much as she did in the only known photograph of her, although the suffering was more clearly etched in her face and her hair had started to go grey. But Klara Hitler remained a beautiful woman to the day of her death. Whenever I saw her I had – I do not know why – a feeling of sympathy for her, and felt that I wanted to do something for her. She was glad that Adolf had found a friend whom he liked and trusted, and for this reason Frau Hitler liked me too. How often did she unburden to me the worries which Adolf caused her. And how fervently did she hope to enlist my help in persuading her son to follow his father's wishes in the choice of a career. I had to disappoint her, yet she did not blame me, for she must have felt that the reasons for Adolf's behaviour were much too deep, far beyond the reach of my influence.

Just as Adolf frequently enjoyed the hospitality of my parents' home, I went often to see his mother and, on taking leave, was unfailingly asked by Frau Hitler to come again. I considered myself as part of the family – there was hardly anybody else who visited them.

Often when I finished work early, I would have a quick wash, change and make my way to Humboldtstrasse. No. 31 was a three-storeyed, not unpleasant tenement building. The Hitlers lived on the third floor. I would run up the steps and ring the bell, Frau Hitler would open the door and give me a warm welcome. This heartfelt friendliness seemed to lighten a little the suffering one could read in her features. Every smile which crossed that serious face gave me joy.

I can still visualise the humble apartment. The small kitchen, with green painted furniture, had only one window which looked out on to the courtyard. The living room, with the two beds of his mother and little Paula, overlooked the street. On the side wall hung a portrait of his father, with a typical civil servant's face, impressive and dignified, whose rather grim expression was mitigated by the carefully groomed whiskers in the style of the Emperor Franz Josef. Adolf lived and studied in the box room, off the bedroom.

Paula, Adolf's little sister, was nine when I first met the family. She was a rather pretty girl, quiet and reserved, but unlike either her mother or Adolf facially. I never saw her giggly. We got on rather well with each other but Adolf was not particularly close to her. This was due perhaps to the difference in age – he always referred to her affectionately as 'the kid'.

Another acquaintance I made in the Hitler family was a striking-looking woman of just over twenty, called Angela, whose place in the family puzzled me at first, although she addressed Klara Hitler as 'mother' just as Paula did. Later, I learned the solution of the mystery. Angela, born on 28 July 1883, that is to say six years before Adolf, was a child of their father's previous marriage. Her mother, Franziska Matzelsberger, died the year after her birth. Five months later her father married Klara Pölzl. Angela, who naturally had no recollection of her own mother, looked upon Klara as her mother. In September 1903, a year before I became acquainted with Adolf, Angela had married a Revenue official called Raubal. She lived with her husband in the Zum Waldhorn Inn in the Bürgerstrasse nearby and often came to visit her stepmother, but never brought Herr Raubal with her; at any rate I never met him. Angela was quite unlike Frau Hitler, a jolly person who enjoyed life and loved to laugh. She brought some life into the family. She was very handsome with her regular features and wore her beautiful hair, which was as dark as Adolf's, in pigtails.

From Adolf's description, but also from some hints of his mother's, I gathered that Raubal was a drunkard. Adolf hated him. He saw in him a personification of everything he despised in a man. He spent his time in bars, drank and smoked, gambled his money away, and – on top of that – he was a civil servant. And as though that were not enough, Raubal thought it was his duty to support his father-in-law's views by urging Adolf to become a civil servant himself. This was enough to antagonise Adolf completely. When Adolf talked of Raubal his face assumed a truly threatening aspect. Perhaps it was Adolf's pronounced hatred of his half-sister's husband that kept Raubal away from the Humboldtstrasse. At the time of Raubal's death, only a few years after his marriage to Angela, the break between him and Adolf was already complete. Angela remarried later, an architect in Dresden, and died in Munich in 1949.

I learned from Adolf that from his father's second marriage there was also a son, Alois, who spent his childhood with the Hitler family but left them while they were living in Lambach. This half-brother of Adolf's – born on

13 December 1881 in Braunau – was seven years older than Adolf. While his father was still alive he came to Leonding a couple of times, but as far as I know he never appeared in the Humboldtstrasse. He never played any important part in Hitler's life, nor did he take any interest in Adolf's political career. He turned up once in Paris, then in Vienna, later in Berlin. His first marriage was to a Dutchwoman and they had a son, William Patrick Hitler, who in August 1939 published a pamphlet *My Uncle Adolf*; a son from his second marriage, Heinz Hitler, fell as an officer on the Eastern Front.

Frau Hitler did not like to talk about herself and her worries, yet she found relief in telling me of her doubts about Adolf. Naturally she did not get much satisfaction from the vague and, for her, meaningless utterances of Adolf about his future as an artist. Her preoccupation with the well-being of her only surviving son depressed her increasingly. Often I sat together with Frau Hitler and Adolf in the tiny kitchen. 'Your poor father cannot rest in his grave', she used to say to Adolf, 'because you do absolutely nothing that he wanted for you. Obedience is what distinguishes a good son, but you do not know the meaning of the word. That's why you did so badly at school and why you're not getting anywhere now.'

Gradually I learned to understand the suffering this woman endured. She never complained, but she told me about the hard time she had in her youth.

So I came to know, partly by experience, partly by what I was told, the circumstances of the Hitler family. Occasionally mention was made of some relations in the Waldviertel, but it was difficult for me to understand whether these were his father's relations or his mother's. In any case, the Hitler family had relations only in the Waldviertel, quite unlike other Austrian civil servants who had relatives scattered all over the country. Only later did I come to realise that Hitler's paternal and maternal lineage merged in the second generation, so that from the grandfather upwards Adolf had only one set of forbears. I remember that Adolf did visit some relatives in the Waldviertel. Once he sent me a picture postcard from Weitra, which is in the part of the Waldviertel nearest to Bohemia. I do not know what had taken him there. He never spoke very willingly about his relations in that part of the country, but preferred to describe the landscape, poor, barren country, a striking contrast to the rich and fertile Danube valley of the Wachau. This raw, hard, peasant country was the homeland of both his maternal and paternal ancestors.

Frau Klara Hitler, née Pölzl, was born on 12 August 1860 in Spital, a poor village in the Waldviertel. Her father, Johann Baptist Pölzl, was a simple peasant. Her mother's maiden name was Johanna Hüttler. The name Hitler is spelt differently in the various documents. There is the spelling of Hiedler and Hüttler, whilst Hitler is used for the first time by Adolf's father. This Johanna Hüttler, Adolf's maternal grandmother, was, according to the documents, a daughter of Johann Nepomuk Hiedler. Thus Klara Pölzl was directly related to the Hiedler-Hüttler family, for Johann Nepomuk Hiedler was the brother of that Johann Georg Hiedler who appears in the baptismal register of Döllersheim as Adolf's father's father. Klara Pölzl was, therefore, a second cousin of her husband. Alois Hitler always referred to her before their marriage simply as his niece.

Klara Pölzl had a miserable childhood in the poor and wretched home where she was amongst the youngest of the family's twelve children. I often heard talk of her sister Johanna. This aunt looked after Adolf quite often after he was orphaned. Later I also got to know another of her sisters, Amalia. In 1875, when she was fifteen years old, Klara's relative, the customs official Alois Schicklgruber, at Braunau, invited her to come and help his wife in the house. Alois Schicklgruber, who only in the following year assumed the name Hiedler, which he changed into Hitler, was then married to Anna Glasl-Hörer. This first marriage of Alois Hitler with a woman fourteen years older than himself remained without issue and they finally separated.

When his wife died in 1883, Alois Hitler married Franziska Matzelsberger, who was twenty-four years his junior. The children of this marriage were Adolf's half-brother Alois and half-sister Angela. Klara, who had worked in the house during the time he was separated from his first wife, left on the second marriage and went to Vienna. When Franziska, the second wife, fell gravely ill after the birth of her second child, Alois Hitler called his niece back to Braunau. Franziska died on 10 August 1884, barely two years after her marriage. (Alois, the first child of this union, had been born out of wedlock and adopted by his father.)

On 7 January 1885, six months after the death of his second wife, Alois Hitler married his niece Klara, who was already expecting a child by him, the first son, Gustav, who was born on 17 May 1885, that is to say five months after the marriage, and who died on 9 December 1887.

Although Klara Pölzl was only a second cousin, the couple needed an ecclesiastical dispensation to marry. The application for this, in the clean, copper-plate handwriting of an Austro-Hungarian civil servant, still exists in the archives of the episcopate in Linz under the reference 6. 911/II/2 1884. The document reads as follows:

Application of Alois Hitler and his fiancée, Klara Pölzl, for permission to marry.

Most reverend episcopate,
    Those, in humblest devotion undersigned, have decided to marry. According to the enclosed family tree they are prevented by the canonical impediment of collateral affinity in the third degree touching the second. They therefore humbly request the reverend episcopate graciously to procure them dispensation on the following grounds: According to the enclosed death certificate the bridegroom has been a widower since 10 August of this year and is father of two infant children, a boy of two-and-a-half (Alois) and a girl of one year and two months (Angela) for whose care he needs a woman's help as he, being a customs official, is away from his home the whole day and also often at night, and therefore hardly able to supervise the education and upbringing of the children. The bride has looked after the children ever since the death of the mother and they are very fond of her, so that it may be justifiably assumed that the upbringing would be successful and the marriage a happy one. Moreover the bride is without means and it is therefore unlikely that she will ever have another opportunity of a good marriage.

    For these reasons the undersigned repeat their humble petition for the gracious procurement of dispensation from the impediment of affinity.

    Braunau, 27 October 1884

    *Alois Hitler*, Bridegroom    *Klara Pölzl*, Bride

The family tree that accompanied the application was as follows:

| Johann Georg Hiedler | Johann Nepomuk Hiedler |
|:---:|:---:|
| / | / |
| Alois Hitler | Johanna Hiedler (married Pölzl) |
| | / |
| | Klara Pölzl |

    The Linz episcopate declared itself not competent to issue the dispensation and forwarded the application to Rome where it was granted by papal decree.

    Alois Hitler's marriage with Klara was described by various

acquaintances as very happy, which was presumably due to the submissive and accommodating nature of the wife. Once she said to me in this respect, 'What I hoped and dreamed of as a young girl has not been fulfilled in my marriage,' and added resignedly, 'but does such a thing ever happen?'

The birth of the children in quick succession was a heavy psychological and physical burden for this frail woman: in 1885 the son Gustav was born, in 1886 a daughter, Ida, who died after two years, in 1887 another son, Otto, who only lived three days, and on 20 April 1889 again a son, Adolf. How much suffering is hidden behind these bare figures! When Adolf was born the three other children were already dead. With what care the sorely tried mother must have looked after this fourth child. She told me once that Adolf was a very weak child and that she always lived in fear of losing him, too.

Perhaps the early death of the three children was due to the fact that the parents were blood relations. I leave it to the experts to give the final verdict. But in this connection I would like to draw attention to one point to which, in my opinion, greatest importance should be attached.

The most outstanding trait in my friend's character was, as I had experienced myself, the unparallelled consistency in everything that he said and did. There was in his nature something firm, inflexible, immovable, obstinately rigid, which manifested itself in his profound seriousness and was at the bottom of all his other characteristics. Adolf simply could not change his mind or his nature. Everything that lay in these rigid precincts of his being remained unaltered for ever. How often did I experience this. I remember what he said to me when we met again in 1938 after an interval of thirty years. 'You haven't changed, Kubizek, you have only grown older.' If this was true of me, how much more was it of him. He never changed.

I have tried to find an explanation for this fundamental trait in his character. Influence of surroundings and education can hardly account for it, but I could imagine – although a complete layman in the field of genetics – that the biological effect of the intermarriage in the family was to fix certain spheres and that those 'arrested complexes' might have produced that particular type of character. It was just that inflexibility that was responsible for Adolf Hitler causing such innumerable sorrows to his mother.

Once more the mother's heart was sorely tried by destiny. Five years after Adolf's birth, on 24 March 1894, she gave birth to a fifth child, a son, Edmund, who also died young on 29 June 1900, in Leonding. Whilst, naturally, Adolf had no recollection of the first three children born in Braunau and never spoke of them, he could clearly remember his brother

Edmund, at the time of whose death he was already eleven years old. He told me once that Edmund had died of diphtheria. The youngest child, a girl called Paula, born on 21 January 1896, survived.

Thus, an early death had deprived Klara Hitler of four of her six children. Perhaps her mother's heart was broken by these terrible trials. Only one thing remained, the care of the two surviving children, a care which she had to bear alone after the death of her husband. Small comfort that Paula was a quiet, easily led child; all the greater was the anxiety over the only son, an anxiety that only ended with her death.

Adolf really loved his mother. I swear to it before God and man. I remember many occasions when he showed this love for his mother, most deeply and movingly during her last illness; he never spoke of his mother but with deep affection. He was a good son. It was beyond his power to fulfill her most heartfelt wish to see him started on a safe career. When we lived together in Vienna he always carried his mother's portrait with him in a locket. In *Mein Kampf* he wrote definitively of his parents: 'I honoured my father, but I loved my mother.'

# Chapter 5

# Portrait of His Father

Although his father had been dead nearly two years when I first met Adolf, he was still 'ever present' to his family. The mother perpetuated his personality in every way, for with her malleable nature she had almost entirely lost her own, and what she thought, said and did was all in the spirit of the dead father. But she lacked the strength and energy to put into effect the father's will. She, who forgave everything, was handicapped in the upbringing of her son by her boundless love for him. I could imagine how complete and enduring the influence of this man had been on his family, a real partriarchal father-of-the-family, whose authority was unquestioningly respected. Now his picture hung in the best position in the room. On the kitchen shelves, I still remember, there were carefully arrayed the long pipes which he used to smoke. They were almost a symbol in the family of his absolute power. Many a time, when talking of him, Frau Hitler would emphasise her words by pointing to these pipes as though they should bear witness how faithfully she carried on the husband's tradition.

Adolf spoke of his father with great respect. I never heard him say anything against him, in spite of their differences of opinion about his career. In fact he respected him more as time went on. Adolf did not take it amiss that his father had autocratically decided on his son's future career, for this he considered his right, even his duty. It was quite a different matter when Raubal, his step-sister's husband, this uneducated person, who was himself only a little revenue official, arrogated to himself this right. Adolf would certainly not permit him to interfere in his personal affairs. But the authority of his father still remained, even after his death, the force in the struggle with which Adolf developed his own powers. His father's attitude had provoked him first to secret, then to open, rebellion. There were violent scenes, which often ended in the father giving him a good hiding, as Adolf told me himself. But Adolf matched this violence with his own youthful obstinacy, and the antagonism between father and son grew sharper.

51

The customs official, Alois Hitler, showed a marked sense of ceremony all his life. Consequently we have good pictures showing him at various stages of his life. Not so much at his weddings, which were always under an unlucky star, but at the various promotions in his career when he had his picture taken. Most of the pictures show him, with his dignified civil servant's face, in gala uniform of white trousers and dark tunic, on which the double row of highly polished buttons gleamed. The man's face is impressive with a broad, massive head, the most notable feature being the side-whiskers, modelled on those of his supreme master, the Emperor. The expression of the eyes is penetrating and incorruptible, the eyes of a man who, as a customs official, is obliged to view everything with suspicion. But in most pictures dignity prevails over the 'inquisitiveness' of the gaze. Even the pictures taken at the time when Alois Hitler had already retired, show that this man was, in spirit, still on duty. Although he was past sixty he did not show any of the typical signs of age. One of the pictures, probably the last one, which can also be seen on his grave at Leonding, shows Alois Hitler as a man whose life consisted of service and duty. To be sure there is also an earlier photograph, dating from his Leonding days which, emphasising his private life, depicts him as a comfortable well-to-do citizen, fond of good living.

Alois Hitler's rise from the illegitimate son of a poor servant girl to the position of a respected civil servant is the path from insignificance and inferior status to the highest rank open to him in the service of the state.

In *Mein Kampf*, Hitler wrote of his father:

> As the son of a poor, small trader he had never thought of following in his father's footsteps. When still only thirteen, he left the Waldviertel and, ignoring the advice of 'worldly' villagers, made his way to Vienna to learn a craft. That was in the 1850s. It must have been a desperate decision to set out for the unknown with just three guides for upkeep. By the age of seventeen he had served his apprenticeship but this gave him no satisfaction, rather the opposite. The long period of poverty and unending misery gave him a resolve to look for something 'higher'. Where once the village priest had seemed to the poor to be the incarnation of the highest possible achievement, in the capital this role was filled by the civil servant. With the tenacity of a boy 'grown old' in late childhood, the seventeen-year-old immersed himself in his new endeavour – and became a civil servant. I think it took him

twenty-three years before he had met the conditions he had laid down for his return – he had sworn never to go back to the village until he had 'made something of himself'. He was pensioned off by decree on 25 June 1895 at the age of fifty-eight after nearly forty years of uninterrupted service.

His colleagues in the customs service describe him as a precise, dutiful official who was very strict and had his 'weak spots'. As a superior Alois Hitler was not very popular. Out of office he was considered a liberal-minded man who did not conceal his convictions. He was very proud of his rank. Every day he would pay his morning visit to the inn with an official's punctuality. His regular drinking companions found him good company but he could flare up over trifles and become rude, displaying both his inborn violence and the sternness that he had acquired in his job.

Outwardly the father's civil service career had been no different from that of thousands of others who worked within the discipline of the Austro-Hungarian customs service, but when the private side is looked at, another picture emerges. *Mein Kampf* was a political tome and not an autobiography, and in it Adolf Hitler said only as much about himself as seemed appropriate for the political purposes of the book. Understandably he might wish to gloss over the fact that he was a child of his father's third marriage; that his father was illegitimate; that his mother was a niece once removed of his father; that he was the progeny of inbreeding; that he was not the first born but the fourth child of his parents; and was one of two survivors of six siblings.

The illegitimate birth of Alois Hitler is conclusively proved by the church register of the Strones parish, according to which the 42-year-old servant maid Anna Maria Schicklgruber gave birth to a son on 7 July 1837 christened Alois. The godfather was her employer, the peasant Johann Trummelschlager, in Strones. As far as is known the child was her first and only one. The identity of the father was not revealed by the mother.

Anna Maria Schicklgruber married the mill worker Johann Georg Hiedler in 1842 when the illegitimate child was already five years old. The Döllersheim church register contains the following entry:

> The undersigned hereby confirm that Georg Johann Hiedler [*sic*], who is well known to the undersigned witnesses, has acknowledged paternity of the child Alois of Anna Maria Schicklgruber and requests that his name be entered in the baptismal register.

The entry is signed by the parish priest and four witnesses.

Johann Georg Hiedler again acknowledged his paternity in an official document concerning some inheritance in 1876 before the notary in Weitra. He was then eighty-four years old, the child's mother had been dead for over thirty years and Alois Schicklgruber himself had been a customs official in Braunau for many years.

As the boy was not officially adopted after his mother's wedding, his name remained Schicklgruber. He would have kept this name throughout his life had not Johann Nepomuk Hiedler, Johann Georg's younger brother, made a will and left a modest sum to the illegitimate son of his brother. But he made it a condition that Alois should assume the surname Hiedler, and on 4 June 1876 the name Alois Schicklgruber in the Döllersheim parish register was altered to Alois Hiedler; the local government authority in Mistelbach ratifying this alteration on 6 January 1877. From now on Alois Schicklgruber called himself Alois Hitler, a name which meant as little as the other, but which secured him his legacy.

Once when we were talking about his relatives Adolf told me the story of his father's change of names. Nothing the 'old man' ever did pleased him as much as this, for Schicklgruber seemed to him so uncouth, so boorish, apart from being so clumsy and unpractical. He found 'Hiedler' too boring, too soft; but 'Hitler' had a good ring to it and was easy to remember.

It is typical of his father that instead of accepting the version 'Hiedler' as did the rest of his relations, he invented the new spelling 'Hitler'. It was in keeping with his mania for ceaseless change. His superiors had nothing to do with this, for in all his forty years of service he was transferred only four times. The towns to which he was posted, Saalfelden, Braunau, Passau and Linz, were so favourably situated that they formed the ideal setting for a customs official's career. But hardly had he settled down in one of these places than he began to move house. During his period of service in Braunau there are recorded twelve changes of address; probably there were more. During the two years in Passau he moved house twice. Soon after his retirement he moved from Linz to Hafeld, from there to Lambach – first in the Leingarner Inn, then to the mill of the Schweigbach forge, that is to say two changes in one year – then to Leonding. When I first met Adolf he remembered seven removals and had been to five different schools. It would not be true to say that these constant changes were due to bad housing conditions. Surely the Pommer Inn – Alois Hitler was very fond of living in inns – where Adolf was born was one of the finest and most presentable buildings in the whole of Braunau. Nevertheless, the father left there soon after Adolf's birth. Actually he often moved from a decent dwelling into a poorer one. The house was not the important thing, but the moving. How can one explain this strange mania?

Perhaps Alois Hitler simply hated to remain in one spot, and as his service forced on him a certain stability, he at least wanted some change in his own sphere. As soon as he had got used to certain surroundings, he grew weary of them. To live meant to change one's conditions, a trait which I experienced in Adolf too.

Three times Alois remodelled his family. It is perhaps true that this was due to outside circumstances. But if so, certainly fate played strangely into his hands. We know that his first wife, Anna, suffered very much from his restlessness, which eventually led to their separation and was partly responsible for her unexpected death. For while his first wife was still alive, Alois Hitler already had a child by the woman who became his second wife. And again when his second wife fell gravely ill and died, Klara, the third wife, was already expecting his child. Just sufficient time elapsed for the child to be born in wedlock. Alois Hitler was not an easy husband. Even more than from Frau Hitler's occasional hints, could one gather this from her weary, drawn face. This lack of inner harmony was perhaps partly due to the fact that Alois Hitler never married a woman his own age. Anna was 14 years older, Franziska 24 years younger, and Klara 23 years younger.

This strange and unusual habit of the father's, always to change his circumstances, is all the more remarkable as those were peaceful, comfortable times without any justification for such change. I see in the father's character an explanation of the strange behaviour of the son, whose constant restlessness puzzled me for so long. When Adolf and I strolled through the familiar streets of the good, old town – all peace, quiet and harmony – my friend would sometimes be taken by a certain mood and begin to change everything he saw. That house there was in a wrong position; it would have to be demolished. There was an empty plot which could be built up instead. That street needed a correction in order to give a more compact impression. Away with this horrible, completely bungled tenement block! Let's have a free vista to the castle. Thus he was always rebuilding the town. But it was not only a matter of building. A beggar, standing before the church, would be an occasion for him to hold forth on the need for a state scheme for the old, which would do away with begging. A peasant woman coming along with her milk cart drawn by a miserable dog – occasion to criticise the society for the prevention of cruelty to animals for their lack of initiative. Two young lieutenants sauntering through the streets, their sabres proudly clanking, sufficient reason for him to inveigh against the shortcomings of a military service which permitted such idleness. This inclination to be dissatisfied with things as they were, always to change and improve them, was ineradicable in him.

And this was by no means a peculiarity which he had acquired through external influences, by his upbringing at home or at school, but an innate quality which was also apparent in his father's unsettled character. It was a supernatural force, comparable to a motor driving a thousand wheels.

Nevertheless, father and son were affected by this quality in different ways. The father's unruly nature was bridled by one steadying factor – his position. The discipline of his office gave his volatile character purpose and direction. Again and again he was saved from complications by the hard exigencies of his duties.

The uniform of the customs official served as a cover for anything that may have gone on in the stormy sphere of his private life. In particular, being in the service, he unreservedly accepted the authority on which the service was built. Although Alois Hitler was inclined to liberal views – which was not uncommon in the Austrian civil service – he would never have questioned the authority of the state, symbolised in the person of the Emperor. By fully submitting to this accepted authority, Alois Hitler was able to steer safely through all the dangerous reefs and sandbanks of his life on which otherwise he might have foundered.

This also throws a different light on his obstinate efforts to make a civil servant of Adolf. It was for him more than a father's usual preoccupation for his son's future. His purpose was rather to direct his son into a position which necessitated submission to authority. It is quite possible that the father himself did not realise the inner reason for his attitude. But his determination in insisting on his point of view shows that he must have felt how much was at stake for his son. So well did he know him.

But with equal determination Adolf refused to comply with his father's wishes, although he himself had only very hazy ideas about his future. To become a painter would have been the worst possible insult to his father, for it would have meant just that aimless wandering to which he (the father) was so much opposed.

With his refusal to enter the civil service Adolf Hitler's path diverged sharply from that of his father; it took a different course, final and irrevocable. It was, indeed, the great decision of his life. The years that followed it I spent at his side. I could observe how earnestly he tried to find the right path for his future, not merely a job that would provide a livelihood, but real tasks for which his talents were fitted.

Shortly before his death, his father had taken the thirteen-year-old Adolf to the Linz customs office in the vain hope of showing his son his future work environment. At heart, beyond the stubborn refusal to follow his father's career, stood Adolf's rejection of the existing state's authority and therefore that power which was absolute in the eyes of the father. The path beyond it led into the unknown and ended with Adolf Hitler becoming the embodiment of all state authority in a country whose soil was not his own. It seems as if the dual qualities which shaped his character, the remorseless march down one path on the one hand, and the mania to change the existing order on the other, are contradictory. But they were really complementary. Although he brought everything around him into a state of flux, he remained in the eye of the whirlwind, unchanged.

Alois Hitler died suddenly. On 3 January 1903 – he was sixty-five and still strong and active – he went, as usual, punctually at ten o'clock in the morning to have his drink. Without warning he collapsed in his chair. Before a doctor or priest could be called, he was dead.

When the fourteen-year-old son saw his dead father he burst out in uncontrollable weeping, proof that Adolf's feelings for his father went much deeper than is commonly assumed.

Chapter 6

# Adolf's Schooldays

When I first met Adolf Hitler he had already abandoned his education. Actually he was still attending the Realschule at Steyr, from where he made visits home on Sundays, but it was only for his mother's sake that he had agreed to undertake this 'last ditch effort' to make something of his schooldays.

From school sources there is abundant authentic material describing his school performance. In primary school he was always near the top of the class. He learnt quickly and made good progress without much effort. His schooling, as I was once briefly informed, was as follows:

**Fischlham bei Lambach, age 6, single-class primary school, started 2 May 1895**

Teacher Karl Mittermaier gave him a report full of grade As. Mittermaier was still alive in 1938 and, when asked for his recollections of his former pupil, said that he remembered the pale, weakly little boy brought to school every day from Hafeld by his twelve-year-old half-sister Angela; little Adolf did as he was told and kept his things tidy, otherwise he had nothing to add. In 1939, as Reich Chancellor, when Hitler revisited the single-class school he sat at the same desk where he had learned to read and write. Of course, he had to change everything, and so bought the old, well-maintained schoolhouse and ordered a new building to be erected there. The lady teacher who had taken over from old Mittermaier was invited to visit Obersalzberg with her class.

**1895–6 Lower form, above school, Hafeld**

**1896–8 Volksschule, Lambach, Forms 2 and 3**

At Lambach, too, Hitler received all grade As from teacher Franz Rechberger. He also sang in the boys' choir at the monastery.

**1898–1900 Volksschule, Leonding, Forms 4 and 5**

Teachers Sixtl and Brauneis could think of nothing exceptional to say when asked, and could give no background information, although Sixtl remembered that in history and geography Adolf Hitler knew more than many teachers did.

## 1900–1 Austro-Hungarian State Realschule, Steingasse, Linz.

## Form 1

Things changed for the worse once Hitler began his secondary education. In *Mein Kampf* he said of those years: 'My manifest failure at school was assured from the outset. What I liked I learnt, this was in the main that which I thought would be useful for a painter. Whatever looked irrelevant or did not appeal to me I sabotaged completely. My school reports of the period varied from "praiseworthy" and "outstanding" down to "satis-factory" and "unsatisfactory". My best subjects were geography and world history. These were my favourite subjects, in which I led the class.'

On the basis of this self-portrait one may obtain a false picture about his schooldays. Although he spoke of them reluctantly, and with irritation, nevertheless our friendship lay to a certain extent in their shadow. Thus the impression I gained at the time differs from what he represented in his book fifteen years later.

At first the eleven-year-old boy found it very difficult to merge into the unaccustomed surroundings. Each day he had to make the long journey from Leonding in the town to the Realschule in the outlying Steingasse. He told me often, when we used to wander up to the old fortress tower on a high point about halfway between Linz and the school, that the trek was the most wonderful thing about those years. It took him more than an hour to walk it and gave him a sense of freedom which he treasured.

His classmates, mostly from solid, good-class Linz families, cold-shouldered the strange boy who arrived daily 'from amongst the peasants', and the professors took only that measure of interest in him that the school curriculum demanded. This differed greatly from primary school with its sympathetic staff who knew each child quite intimately and spent the evenings with the fathers over a drink at the inn. In primary school, Hitler had strolled through the school year without any appreciable effort. Initially at secondary school he tried to get through by improvisation. This was necessary because he did not like having to learn those things which the professors considered important, but his usual twists and turns could not serve him here. Accordingly he withdrew into his shell and let the waters wash over him.

In class he rarely came to anybody's notice. He had no friends, contrary to primary school, and wanted none. Occasionally one of the class snobs would let him know that 'boys coming up from the town' were not really suitable for the Realschule. That encouraged him to isolate himself even more from the other pupils. It is noteworthy that no single classmate from this period ever claimed to have established any kind of intimacy or friendship with him, not even long afterwards.

Headmaster Hans Commenda, who taught the first form mathematics, gave Hitler an 'unsatisfactory', as did the natural history master Max Engstler, feared by everyone. Thus did Realschule-schoolboy Hitler end his first year with two 'unsatisfactory' categories with the result that he had to re-sit the year. Adolf never told me what his father's reaction was, but I can easily imagine it.

### 1901–2 Realschule, Linz, repeated Class 1

Thus he had to start all over again. His form-master was now Professor Eduard Huemer, who taught German and French, this latter being the only language which Adolf took up, or rather was forced to take up. But here at least he acclimatised somewhat, re-sat Class 1 and passed.

### 1902–3 Realschule Linz, Class 2

He got through this year with difficulty, and again his father was obliged to sign a school report in which mathematics was 'unsatisfactory': Adolf had not been taught in this subject by Professor Heinrich Drasch before, and so he could not argue that his poor grade was a rebellion against the teacher. He hated mathematics because it was too dry and required systematic application. We often discussed it. In Vienna, Hitler realised he would need mathematics if he wanted to be an architect, but he was unable to overcome his inner dislike of the subject.

### 1903–4 Realschule Linz, Class 3

Class 3 finished with two 'unsatisfactory' grades, mathematics and German, even though later he placed Professor Huemer amongst the three teachers for whom he had some regard. In this year his father died. Professor Huemer made it clear to Frau Hitler that the boy could only progress to Class 4 by transferring to an outlying Realschule. It is therefore not true to say that he was expelled from the Realschule at Linz; he was merely 'farmed out'.

### 1904–5 Realschule Steyr, Class 4; autumn 1905 repeated school-leaving certificate

Hitler himself was outraged at his treatment. He was determined that his final year at Steyr would fail; he decided that he had had quite enough of school and was convinced that it no longer served his purpose. What he lacked in knowledge he would make up with self-tuition. Art had long had a place in his life; with youthful passion he was convinced that he was called to be an artist. In contrast to art, the school machine was grey and monotonous. He wanted to be free of all compulsion and forge ahead on his own. He despised his contemporaries who were unable to do the same. What the uninteresting acquaintances of the Realschule classrooms had denied him he now expected from his friend.

Whereas it had been his father's orders that kept him at school previously, now it was his love for his mother which kept him at his studies. He was at Steyr under protest, and after reading Dante's *Divine Comedy* labelled the school 'The Place of the Damned'. At Steyr, Hitler lodged at the house of a court official, Edler von Cichini at Grünmarkt 19, but returned to Linz whenever the opportunity presented itself. The outcome was bad, and he achieved nothing more by re-sitting the school-leaving certificate between 1 and 15 September 1905, acquiring an extra 'unsatisfactory' in geometry to go with his customary 'unsatisfactory' in mathematics.

Another, more substantial struggle ran parallel with the constant skirmishing with the professors: the spiritual conflict with his mother. The fact is, as I myself observed, that Adolf tried as far as he could to spare her, she who was the whole world to him, but it became impossible once his failure was definitive and he departed from the career path which his father had anticipated for him. He was unable to convince her why he had to follow another, unsignposted, road to his future profession. What his bad reports meant for Adolf we cannot be sure but they demonstrated to his mother that he would not matriculate. What the 'other road' he had chosen might be he was not even certain himself, and he remained uncertain for many years after her death. Thus she took her major concerns about her son's future with her to the grave.

In that dark autumn of 1905, things were on a knife edge for Adolf. Outwardly, the decision which he had to face was whether to re-sit Class 4 at the Steyr Realschule, or abandon formal education altogether, but in reality he had to decide between continuing, for his mother's sake, on a path he held false and purposeless, or accept that he must strike her a hard blow and choose 'the other way' of which all he could say was that it led to art. All things being equal, there was no decision in the real sense because he had already elected to leave school and follow the second path. So far as his mother was concerned, I know that it tore him apart.

Adolf survived a severe crisis in those autumn months of 1905, the worst in my experience of our friendship. This found its outward expression in a serious illness. In *Mein Kampf* he talks of a respiratory disease. His sister Paula described it as a haemorrhage; others maintain the problem was in his stomach. I went nearly every day to visit his bedside in the Humboldt-strasse, mainly because I had to keep him informed about Stefanie. To the best of my recollection it was a pulmonary infection, probably pneumonia. I know that long afterwards he used to cough a lot, and bring up matter from his chest, especially when the weather was damp and misty.

It was on account of this malady that his mother absolved him of the responsibility of attending school, and in that respect it was a rather timely illness. It is impossible to say whether he exaggerated the symptoms, whether it was to some degree psychosomatic or he was predisposed to suffer the condition. When at last he arose from his sick bed he had long since got things straight in his mind. His schooldays were behind him, and without the least doubt or compunction he had set his sights on a career as an artist.

There now followed two years without an apparent goal. 'In the hollowness of the empty life' he describes this phase with some discomfort in *Mein Kampf*. It is a good description. He no longer attended school; did nothing to get himself job training; lived with his mother and let her keep him. But he was not idle: this period of his life was filled with restless activity. He sketched, he painted, he wrote poetry, he read. I cannot remember a time when he had nothing to do or was bored. If it happened that he did not like a performance we went to he would leave and throw himself with great zeal into some activity or other. Admittedly it was difficult to see what system there was in it, for no objective or clear goal was apparent; he just accumulated impressions, experiences and material around himself. The purpose of it all was never explained to me. He just searched, everywhere, constantly.

In this manner, however, Adolf found a way to prove to his mother that schooling had no useful end – 'one can learn so much more by oneself' he explained to her. He joined the People's Educative Society bookshop in the Bismarckstrasse, also the Museal Society so as to be able to borrow their books. And he frequented the lending library of the Steurer and L. Hasslinger book companies. From this time on I remember Adolf as always surrounded by piles of books, in particular by the numerous volumes of his favourite work *Die Deutschen Heldensage* – 'The Sagas of the German Heroes' – which he was never without. How often he asked me, as soon as I came home from the noisy upholstery machinery, to study this or that book so that he could discuss it with me. Suddenly, everything he had lacked at school –

industry, interest, joy in learning – returned. As he boasted, he had overcome school with its own weapons.

At Adolf Hitler's trial for high treason following the failed putsch attempt of 1923, Professor Huemer, his form master at Linz Realschule for three full years, appeared as a character witness. He deposed:

> (As a schoolboy), Hitler was undoubtedly gifted, if in a one-sided way. He had little in the way of self-discipline, and since he insisted on swimming against the current as well as being arbitrary, egotistical and irascible, he would obviously have struggled to fit into a school framework. He was also lazy, for otherwise with his undoubted capacity he would have achieved far better results.

At the end of this adverse opinion, Professor Huemer spoke from the heart and added:

> All the same, as experience teaches us, our schooldays do not provide us with much useful for life itself, and while the rising stars often disappear without trace, school grades do not mean much until one has sufficient elbow room. It seems to me that my former pupil Hitler fits into this latter category, and from the heart I wish that he soon recovers from the tension and excitement of recent events and yet still experiences the fulfillment of those ideals which he cherishes in his breast, and which would do honour to every German.

These words, written in 1924, are free of any 'political' praise which might have tainted them post-1933. They indicate a striking solidarity between teacher and former pupil. There is a hint in what Professor Huemer says that the ideals, as a result of which Adolf Hitler was indicted, originated in his schooling. Hitler was not a good pupil even in the German classes of Professor Huemer, as the grammatical errors to be found in the letters and postcards he sent me prove.

Another of the teachers judged positive by Hitler, on the basis of their political opinions rather than their scholarship, was natural history master Theodor Gissinger, who had replaced Professor Engstler. Gissinger was a great enthusiast for the outdoors who loved long rambles and mountain climbing. He was the most radical of the teachers in the nationalist camp. The political divisions of the time revealed themselves more acutely within the teaching staff than in public. This atmosphere, charged with political tensions, was more decisive for Hitler's mental development than the school curriculum; so, it appears, the atmosphere rather than the teaching materials determines the worth or otherwise of the school. Professor Gissinger wrote in retrospect of his former pupil:

> At Linz, Hitler made neither a good nor a bad impression on me. He was also not a leader in class. He was slim and upright, his face mostly pale and gaunt, and there was almost a consumptive look about him, his gaze enormously open, his eyes luminous.

The third and last of his teachers judged as 'positive' by Hitler was professor of history Dr Leopold Pötsch, the only one of almost a dozen teachers of whom he admitted admiration at the time. The words which he devoted to this man in *Mein Kampf* are well known:

> It was perhaps decisive for my whole later life that fate gave me as my history teacher one of the very few who knew how to get across the important things in class and examinations, and to dismiss the unimportant. In my history professor Dr Leopold Pötsch at the Linz Realschule, this necessity was incorporated in the ideal manner. An aged gentleman of kindly but determined manner, he succeeded especially by his gift of radiant eloquence, leaving us not only spellbound, but also enthusiastic. Even today I remember with emotion the greying man who could make us forget the present with the fire of his presentation, charm us back through past ages and, in the mists of the centuries, give living reality to things of dry historical memory. We used to sit, often overcome, sometimes even moved to tears.

Leopold Pötsch is the only personality mentioned by name in *Mein Kampf*, and Hitler devotes two and a half pages to him. Such devotion is surely exaggerated, and the proof thereof is that Hitler finished his school career with only a 'satisfactory' in history, which was perhaps partly attributable to the changes of school. Even so, one should not under-estimate the impression this professor made on a very receptive young mind, and if one says that the most valuable adjunct to the study of history is the enthusiasm which the subject breeds, then Dr Pötsch certainly fulfilled his mission in this particular case.

Pötsch came from the Austrian southern borderland and before arriving at Linz had taught at Marburg an der Drau (in present-day Yugoslavia)* and

---

* Now Maribor in Slovenia.

other localities on the linguistic divide. He therefore brought a lively experience to the racial battle. I believe that that unconditional love for the German-speaking peoples, which Pötsch combined with his contempt for the Habsburg state, was decisive in winning over young Hitler. Hitler remained eternally grateful to his old history teacher, and this gratefulness tended to grow in size the longer was the time since Hitler's departure from education. On his 1938 visit to Klagenfurt, Hitler met Pötsch again, in retirement at St Andrä in Lavantthal, spending an hour with him alone. There were no witnesses to the conversation, but when Hitler left the room, he told his escort, 'You have no idea what I owe to that old man.'*

To what extent these opinions held by Hitler with regard to his former professors can be relied upon is as open a question as that of the contradictory opinions about Hitler by his former classmates. The fact is, however, and I am a witness to it, that Adolf gave up school loathing it. Though I always took care to steer any conversation away from the subject of his schooldays, he now and again he would fire off a violent broadside. He made no attempt to remain in contact with any of the teachers, not even Professor Pötsch – on the contrary! He avoided them, and ignored them when they came face to face in the street.

---

* Following the conclusion of the Greek/Yugoslav campaign, Hitler again visited Pötsch at Klagenfurt on 27 April 1941. See Seidler and Zeigert, *Die Führerhauptquartiere*, Herbig 2000, p. 134. [Ed.]

# Chapter 7

# Stefanie

To tell the truth, it is not very agreeable to be the only witness – apart from Stefanie herself – who can tell of my friend's youthful love, which lasted four years from the beginning of his sixteenth year. I fear that by giving a picture of the actual facts, I shall disappoint those who are expecting sensational disclosures. Adolf's relations with this girl from a much-respected family were confined to those permitted by the prevailing code of morals and were absolutely normal, unless today's conception of sexual morality is so upside-down that one considers it abnormal if two young people, as these were, have an affair and – to put it briefly – 'nothing happens'.

I must ask to be excused from mentioning this girl's surname as well as her later married name. Occasionally I have revealed it to persons engaged in research on Hitler's youth, who had satisfied me as to their bona fides. Stefanie, who was one, or perhaps, two years older than Adolf, later married a high-ranking officer and lived after the Second World War as a widow in Vienna. The reader will, therefore, understand my discretion.

One evening in the spring of 1905, as we were making our usual stroll, Adolf gripped my arm and asked me excitedly what I thought of that slim, blonde girl walking along the Landstrasse arm-in-arm with her mother. 'You must know, I'm in love with her,' he added resolutely.

Stefanie was a distinguished-looking girl, tall and slim. She had thick, fair hair which she mostly wore taken back in a bun. Her eyes were very beautiful – bright and expressive. She was exceptionally well-dressed and her bearing indicated that she came from a good, well-to-do family.

The photograph by Hans Zivny, taken in Urfahr, on her leaving school was somewhat earlier than this meeting and Stefanie could only have been then seventeen or, at the most, eighteen years old. It shows a young girl with pretty, regular features. The expression of the face is completely natural and open. The abundant hair, still worn in the Gretel fashion, serves to strengthen this impression. A freshness and lack of affectation show in the girl's healthy countenance.

The evening stroll along the Landstrasse was, in those years, a favourite habit with the Linzers. The ladies looked at the shop windows and made little purchases. Friends met, and the younger generation amused themselves in innocent ways. There was a lot of flirting and the young Army officers were particularly good at it. It seemed to us that Stefanie must live in Urfahr, for she always came from the bridge up the main square, and strolled down the Landstrasse arm-in-arm with her mother. At five o'clock, almost precisely, mother and daughter appeared – we stood waiting at the Schmiedtoreck. It would have been improper to salute Stefanie, as neither of us had been introduced to the young lady. A glance had to take the place of a greeting. From then on, Adolf did not take his eyes off Stefanie. In that moment he was changed, no longer his own self.

I found out that Stefanie's mother was a widow and did, indeed, live in Urfahr, and that the young man who occasionally accompanied them, to Adolf's great irritation, was her brother, a law student in Vienna. This information eased Adolf's mind considerably. But from time to time the two ladies were to be seen in the company of young officers. Poor, pallid youngsters like Adolf naturally could not hope to compete with these young lieutenants in their smart uniforms. Adolf felt this intensely and gave vent to his feelings with eloquence. His anger, in the end, led him into uncompromising enmity towards the officer class as a whole, and everything military in general. 'Conceited blockheads', he used to call them. It annoyed him immensely that Stefanie mixed with such idlers who, he insisted, wore corsets and used scent.

To be sure, Stefanie had no idea how deeply Adolf was in love with her; she regarded him as a somewhat shy but, nevertheless, remarkably tenacious and faithful admirer. When she responded with a smile to his enquiring glance, he was happy and his mood became unlike anything I had ever observed in him; everything in the world was good and beautiful and well-ordered, and he was content. But when Stefanie, as happened just as often, coldly ignored his gaze, he was crushed and ready to destroy himself and the whole world.

Certainly such phenomena are typical of every first great love, and one might perhaps be tempted to dismiss Adolf's feelings for Stefanie as calf love. This may have been true as far as Stefanie's own conception of them was concerned. But for Adolf himself, his relation to Stefanie was more than calf love. The mere fact that it lasted more than four years, and even cast its splendour over the subsequent years of misery in Vienna, shows that Adolf's feelings were deep, true and real love. Proof of the depth of his feelings is that for Adolf, throughout these years, no other woman but Stefanie existed – how unlike the usual boy's love, which is always changing its object. I cannot remember that Adolf ever gave any thought to another girl. For him, Stefanie embodied the whole of femininity. Later, in Vienna, when Lucie Weidt roused his enthusiasm in the part of Elsa in *Lohengrin*, the highest praise he could give her was that she reminded him of Stefanie. In appearance, Stefanie was ideally suited for the part of Elsa, and other female roles of Wagner's operas, and we spent much time wondering whether she had the necessary voice and musical talent. Adolf was inclined to take it for granted. Just her Valkyrie-like appearance never failed to attract him and to fire him with unbounded enthusiasm. He wrote countless love-poems to Stefanie. *Hymn to the Beloved* was the title of one of them, which he read to me from his little black notebook: Stefanie, a high-born damsel, in a dark-blue, flowing velvet gown, rode on a white steed over the flowering meadows, her loose hair fell in golden waves on her shoulders; a clear spring sky was above; everything was pure, radiant joy. I can still see Adolf's face glowing with fervent ecstasy and hear his voice reciting these verses. Stefanie filled his thoughts so completely that everything he said, or did, or planned for the future, was centred around her. With this growing estrangement from his home, Stefanie gained more and more influence over my friend, although he never spoke a word to her.

My ideas about these things were much more prosaic, and I remember very well our repeated arguments on the subject – and my recollections of Adolf's relationship to Stefanie are particularly distinct. He used to insist that, once he met Stefanie, everything would become clear without as much as a word being exchanged. For such exceptional human beings as himself and Stefanie, he said, there was no need for the usual communication by word of mouth; extraordinary human beings would understand each other by intuition. Whatever the subject we might discuss at any time, Adolf was always sure that Stefanie not only knew his ideas exactly, but that she shared them enthusiastically. If I dared to comment that he had not spoken to Stefanie about them, and to express my doubts as to whether she was at all interested in such things, he became furious and shouted at me: 'You simply don't understand, because you can't understand the true meaning of extraordinary love.' In order to quieten him down, I asked him if he could transmit to Stefanie the knowledge of such complicated problems simply by gazing at her. He only replied, 'It's possible! These things cannot be explained. What is in me, is in Stefanie too.' Of course, I took great care not to push these delicate matters too far. But I was pleased that Adolf trusted me so much, for to nobody else, not even to his mother, had he talked about Stefanie.

He expected Stefanie to reciprocate his love for her to the exclusion of all others. For a long time he put up with the interest she took in other young men, especially the officers, because he regarded it as a sort of deliberate diversion to conceal her own tempestuous feelings for him. But this attitude often gave way to fits of raging jealousy; then Adolf would be desperate when Stefanie ignored the pale youth who was waiting for her, and concentrated her attention instead on the young lieutenant escorting her. Why, indeed, should a lively young girl have been satisfied with the anxious glances of a secret admirer, whilst others expressed their admiration so much more gracefully? But I, of course, would never have dared to express such a thought in Adolf's presence.

One day he asked me, 'What shall I do?' Never before had he asked for my advice and I was extremely proud that he did; at last, for a change, I could feel superior to him. 'It's quite simple,' I explained. 'You approach the two ladies and, raising your hat, introduce yourself to the mother by giving your name, and ask her permission to address the daughter and escort them.'

Adolf looked at me doubtfully and pondered my suggestion for quite a while. In the end, however, he rejected it. 'What am I to say if the mother wants to know my profession? After all, I have to mention my profession straight away; it would be best to add it to my name – "Adolf Hitler, academic painter" or something similar. But I am not yet an academic painter, and I can't introduce myself until I am. For the mama, the profession is even more important than the name.'

I thought, for a long time, that Adolf was simply too shy to approach Stefanie. And yet, it was not shyness that held him back. His conception of the relationship between the sexes was already then so high that the usual way of making the acquaintance of a girl seemed to him undignified. As he was opposed to flirting in any form, he was convinced that Stefanie had no other desire but to wait until he should come to ask her to marry him. I did not share this conviction at all, but Adolf, as was his habit with all problems that agitated him, had already made an elaborate plan. And this girl, who was a stranger to him and had never exchanged a word with him, succeeded where his father, the school and even his mother had failed: he drew up an exact programme for his future which would enable him, after four years, to ask for Stefanie's hand.

We discussed this difficult problem for hours, with the result that Adolf commissioned me to collect further information about Stefanie.

In the Music Society there was a cellist whom I had occasionally seen talking to Stefanie's brother. Through him I learned that Stefanie's father, a higher government official, had died some years earlier. The mother had a comfortable home and was in receipt of a widow's pension, which she used to give her two children the best possible education. Stefanie had attended the girls' high school and had already matriculated. She had a great number of admirers – small wonder, beautiful as she was. She was fond of dancing and, the previous winter, had gone with her mother to all the important dances of the town. As far as he knew, the cellist added, she was not engaged.

Adolf was highly satisfied with the result of my investigations – that she was not engaged he had, anyhow, taken for granted. There was only one point in my report that disturbed him greatly: Stefanie danced, and according to the cellist's assurance, she danced well, and enjoyed it. This did not fit at all into Adolf's own image of Stefanie. A Valkyrie who waltzed round the ballroom in the arms of some 'blockhead' of a lieutenant was, for him, too terrible to be contemplated.

What was the origin of this strange, almost ascetic trait in him which made him reject all the pleasures of youth? Adolf's father, after all, had been a man who enjoyed life and who, as a good-looking customs official, had certainly turned many a girl's head. Why was Adolf so different? After all, he was a most presentable young man, well-built, slender, and his somewhat severe and exaggeratedly serious features were enlivened by his extraordinary eyes, whose peculiar brilliance made one forget the sickly pallor of his face. And yet – dancing was as contrary to his nature as smoking or drinking beer in a bar. These things simply did not exist for him, although nobody, not even his mother, encouraged him in this attitude.

After having been his butt for so long, at last I had a chance of pulling his leg. I proclaimed with a straight face, 'You must take dancing lessons, Adolf.' Dancing immediately became one of his problems. I well remember that our lonely perambulations were no longer punctuated by discussions on 'the theatre' or 'reconstruction of the bridge over the Danube' but were dominated by one subject – dancing.

As with everything that he couldn't tackle at once, he indulged in generalisations. 'Visualise a crowded ballroom', he said once to me, 'and imagine that you are deaf. You can't hear the music to which these people are moving, and then take a look at their senseless progress, which leads nowhere. Aren't these people raving mad?'

'All this is no good, Adolf,' I replied, 'Stefanie is fond of dancing. If you want to conquer her, you will have to dance around just as aimlessly and idiotically as the others.' That was all that was needed to set him off raving. 'No, no, never!' he screamed at me, 'I shall never dance! Do you understand! Stefanie only dances because she is forced to by society on which she unfortunately depends. Once she is my wife, she won't have the slightest desire to dance!'

Contrary to the rule, this time his own words did not convince him; for he brought up the question of dancing again and again. I rather suspected that, secretly at home, he practised a few cautious steps with his little sister. Frau Hitler had bought a piano for Adolf; perhaps, I thought, I might soon be asked to play a waltz on it, and then I would chaff Adolf about being deaf while he danced. He did not need music for his movements. I also intended to point out to him the harmony between music and bodily movements, of which he did not seem to have any conception.

But it never got as far as this. Adolf went on brooding for days and weeks, trying to find a solution. In his depressed mood, he hit on a crazy idea: he seriously contemplated kidnapping Stefanie. He expounded his plan to me in all its details and assigned me my role, which was not a very rewarding one, for I had to keep the mother engaged in conversation whilst he seized the girl. 'And what are you both going to live on?' I asked prosaically. My question sobered him up a little and the audacious plan was abandoned.

To make matters worse, Stefanie was, at that time, in an unfriendly mood. She would pass the Schmiedtoreck with her face averted, as though Adolf did not exist at all. This brought him to the verge of despair. 'I can't stand it any longer!' he exclaimed. 'I will make an end of it!'

It was the first and, as far as I know, the last time that Adolf contemplated suicide seriously. He would jump into the river from the Danube bridge, he told me, and then it would be over and done with. But Stefanie would have to die with him – he insisted on that. Once more a plan was thought up, in all its details. Every single phase of the horrifying tragedy was minutely described, including the part I would have to play; even my conduct as the sole survivor was ordained. This sombre scene was with me, even in my dreams.

But soon the sky was blue again and for Adolf came that happiest of days in June 1906, which I am sure remained in his memory as clearly as it did in mine. Summer was approaching and a flower festival was held in Linz. As usual, Adolf waited for me outside the Carmelite church, where I used to go every Sunday with my parents; then we took up our stand at the Schmiedtoreck. The position was extremely favourable, as the street here is narrow and the carriages in the festival parade had to pass quite close to the pavement. The regimental band led the string of flower-decked carriages, from which young girls and ladies waved to the spectators. But Adolf had neither eyes nor ears for any of this; he waited feverishly for Stefanie to appear. I was already giving up hope of seeing her, when Adolf gripped my arm so violently that it hurt. Seated in a handsome carriage, decorated with flowers, mother and daughter turned into the Schmiedtorstrasse. I still have the picture clearly in my mind. The mother, in a light grey silk dress, holds a red sunshade over her head, through which the rays of the sun seem to cast, as though by magic, a rosy glow over the countenance of Stefanie, wearing a pretty silk frock. Stefanie has adorned her carriage, not with roses as most of the others, but with simple, wild blossoms – red poppies, white marguerites and blue cornflowers. Stefanie holds a bunch of the same flowers in her hand. The carriage approaches – Adolf is floating on air. Never before has he seen Stefanie so enchanting. Now the carriage is quite close to us. A bright glance falls on Adolf. Stefanie sends him a beaming smile and, picking a flower from her posy, throws it to him.

Never again did I see Adolf as happy as he was at that moment. When the carriage had passed he dragged me aside and with emotion he gazed at the flower, this visible pledge of her love. I can still hear his voice, trembling with excitement, 'She loves me! You have seen! She loves me!'

During the following months, when his decision to leave school had caused conflict with his mother, and he was ill, his love for Stefanie was his only comfort and he always kept her flower in his locket. Adolf was never in greater need of my friendship, for as I was the only person who shared his secret, it was only through me that he could get news about her. I had to go every day to the usual spot at the Schmiedtoreck and to report to him all my observations and tell him, in particular, who had spoken to mother and daughter. That I stood alone at the familiar corner, Adolf felt, would naturally upset Stefanie immeasurably. It did not, but I kept it from him. Fortunately, it had never occurred to Adolf that I might fall in love with Stefanie, for the slightest suspicion in this respect would have meant the end of our friendship, and as there was no real reason for it, I was able to give my reports to my poor friend wholly disinterestedly.

Adolf's mother had been aware for a long time of the change in her son. One evening – I remember it well because it embarrassed me considerably – she asked me straight out: 'What's the matter with Adolf? He's so impatient to see you.' I muttered some excuse and hurried into Adolf's room.

He was happy when I brought him some new fact concerning Stefanie. 'She has a good soprano voice,' I told him one day. He jumped up. 'How do you know that?' 'I followed her very closely for some time and I heard her speak. I know enough music to be able to tell that somebody with such a clear and pure voice must be a good soprano.' How happy this made Adolf. And I was pleased that he, languishing in his bed, had a moment of happiness.

Every evening I had to get back to the Humboldtstrasse from the evening stroll by the quickest route. I would often find Adolf sketching a big blueprint. 'Now I have made up my mind,' he said in dead earnest, after having heard my report, 'I have decided to build the house for Stefanie in Renaissance style.' And then I had to give my opinion, especially as to whether I was satisfied with the shape and size of the music room. He had paid special attention to the acoustics of the room, he said, and he asked me to say where the piano should go, and so on and so on. All this in a manner as though there were not the slightest doubt that the plans would be carried out. A timid enquiry about the money brought forth the rude reply, 'Oh, to hell with the money!' – an expression which he frequently employed.

We had some arguments as to where this villa would be built; as a musician I was all for Italy. But Adolf insisted that it could only be built in Germany in the neighbourhood of a big city, so that he and Stefanie could go to the opera and concerts.

As soon as he could leave his bed, he went to town and took up his position at the Schmiedtoreck; he was still very pale and ill. Punctual as usual, Stefanie and her mother appeared. Seeing Adolf, pale-faced and hollow-eyed, she smiled at him. 'Did you notice?' he asked me happily. From that moment on, his health improved rapidly.

In spring 1906, when Adolf left for Vienna, he gave me detailed instructions how I should behave *vis-à-vis* Stefanie; for he was convinced that she would soon ask me whether my friend was ill again, as I was there alone. Then I was to answer as follows: 'My friend is not ill, but he had to go to Vienna to take up his studies at the Academy of Art. When his studies are finished he will spend a year travelling, abroad, of course.' (I insisted on being allowed to say 'in Italy'. 'Very well then, Italy.') 'In four years time he will return and ask for your hand in marriage. In case of an affirmative answer, the preparations for the wedding would be put in hand forthwith.'

Whilst Adolf was in Vienna, I naturally had to send him regular written reports about Stefanie. As it was cheaper to send postcards than letters, Adolf gave me a code word for Stefanie before he left. It was Benkieser, the name of a former classmate. A picture postcard which he sent me on 8 May from Vienna shows how much this Benkieser was still on his mind in spite of his many new and varied impressions in Vienna. 'I am longing to return to my beloved Linz and Urfahr,' it reads. The underlining alludes, of course, to Stefanie, who lived there. 'I have to see Benkieser again. I wonder what he's doing.'

A few weeks later Adolf returned from Vienna and I met him at the station. I still remember how we took turns carrying his bag and he urged me to tell him all about Stefanie at once. We were in a hurry because the evening stroll would begin in an hour's time. Adolf would not believe that Stefanie had not asked after him, for he took it for granted that she was longing for him just as much as he was for her. But, at heart, he was glad that I had not had the opportunity to tell Stefanie about his grandiose plans for the future, as his prospects at the moment were not very bright. We hardly stopped in the Humboldtstrasse to greet his mother before hurrying off to the Schmiedtoreck. Full of excitement, Adolf waited. Punctually Stefanie and her mother appeared. She threw him a surprised glance. That was sufficient – he did not want more. But I got impatient. 'You can see that she wants you to talk to her,' I said to my friend. 'Tomorrow,' he answered.

But the morrow never came, and weeks, months and years passed without his taking any steps to change this state of affairs which caused him so much unrest. It was natural that Stefanie did nothing beyond that first phase of exchanging glances. The most Adolf could have expected of her, was the flower, thrown at him with a roguish smile in the carefree atmosphere of the flower festival. Besides, any move of hers beyond the rigid limits of convention would have destroyed the picture of her which Adolf kept in his heart. Perhaps even this strange timidity was prompted by the fear that any closer acquaintance might destroy this ideal. For, to him, Stefanie was not only the incarnation of all womanly virtues, but also the woman who took the greatest interest in all his wide and varied plans. There was no other person, apart from himself, whom he credited with so much knowledge and so many interests. The slightest divergence from this picture would have filled him with unspeakable disappointment.

Of course, I am convinced the first words he exchanged with Stefanie would have caused that very disappointment, because she was fundamentally a young, happy girl, like thousands of others, and certainly had the same kind of interests. Adolf would have sought in vain for those grandiose thoughts and ideas which he had lent her to such an extent as to

74

make her the female image of himself. Only the most rigid separation could preserve his idol.

It is most revealing that the young Hitler, who so thoroughly despised bourgeois society, nevertheless, as far as his love affair was concerned, observed its codes and etiquette more strictly than many a member of the bourgeoisie itself. The rules of bourgeois conduct and etiquette became for him the barricade behind which he built up his relationship to Stefanie. 'I have not been introduced to her' – how often have I heard him say these words, although in the ordinary way he would make light of such obstacles. But this strict observance of social customs was part of his whole nature. It was apparent in his neat dress, and in his correct behaviour, as much as in his natural courtesy, which my mother liked so much about him. I have never heard him use an ambiguous expression or tell a doubtful story.

So, in spite of all apparent contradictions, this strange love of Hitler for Stefanie falls into the pattern of his character. Love was a field where the unforeseeable might happen, and which might become dangerous. How many men who had set out with great intentions had been forced off their path by irregular and complicated love affairs. It was imperative to be on one's guard!

Instinctively the young Hitler found the only correct attitude in his love for Stefanie: he possessed a being whom he loved, and at the same time, he did not possess her. He arranged his whole life as though he this beloved creature was already entirely his. But, as he himself avoided any personal meeting, this girl, although he could see that she walked the earth, remained a creature of his dream world, towards whom he could project his desires, plans and ideas. And thus he kept himself from deviating from his own path; indeed, this strange relationship, through the power of love, increased his own will. He imagined Stefanie as his wife, built the house in which they lived together, surrounded it with a magnificent garden and arranged his home with Stefanie, just as, in fact, he did later on the Obersalzberg, though without her. This mixing of dream and reality was characteristic of the young Hitler. And whenever there was a danger that the beloved would entirely escape into the realm of fantasy, he hurried to the Schmiedtoreck and made sure that she really walked the earth. Hitler was confirmed in the choice of his path, not by what Stefanie actually was, but by what his imagination made of her. Thus, Stefanie was two things for him, one part reality and one part wish and imagination. Be that as it may, Stefanie was the most beautiful, the most fertile and purest dream of his life.

Chapter 8

# Enthusiasm for Richard Wagner

I have paired deliberately the chapters about Hitler's first amour and his passionate enthusiasm for Richard Wagner. They belong together, because Stefanie embodied for Hitler all femininity in one ideal female – this determined the path he would follow for many years; Richard Wagner, the man as well as his work, embodied what German art signified. Stefanie could never have fulfilled the role his ideas and aspirations demanded had she not, by her appearance, conduct and bearing, been the equal of that female ideal represented by Richard Wagner in his great musical dramas. Hitler saw his love as Elsa, as Brünhilde, as Eva of the *Meistersinger*; in a sense she was a creation of the inspired master himself, and had descended as preordained from Wagner's dream world into reality.

The relationship of Hitler to Stefanie was an aspect of his fascination for Wagner. Looked at from another angle, from the first moment he saw Stefanie, his feelings towards Richard Wagner became a true passion, but not until his love for the girl blossomed did his artistic sensibilities extend to devotion. The fact that this love was one-sided and was never seriously returned, and therefore unrequited, drove him ever more forcefully towards the great master in whose work he could find that comfort and consolation which his bitter-sweet love denied him. From his earliest youth until death, Hitler remained loyal to the man from Bayreuth. Just as Stefanie in the course of this strange romance, which was no such thing in the usually understood concept of the term, became a creation of his fantasies, by stages over the years Adolf Hitler probably created his own 'personal' Wagner by adding to his perception of the man much that was imaginary.

Hitler's musical education was very modest. Aside from his mother, pride of place goes to Father Leonhard Gruner of the choir of the Benedictine monastery at Lambach, who trained Adolf as a chorister for two years. The boy was eight when he joined, and therefore at a highly receptive age. Those who know the culture level of these old Austrian institutions will appreciate that there was scarcely a better musical training to be had than that in a well-led choir. Unfortunately this promising beginning was discontinued even though the young Hitler's clear, sure voice brought delight to all who heard him sing. His father presumably had little interest in it. The boy's primary school reports were always endorsed 'outstanding' for singing, but the Realschule offered no musical instruction at all. Whoever wished to pursue it had to pay for private tuition or go to music school. Because he spent more than two hours daily on the trek between Leonding and the Realschule, Adolf would have had no time for private musical tuition even if his father had been in favour of it.

Adolf took a great interest in my own musical education, but the fact that I understood more about music than he did left him restless. From our regular conversations about music he was *au fait* amazingly quickly with all the technical terms and expressions. He had taken the low road, so to speak, while I took the high one, yet he could talk about everything under the sun in music without having studied it systematically. Talking about it awoke in him understanding. I can only say that he had a great depth of feeling for music, and this often astonished me, for in reality he knew nothing about it. This self-tuition had its limits of course as soon as he came to the point of actually playing something. Here one needed to have systematic training, constant practice, determination and endurance, qualities for which my friend had little comprehension, although he did not like to be told so. His great empathy, his fantasies and his unlimited self-confidence reduced to insignificance the qualities of which I had spoken; he was sure he could compete. As soon as he put my viola under his chin and took up the bow he was no longer so certain of victory, however. I recall his surprise that it was not so easy as it looked, and when I took the instrument from him to play him a piece, he did not want to listen. It annoyed him that there were things which defeated his will. Naturally, he was already too old for even elementary instruction.

One day he ranted at me: 'Now I am going to see if music is the witch-craft you always say it is!' and with these words he announced his decision to learn the piano, convinced that in no time at all he would have mastered it. He signed up for lessons with Josef Prewratzky and soon realised that without diligence and endurance it could not be done. His experience with Prewratzky was comparable to mine with my old music sergeant Kopetzky. Prewratzky had no time for intuitive ideas and genial improvisations, insisting on 'clean finger-training' and strict discipline. Here Adolf fell into a dilemma. He was far too proud simply to give up on an attempt by which he had set such store, but this stupid 'exercising the fingers' left him raging. I weathered the conflict easily, for in musical matters Adolf could not bamboozle me as he might in others. I noticed that his furious outbursts against Prewratzky's 'crazy musical gymnastics' began to fall off – when I crossed the threshold of the 19 Humboldtstrasse apartment it was increasingly obvious that no important progress on the piano had been made, for he avoided even opening the lid of the good Heitzmann instrument in my presence. Prewratzky's name entered our conversations ever less often and so 'learning to play the piano' was quietly laid to rest. I cannot say how long Adolf braved the course. It was certainly not a year although it seemed that an extraordinarily long time passed during which Prewratzky had young Hitler at his mercy. All the same, in Vienna later when we made an opera – unfortunately never completed! – for our student stage, Adolf took upon himself not only the lyrics but the musical composition as well, although he did at least leave the guiding theme to me. This was his way of proving that, despite all the previous contra-indications, what mattered most in music was inspiration, and not finger exercises.

All the same, Adolf recognised my musical talent without the least envy, and rejoiced or suffered with me in my successes or setbacks as if they were applicable to himself. I found him very supportive and the great strength behind my ambition. His belief in my virtuosity was the most important thing for me; it welded our friendship. It might be that during the day I was no more than an upholsterer's assistant who repaired moth-eaten old chairs in an atmosphere of dust and humidity, but in the evenings, when I went to the Hitler apartment, I forgot the workshop and found myself transported, with and through him, into the pure, sublime atmosphere of art.

How faithfully he shared with me in the performance of Franz Liszt's glorious oratorio *Die heilige Elisabeth*. My trumpet teacher was Viertelmeister. Imagine my excitement when, during a lesson, he asked me straight out if I would be interested to take part in a performance of the great work. My knees were like jelly. 'Then let's begin!' he exclaimed and without further ado went over the trumpet score with me. Next I practised in the concert hall and got to know August Göllerich the conductor. Even today my heart beats faster when I recall the big day. I was barely seventeen, easily the youngest member of the orchestra. No instrument is so sensitive to poor handling as the trumpet. Below in the tightly-packed stalls I saw my mother sitting next to Adolf, who gave me a smile of encouragement. Everything went off well and I considered that I had merited a portion of the rousing ovation we received. At any rate, Hitler's applause was for me alone. There were tears in my mother's eyes.

After this successful public debut Adolf told me during one of our lonely nocturnal strolls that I should make it my goal to devote myself totally to music. His penetrating words are still with me as though spoken only yesterday: 'You have got to give up the upholstery work, it will kill you. (Shortly before I had been seriously ill.) It is no good either for yourself or your psyche. You have quite definite talent, and not only as a soloist – that is obvious – but also as a stage or concert conductor. I was watching you constantly in the theatre and noticed how you knew the whole score before it was played. Music is your role in life, there you are in your element. There you belong.' Adolf had now put into words what I had long felt for myself. To become a musical conductor was the finest life's ambition I could imagine.

That he shared my opinion of myself filled me with endless joy. Our conversations became ever more intense about this plan for the future even though the sober facts militated against it. My father was ill. I was his only son and had learnt the upholstery trade so that eventually I should take over a business which, with a great deal of hard work, he had developed from small beginnings. All his hopes, his life energy, were concentrated into his desire to be able to hand over the business to me as a going concern. The fact that, unlike Adolf's father, he did not attempt to force it on me would make my departure from the path planned for me all the more difficult. He rarely spoke of his concerns for me, but I felt keenly how much his life's work meant to him.

In this emotional conflict, Adolf Hitler proved a reliable friend. He had put backbone into my idea of choosing music as my profession, and was very clever at how he went about making it possible. For the first and only time I discovered in him a quality of which I was unaware and which I never experienced in him later: patience. He saw clearly that my father could not be won over for such an enormous decision by a frontal assault, no matter how determined, and had identified the weak point where he should concentrate his attack. My mother had a natural affinity for music and would be receptive to his overtures even though she had a pretty good idea of how much a musical education was going to cost. The road to the father led through the mother. All that would be needed to carry the day, Adolf considered, was a skilful approach.

In all the difficult situations through which Adolf and I were obliged to struggle, it was to music that we owed our inner development. It must be remembered that in those days there was no cinema or radio and that a chance to listen to music required visiting a concert hall, something that today has become a rarity for most people. For us it was the centre of our world. Everything that motivated and interested us revolved in some way or other around the concert hall. While I fantasised about conducting a great orchestra, Adolf busied himself with designing truly impressive theatres of the most grandiose proportions.

Additionally, we had met in the auditorium at Linz, and our friendship had developed from that acquaintanceship. The friendship which began from the lowly little provincial theatre would continue to the Vienna Opera and the Burg Theatre and be crowned finally at Bayreuth, where I sat through Wagner Festivals as a guest of Reich Chancellor Adolf Hitler.

Hitler had a natural joy and passion for the concert hall. I am convinced that it had to do with his early childhood impressions, particularly at Lambach. I cannot remember for sure if he ever told me anything about the Benedictine choral performances, here my memory fails me, but I think that on closer investigation one would find that he was probably ever-present. As a choirboy he had access everywhere and perhaps he took an interest in other musical presentations too. The fine Baroque stage was a jewel of its kind, and I can imagine that to sing in a choir there would make one enthusiastic for music generally.

As a twelve-year-old he went to the Landestheater in Linz from Leonding, as he describes in *Mein Kampf*:

> The provincial capital of Upper Austria had at that time a concert hall which was not bad, relatively speaking. Everything was performed there. When I was twelve, I saw *Wilhelm Tell* for the first time and a few months later my first opera, *Lohengrin*. At a stroke I was hooked. My youthful enthusiasm for the master of Bayreuth knew no bounds. Again and again I was attracted to his work and I consider it today to have been my especial good fortune to have experienced the modesty of the provincial presentation, for I knew it could only get better.

Very nicely put! If asked for my own opinion I would not have spoken about the Linz Landestheater so kindly. Perhaps because I felt I was destined to be its future musical conductor I was more critical in my evaluation of everything there, including the orchestra, than he was. Probably, however, I lacked that intense empathy which made it possible for him to overlook the obvious inadequacies of the place and maintain the

80

illusion of the work being performed. I often had the impression that no matter how defective the presentation might be he saw only the artistic content of the work itself. When, as the result of a stage-hand's incompetence, Lohengrin fell out of the longboat and, covered in sawdust, arose from the 'sea' to clamber back aboard for the remainder of his swan-voyage – which had not only the audience but also Elsa in stitches – even this did not detract from the beauty of the presentation for him. After all, what had these amusing episodes to do with the high idea the great master had had when composing the opera? But, despite his unusual capacity to disregard the irrelevant in this respect, he could be a harsh, strong critic as well.

The Landestheater was a very dignified building, but the stage was far too small for the performance of Wagner operas, inadequate in every respect. The technical installations needed for a worthy standard of presentation of these works were not fitted. There was a major shortage not only of suitable costumes, but of wardrobe in general. The orchestra was too short-handed to reach the sound levels required. To provide just one example, when *Die Meistersinger* was staged, a number of instrumental parts were discarded, these being, as I established as a 'technical expert', the bass clarinet, the English horn and the contra-bassoon in the woodwind section and the so-called Wagner horn in the brass while the string section was short of three players. But even if there had been available the instrumentalists necessary to make up the numbers, there would still have been nowhere near enough space in the narrow orchestra pit to put them all. This was the truly pitiful state of affairs confronting the conductors. To attempt a Wagner performance with a twenty-man orchestra was thus something of an adventure. The choir, needless to say, was a disgrace, turned out in completely unsuitable costume and often requiring the indulgence of the public as for example in *Die Meistersinger* when the males were all equipped with English-style false moustaches which made Hitler hit the roof. For a provincial stage the soloists were not bad, but there were only a handful of real Wagner-singers amongst them.

The stage scenery came in for constant criticism. The backdrop flapped with every footstep; this was particularly annoying when it was supposed to represent a rocky landscape. My hair stands on end when I remember the fire at the capitol which brought one *Rienzi* performance to its conclusion. The palazzo stood centre-stage with a projecting balcony upon which Rienzi and Irene stepped forward to pacify the mob. To the right and left of them was some burning resin representing the beginnings of the 'conflagration'. A stage hand had to let down a huge prop depicting the palazzo with bright flames licking it to destruction. This prop was hung to one side from a braced strut. When someone loosened the strut, the prop rustled to the floor. One always had to reckon with this kind of accident. It was all well and good for Hitler to say that these 'modest' presentations held the promise of something better, such as we were later to find at the Viennese Hof Opera, but it amazes me today that such woefully inadequate performances could possibly 'inspire' or 'transport' us. The idealism in our young hearts ensured that we were never spiteful in our criticism of the performances.

The theatre was always sold out for Wagner. We would often queue for up to two hours waiting for the doors to open if we intended to fight for a column in the standing area. The intervals were interminable. As we glowed with enthusiasm, desperate for a cooling drink, an old usher with a white beard would sell us a glass of water, allowing us to remain in occupation of our conquered territory around the pillars. We would put a small coin in the empty glass and return it to the usher. Often the performance would go on until midnight. Then I would accompany Adolf home, but the walk there was too short to allow us to shake off the powerful vibrations of the evening and so he would accompany me to my home in the Klammstrasse. During this period he would really get into the spirit of the thing, and we would then return together to the Humboldtstrasse. I do not recall that Adolf ever got tired; the night seemed to fire him up and he rarely had anything much to do in the morning. Thus it would happen after a performance that we strolled back and forward between our two homes until I started yawning and found it difficult to keep my eyes open.

From his childhood, Adolf had been intoxicated by tales of the ancient German heroes. As a boy he could not read enough about them. He had a book by Gustav Schwab which presented these sagas of early German history in a popular format. This book was his favourite, and at Humboldtstrasse had pride of place in his library where it was always to hand. On his sickbed, he engrossed himself with true fervour in the mysterious world of myth which this book had opened up for him. In our Viennese student rooms, I remember that Adolf had an especially fine edition of the German *Heldensagen* to which he had frequent and eager recourse despite the pressing day-to-day problems which beset him at that time.

His familiarity with these sagas was by no means the passing fad which it might be with other people. It was essentially the thing which captivated him, and in his historical and political considerations you could be sure it was never far from his thoughts, for this was the world in which he felt he belonged. He could not imagine for himself a finer existence than that lived by these radiant heroes of early German history. He identified himself with the great men of this vanished epoch. Nothing appeared more worthy of the struggle than a life like theirs, full of brave acts of great consequence, the most heroic life possible, and from there to enter Valhalla* and so become an immortal of myth, joining those already present whom he so venerated. This strange, romantic perspective of Hitler's thinking should not be overlooked. In a world of harsh political reality, the tendency will be to reject these youthful musings as fantasies, but the fact remains, despite everything at this time of his life, that Adolf Hitler's personality dwelt only in the truly pious beliefs to which the German heroic sagas had introduced him.

In conflict with a bourgeois world, which with its deceit and false rectitude had nothing to offer him, he sought instinctively his own world and found it in the origins and early history of his own peoples. He considered it their finest era, and this long-vanished epoch, known only from a very patchy historical record, became for the fiery young Hitler the full-blooded present. The intensity with which he lived this age 1,500 years previously was such that it often made my head spin, entrenched as I was in the early twentieth century. Did he really live amongst the heroes of that misty dark age, of whom he spoke as if they were camped out in the woods through which we took our nightly rambles? Was the dawning century in which we found ourselves no more than a waking dream for him? This century-shift often concerned me to the extent that I feared for his sanity: maybe one day he might find himself unable to escape from the time warp he had created for himself.[†]

---

* Valhalla, according to Professor Heinrich Niedner in his *Nordic Mythology*, Section XVI, was the glorious destination for those select who fell in battle. The word means 'place of the dead warriors'. It was ruled over by the god of war Odin (also known as Wotan), whose daughters, the Valkyries, were sent to choose those who were to be admitted. [Ed.]

† In the First World War, Hitler always carried with him in his gas-mask canister not *Die Deutschen Heldensage* but the five volumes of Schopenhauer (Heims: Adolf Hitler, *Monologe im Führerhauptquartier*, Orbis, Munich, 2000, entry for 19 May 1944). Since he also stated (*Monologe*, 14 October 1941) that 'our mythology of the gods was already defunct when Christianity came' and that it seemed 'utterly stupid to resurrect the cult of Wotan', it is logical to infer that by 1914 his religious–philosophical ideas had gone through a metamorphosis. [Ed.]

The constant, intensive preoccupation with the heroes of German mythology appeared to have made him peculiarly receptive to the life work of Richard Wagner. As soon as the twelve-year-old heard *Lohengrin*, which translated his boyish dreams into poetry and music, his longing for the sublime world of the German past manifested itself within him and, from the moment Wagner entered his life, the dead genius never set him free. In Wagner's work, Hitler saw not only a confirmation of his path of spiritual 'transmigration' into early German history, but it fortified the idea that this long-gone era must have something in it of use for the future.

In the years of my friendship with Adolf Hitler I lived through the first phase of his development into adulthood. As an enthusiastic musician I also had idols whom I attempted to emulate, but what my friend looked for in Wagner was much more than a role model. I can only say that he 'put on' the personality of Wagner just as though it were possible for his ghost to possess him.

He read avidly everything he could get hold of concerning Wagner, the good and the bad, written by those in favour and those against. He was particularly keen on biographical literature about him, read his notes, letters, diaries, his self-appraisal, his confessions. Day by day he penetrated ever deeper into the man's life. He was well-informed about the most trivial details and unimportant episodes. It might happen that on one of our rambles Adolf would suddenly abandon the subject upon which he had been up to that moment holding forth – perhaps the supply of an inventory needed by a poor provincial concert hall from a notional state fund set aside for such deserving cases – and recite the text of some note or letter by Wagner, or maybe a thesis – *Kunstwerk und Zukunft* ('Artistry and the Future') or *Die Kunst und die Revolution* ('Art and the Revolution'). Although it would not always be an easy matter to follow the thread of these I would always pay close attention and look forward to Hitler's concluding observations, which were invariable. 'So you see', he would say, 'even Wagner went through it just like I have. All the time he had to tackle the ignorance of his surroundings.'

These comparisons seemed very exaggerated to me. Wagner lived to be seventy years of age. In such a productive life there were bound to have been ups and downs, successes and failures, but my friend, who saw his own life as a parallel to that of Wagner, was barely seventeen, had created nothing but a few drawings, water-colours and architectural plans and experienced nothing of life except the death of his father and failure at school. Yet he spoke as though he had been the victim of persecution, fought his enemies and been exiled.

Fervently he compiled the decisive episodes from Wagner's life, of which in due course I would be on the receiving end. He described Wagner's stormy sea passage in the Skagerrak with his young wife as the result of which the idea of *Die fliegende Holländer* had been conceived. I heard out the adventurous flight of the young revolutionary Wagner, the years of rejection, the exile. I enthused with my friend over Ludwig II, protector of the arts, who had accompanied Wagner on his last voyage to Venice. It was not that Adolf refused to recognise the human weaknesses of Richard Wagner, his profligate spending and so on, but he forgave him on the grounds of the immortal greatness of his work.

At that time, Wagner had already been dead over twenty years, but the battle to have his work generally recognised and accepted was still in full swing. It is difficult today to imagine the passion this controversy engendered amongst the music-loving youth of those times. For us there were only two categories of people: friends and foes of Richard Wagner. Modern-day debates about music are so tame in comparison they raise only a smile. But in those days, there was no radio, television, cinema or recording equipment, only theatres, and what was presented there was a matter of great import. Whenever a performance was staged, we became as animated as those heroes on the stage itself. We sought ever more means to express our unrestrained passion and enthusiasm, and in conductor August Göllerich, who had worked under Wagner, we had not only a worthy interpreter of the great master's material, but also a veteran guardian of his legacy. In our eyes, he was the keeper of the grail.

We were convinced that we were experiencing the birth of a new German art form. This sort of musical drama was something completely new, scarcely thought of previously, combining for the first time poetry and music and setting them in a mythical world which had become our own.

Adolf's great longing was to visit Bayreuth, the national pilgrimage centre of Germany, to see 'Wahnfried', the house where the genius had lived, to meditate beside his grave and see the performance of his works in the theatre he had constructed. If many dreams and wishes of his life remained unfulfilled, at least this one was satisfied to the uttermost.

These are pleasing memories for a 64-year-old man such as I, memories to make the heart young again, and happy, the same heart that beat so fiercely for the master of Bayreuth! Actually I would not have wanted to miss these youthful experiences, seeing the first phase of Hitler's ecstasy for Wagner. Whereas I was merely an intermediary in his relationship with Stefanie, reporting information, I was more positively involved in his

Wagner experience, having a better musical foundation than he did. The secret of his love for Stefanie certainly brought me closer to him, for nothing forges a friendship better than a secret shared, and in addition we had in common the highest devotion to Richard Wagner.

Chapter 9

# Hitler the Young Volksdeutscher

When I remember the political thoughts and ideas of the youthful Hitler I hear his voice saying to me, 'You don't understand', or 'One can't discuss a thing like that with you', and often he condemned me in even stronger terms as when, for example, during one of his monologues I nodded at the wrong point, he erupted in indignation: 'Politically, Gustl, you are a turkey.'

The fact was, only one thing mattered in my life – music. Adolf had agreed that art should have priority in all areas of life, but in the course of the years we spent together politics gradually gained the upper hand without noticeably compromising his efforts in the direction of art. One can put it this way: the Linz years were under the star of art; those in Vienna under the star of politics. I felt that I was only really useful to him in the arts. The more the stress fell on politics, the less our friendship could give him. Not that he would ever allow me to gain this impression from himself, for he took our friendship far too seriously, or maybe he did not realise the fact.

Politics became critical for our relationship. Politically I had hardly any opinions, and those I did have were not held with enough passion for me to need to defend them or impose them on others, and so in me Adolf had himself a poor partner. He liked to convert by persuasion, but I accepted willingly and uncritically whatever he advocated. I noted things so that now and again I could discuss them with him at quite a skilful level, but I did not extend to being an opposition which he would have found useful for verbal sparring purposes. In essence I was like the deaf man at a symphony concert: I could see that something was being played, but had no idea what it was. Nature had provided me with no bodily organ which could handle politics. This could bring Adolf to despair. He considered it impossible that there ever could be a person with my lack of interest for, and knowledge of, politics. He would not let me off the hook, however. I remember how often he needed me to keep him company for some reason at the parliament even

87

though it had no interest for me and I would rather have remained at the piano. But Adolf would not have it and he forced me to go even though he knew that the parliamentary business bored me to tears. But I dared not say so, of course.

People tend to assume that politicians come from a highly politicised home environment. This was not true of Adolf Hitler – on the contrary. Here we have another of the many contradictions about him. His father liked to talk politics and made no secret of his partiality to free thought, although he would not entertain any talk against the monarchy. As an Austro-Hungarian customs official, he was very hot on this point. When he put on his parade uniform every 18 August, the Habsburg Kaiser's birthday, he was the perfect picture of a servant of the state from the parting in his hair to the soles of his boots.

I think that little Adolf got to hear very little about politics, for in Alois Hitler's opinion they belonged in a bar and not at home. If things got heated at the inn, one knew nothing of it at the hearthside. I can never recall that Adolf ever mentioned his father in connection with any of his own political views.

Even less trace was there to be found of it in the Humboldtstrasse flat. Klara Hitler was a simple, pious woman with no interest in politics. When her husband was alive, she had probably heard him arguing about politics with others but never became involved in it herself or repeated the substance of what she had heard to her children. It probably seemed right and proper to the choleric husband and father that what he thundered out at the inn should be unknown to his quiet little wife and not ruffle the still waters of family life. Nobody would be welcome in the Hitler household who brought politics along with him. I never remember a single occasion in the Hitler family when a political subject was spoken of. Even if some event of great political moment caused ripples through the town, one would remain oblivious of it in this quiet home, for even Adolf respected the rule there.

The only change in family circumstances I witnessed was when Frau Klara moved from Humboldtstrasse to Urfahr in 1906. This had nothing to do with the endless shifting of address which had been the father's custom, but rather a practical consideration. Urfahr, now part of Linz, was then a separate little town of mainly rural character, a favourite choice for retirement on a good pension. As no duty was levied in Urfahr on many things, such as meat, it was cheaper there than in Linz itself. Frau Klara was hoping that her modest pension of 120 crowns monthly, which she split 90:15:15 between herself and her two children, would stretch further, and in any case she felt more at home living within sight of green fields and pasture. The house at Blütengasse 9 is unchanged at the time of writing so that often when I go down that little street off the beaten track beyond which the countryside begins I almost expect to see Frau Klara appear on the elegant little balcony. For Adolf it was a special thing to live 'on the other side of the river' in the same town as Stefanie. Our evening walk home through the outskirts to Urfahr now took longer, although at least it gave Adolf and me additional time to discuss many pressing matters. The route took us over the Danube bridge, and if something was preoccupying us particularly, we would go back and forth across the Danube until the conversation came to an end or more accurately, Adolf exhausted the possibilities of his monologue while I listened.

When I think of the quiet home in which Adolf grew up and recall the political pressures on him, the image that always presents itself is of the whirling tornado, at the centre of which is a place of absolute windlessness and calm, all the more profound the more violent the raging whirlwind. In considering the political genesis of so unusual a person as Adolf Hitler, the external influences have to be kept separate from the inner predisposition, for in my opinion the latter has much greater significance.

At that time, many young people had the same teachers as Adolf, lived through the same political events, were enthusiastic or outraged at what they saw and yet finished up simply as able salesmen, engineer or factory directors without political significance.

The atmosphere at Linz Realschule was decidedly Volksdeutsch. Secretly, Hitler's classmates were opposed to all established institutions, patriotic discourses, dynastic holidays and proclamations; they were against school religious services and and taking part in Corpus Christi processions. Adolf Hitler portrayed this atmosphere, which was more important for him than actual education, in *Mein Kampf*:

> Collections were made for Südmark and Schulverein,* the cause was emphasised by cornflowers† and the black-red-gold colours, 'Heil!' was the greeting and *Deutschland über Alles* was sung instead of the Austrian anthem, despite warnings and punishments.

---

\* The term *Südmark* – 'southern territory' – represents the idea of Austria as a province of Germany: *Schulverein* means the incorporation of schools into the *Deutscher Schulverein*. [Ed.]

† The cornflower is the national flower of Germany. [Ed.]

The struggle for the preservation of the German racial group in the Danube state moved young hearts, and understandably so, for this Germanness in Austria was now lived amongst the Slavs, Magyars and Italians of Austro-Hungary. Linz was basically a German city far from the reintegrated borderlands but in neighbouring Bohemia there was constant unrest; in Prague one disturbance followed another such that a state of emergency had had to be declared. There was outrage in Linz that the Austro-Hungarian police force had admitted that it could not guarantee to protect German houses against the Czech mob should the eventuality arise.

Budweis was then still a Volksdeutsch town, its administration and a majority of deputies being of German origin. Adolf's classmates who originated from Prague, Budweis or Prachatitz jumped up and down with rage when jokingly referred to as 'Bohemians', for they wanted to be Volksdeutsche just like the others were. Gradually, unrest came to Linz, which amongst its population had a few hundred peaceably employed Czechs. These people had never caused trouble, but now a Czech of the Capuchin Order by the name of Jurasek had founded a Sokolverein – Czech cultural organisation – and besides holding religious services in the Martinskirche in Czech was collecting to build a Czech school. This caused consternation in Linz, and many people saw in the activities of the fanatical Capuchins the thin edge of the wedge of a Czech cultural invasion. The whole thing was blown out of proportion, of course, but all the same, these Czech activities gave the sleepy Linzers the feeling of being under some kind of threat, and they all joined in the cultural battle raging around them.

> Whoever knows the soul of youth will understand that it is precisely they who are happiest to hear the call for conflict. In a hundred different forms they take it on ... They are a true reflection of the greater struggle in miniature, but often of higher and more sincere conviction.

This is an accurate observation by Hitler to the extent that one can rely on how he depicts his personal political development in *Mein Kampf*. The Volksdeutsch teachers at his Realschule stood at the forefront of the defensive struggle. Dr Leopold Pötsch, the history teacher, was an active politician. On the municipal council he led the Volksdeutsch group. He hated the Habsburg multi-national empire which is held up to us today – what a turnaround – as the model of a multi-national state, and spoke for youth.

'In the upshot, who could remain true to the Kaiser of a dynasty which, past and present, subordinated the interests of its German peoples to its own advantage?' Hitler asked, and with that the son, won over to the pan-German programme, abandoned finally and irrevocably the path mapped out for him by his father. When Adolf lost his train of thought in long, excited monologues – I was scarcely able to follow most of them – I noticed how one particular term recurred: 'the Reich'. It would always crop up at the end of a long discourse, and if his political contemplations brought him to a dead end, and he could see no way out, he would declare: 'The Reich will resolve this question.' When I enquired who would foot the bill for all the gigantic structures he had designed on his drawing board, the answer was 'the Reich', and the tab for even those things which lacked general interest would be picked up by 'the Reich'. The inadequate fixtures and fittings of the provincial concert hall would become the responsibility of a Reich Stage Designer (and after 1933 there actually was a man with the title of Reichs-bühnenbildner). I remembered that Adolf Hitler coined this term in Linz as a seventeen-year-old. Even the societies for the blind or the protection of animals were to be institutions of 'the Reich'.

In Austria, the word *Reich* usually meant the national territory of Germany, and the people of that state were known as *Reichsdeutsche*. (A person of German stock living elsewhere was a *Volksdeutscher*.) When my friend used the word *Reich*, however, he meant more than just the German state. Though avoiding a more exact definition of his own, it was clear that 'the Reich' contained everything which motivated him politically, and so it was very big indeed.

With the same passion that he loved the German people and 'the Reich', he rejected everything foreign. He had no leaning to know other countries. That urge, so typical of young back-packers even then, found no place in his personality. Even the artist's typical attraction to Italy seemed absent. When he projected his plans and ideas for a country, that country was always 'the Reich'.

In this stormy 'national' struggle, which was clearly aimed against the Austrian monarchy, the unusual facets of his character came to the fore, in particular the iron will. The 'national' ideology was fixed in the 'unchangeable' region of his mind. No failure or setback would ever shift him on it, and he remained to his death what he had always been from at least sixteen years of age: a 'German Nationalist'.

That healthy unconcern which distinguishes young people was completely alien to him. I never saw him 'just flick through' reading matter; everything had to be looked at thoroughly and then examined as though it

91

was to be included amongst the great political aims he had. Traditional political viewpoints meant nothing to him; the world had to be reorganised from the bottom upwards, in all its components.

It would be quite wrong to conclude from this picture that the young Hitler burst upon the political scene, war flags at the masthead. Those important solutions which he found and which needed a public airing he would expound in the evenings to an audience of one, an insignificant and simple person. The relationship of young Hitler to politics is similar to his relationship towards love, if I may make a comparison which some may find lacks taste. The more politics occupied him mentally, the more he held himself aloof from any practical political activities. He joined no party nor political organisation, did not attend political meetings and limited his opinions to myself. What I saw in Linz was a 'first glance' at politics, nothing more, just as though he already suspected what politics would eventually come to mean for him.

Politics for him meanwhile were just a mental exercise. In this reserve I saw his impatience restrained by his ability to wait. Politics remained for him for years something to be observed, criticised, examined, collected.

It is an interesting fact that the young Hitler in those years was very anti-military. This contradicts a passage in *Mein Kampf*:

> Searching through my father's library I came across various books with a military content, amongst them a people's edition about the Franco-Prussian War of 1870–1. It consisted of two volumes of an illustrated newspaper of the time and became my favourite reading matter. Before long the great heroic struggle had become the greatest inner experience for me. From then on I got more and more enthusiastic for everything connected with war and the soldier's life.

I am guessing that this 'memory' was thought to be a useful one to have at the time *Mein Kampf* was written at Landsberg prison in 1924, for during the period when I knew Adolf Hitler he was not the least interested in anything that was in any way 'connected with war'. The lieutenants who escorted Stefanie were a thorn in his side, but his aversion went much deeper. The very mention of military conscription would set him off. No, never would he allow himself to be a soldier by compulsion; if he were to be a soldier, it would be of his own volition, and definitely not in the Austrian Army.

Before closing this chapter on the political development of Adolf Hitler,

I would like to review two matters which appear to me more relevant than anything else in the realm of his politics: young Hitler's attitude to Jewry and the Church.

Respecting the Jewish question during his years at Linz, he wrote:

> It is difficult for me today, if not impossible, to say when the word 'Jew' first gave me occasion to think about the subject specially. In my father's house, I do not remember ever having heard the word mentioned during my father's lifetime. I believe that the old gentleman would have seen a cultural retardedness in special emphasis placed on this word. He had a more or less bourgeois world view which he maintained in the face of the rudest national feelings, and this had rubbed off on me. Neither at school was I under any impetus to change this accepted picture. At Realschule I did get to know a Jewish boy; we did not trust him and he was kept by all of us at a distance, but only because of his taciturn manner which was due to various experiences when he had been baited. I had no more contact with him than any of the others, however. Not until my fourteenth or fifteenth year did I note the word 'Jew' cropping up more frequently, partly in connection with political talk. I felt a slight aversion and could not divest myself of an unpleasant feeling which always crept up on me when religious trouble-makers discussed things in front of me. But otherwise, the question was of no interest to me. Linz had very few Jews . . .

This all sounds very plausible but does not really coincide with my own recollections. The image of his father as a liberal does not seem correct. The debating table at the inn to which the latter habitually repaired had embraced the ideas of Schönerer.* Therefore, Hitler's father would definitely have been anti-Jewish. As regards his schooldays, Hitler fails to mention that the Realschule had teachers who made no secret, even in front of their pupils, of their hatred for the Jews. At Realschule, Hitler must have known something of the political aspects of the Jewish question, and in fact I do not think it could have happened any other way, for when I got to know

---

* Georg Ritter von Schönerer (1842–1918): anti-Habsburg, anti-clerical and anti-Jewish, he advocated Austria being annexed into Greater Germany under Prussian leadership. He was a member of the Austrian Reichsrat 1873–88 and 1897–1907. His extremism led him increasingly into a position of isolation. [Ed.]

him he was already openly anti-Jewish. I remember clearly how once, while we were strolling down Bethlehemstrasse and came to the small synagogue there, he said to me, 'That doesn't belong in Linz.'

I recall that he was already a dyed-in-the-wool anti-semite when he came to Vienna,* but he did not make much of it early on even though his experiences in Vienna on the subject must have made him think in a more radical manner than before. In my opinion, what Hitler is saying in a roundabout way is that even at Linz, where the Jewish populace was small, the question was not an irrelevance, but he began to give serious thought to the question in Vienna only after he saw how large the Jewish population was there.

Rather different are things in the Church sphere. *Mein Kampf* is silent on the subject except for a brief observation about his childhood experience at Lambach:

> Since I had singing lessons in my spare time at the Lambach choristry, I had the best opportunity to fall under the spell of the sumptuous celebrations of Church festivals. What was more natural than that I should see in the same light the lord abbot as once my father had seen the village priest – the highest ideal to be striven for in life. At least at the time, that was the case.

Hitler's forebears were certainly Church people as is usual amongst the peasantry. His family were divided in this respect: the mother pious, devoted to the Church, the father liberal, a lukewarm Christian. Certainly matters pertaining to the Church were closer to him than the Jewish question, for as a state official he could not afford to be seen as anti-clerical in a monarchy where throne and altar were mutually supporting.

So long as little Adolf was close to his mother, her influence ensured that he was committed to all the great and wondrous things that the Church represented. The small, pale choirboy was a pious believer. The little that Hitler says about that period speaks louder than words could. He was familiar with the magnificent building; he felt attracted to the Church and his mother would certainly have gone out of her way to encourage this. The more he leaned towards his father in subsequent years of his childhood, the more did his father's free-thinking attitude gain the upper hand. The

---

* In *Monologe, op. cit.*, on 17 December 1941 Hitler stated in a conversation: 'I came to Vienna as a disciple of Schönerer, and was therefore an opponent of the Christian Socialists.' [Ed.]

Realschule at Linz, where Franz Schwarz taught religion, was no bastion of the Church, for none of the pupils took the teacher seriously.

My own recollections can be set down in a few sentences. For the entire period that I knew Adolf Hitler, I do not think he ever attended mass. He knew that I went every Sunday with my parents. He did not try to dissuade me, but said occasionally that he could not understand it of me. His mother was a Church-going woman but he would not let her force him to go. It was no more than an observation, however, delivered with a certain indulgence which was rare for him. I do not recall that, when he met me at the Carmelite church after mass on Sundays, Adolf ever spoke depracatingly of church attendance or had an attitude about it. To my surprise it was never a subject of debate for him either. All the same, one day he came to me in great excitement and showed me a book about the Church witch-hunts, on another occasion one about the Inquisition, but despite his outrage over the events described in these books he avoided making a political statement on the matter. Perhaps he thought I was not the right public for him.

On Sundays his mother always went to mass with little Paula. Adolf never accompanied her that far even when she begged him. Pious believer that she was, she appeared to have come to terms with the fact that her son wanted to follow another path; perhaps his father had said something to her. All in all I think that the Church was not an irrelevance for Hitler, but that it had nothing to offer him. He was a nationalist, devoted to the German people for whom he lived and beside whom no other people existed.

# Chapter 10

# Adolf Rebuilds Linz

While I was undecided whether to list my friend amongst the great musicians or the great poets of the future, he sprang on me the announcement that he intended to become a painter. I immediately remembered that I had seen him sketching, both at home and on our excursions. As our friendship progressed, I saw many samples of his work. In my job as an upholsterer, I had occasionally to do some sketches, which I always found difficult, so the more was I astonished by my friend's facility. He always carried with him various types of paper. The start had always been the worst part for me – for him, it was the other way round. He would take his pencil and, throwing a few bold strokes on the paper, would express his meaning – where words failed him, the pencil would do the job. There was something attractive about these first, rough lines – it thrilled me to see a recognisable design gradually emerge from their confusion. But he was not so keen on finishing the rough draft.

The first time I went to visit him at home, his room was littered with sketches, drawings, blueprints. Here was 'the new theatre', there the mountain hotel on the Lichtenberg – it was like an architect's office. Watching him at work at the drawing board – he was more careful then and more precise in details than he used to be in moments of happy improvisation – I was convinced that he must, long since, have acquired all the technical and specialised skill necessary for his work. I simply could not believe that it was possible to set down such difficult things on the spur of the moment, and that everything I saw was improvised.

The number of these works is sufficient to allow one to form a judgment of Adolf Hitler's talents. There is, in the first place, a water-colour – rather, water-colour is not the right word, as it is a simple pencil drawing coloured with tempera. But just the rapid catching of an atmosphere, of a certain mood, which is so typical of a water-colour and which, with its delicate touch, imparts to it freshness and liveliness – this was missing completely in Adolf's work. Just here, where he might have worked with fast intuitive strokes, he has daubed with painstaking precision.

Adolf(us) Hitler's birth and baptism certificate. The entries relating to the mother, Klara Hitler, show that her own mother had the maiden name Hitler. Klara was therefore a close relative of her husband.

Klara Hitler, née Pölzl, Adolf Hitler's mother.

Alois Hitler, Adolf Hitler's father.

*Top:* The fourth form of the state primary school at Leonding (*Hitler centre, top row*).
*Above:* The first form of the secondary Realschule at Linz (*Hitler far right, top row*).

The first photograph of Adolf Hitler, taken at Braunau am Inn.

Alois Hitler in impressive pose in his official uniform.

*Above:* Adolf Hitler, aged sixteen: a sketch by a fellow pupil in the fourth form of the secondary school at Linz.

*Right:* Dr Leopold Pötsch, the history teacher at Steyr Realschule, was venerated by Hitler.

August Kubizek at the time of his friendship with Adolf Hitler.

No. 9 Blütengasse, Urfahr near Linz, where Hitler shared a flat with his mother. The two windows to the right of the balcony were those of her bedroom.

A sketch by the eighteen-year-old Hitler for a new concert hall to be built in Linz.

*Above:* A signature of Adolf Hitler's father (*top*) and examples of Adolf's signatures from the years 1906, 1907, 1913 and 1914.

*Above right:* Stefanie, Adolf Hitler's first love.

A wedding photograph of Hitler's half-sister Angela Raubal, whose husband Leo became Adolf's ardent adversary.

*Above:* Extract from the notice of his mother's death, signed by Hitler on 18 January 1908.

*Right:* Hitler's design for the villa he wanted to build for Kubizek.

Hitler's hand-written application to the Austrian authorities asking for an orphan's pension for himself and his sister Paula, after the death of their mother.

*Above & right:* A postcard from Hitler to Kubizek, sent during Adolf's first visit to Vienna and expressing his disapproval of the interior design of the Opera House.

*Above, both:* Another postcard from Hitler to Kubizek, addressing him as 'Gustav', the name of Hitler's favourite brother, as in all their correspondence.

A water colour by Hitler dating from 1906 and showing Pöstlingberg Castle, near Linz.

Hitler's letter to Kubizek of 4 August 1933, using the familiar *Du* form of address and referring to the years he spent with Kubizek as the best of his life.

All I can say about Adolf's artistic activity refers to his first attempts, and the only water-colour of his I possess is one of these. It is still very clumsy, impersonal and really primitive, though perhaps this gives it a special attraction. In vivid colours it depicts the Pöstlingberg, the landmark of Linz. I can still remember when Adolf gave it to me.

His drawings are a different matter, but there are only a few of them in existence. Although he gave me several, only one of them is left, a purely architectural drawing with little meaning. It shows a villa at No. 7 Stockbauerstrasse. It had just been built and it appealed to Adolf. So he drew it and made me a present of it. Apart from revealing his love for architecture, it is of no significance.

Casting my thoughts back to those years, I have to say this: Adolf never took painting seriously; it remained rather a hobby outside his more serious aspirations. But buildings meant much more to him. He gave his whole self to his imaginary buildings and was completely carried away by them. Once he had conceived an idea he was like one possessed. Nothing else existed for him – he was oblivious to time, sleep and hunger. Although it was a strain for me to follow him, those moments remain unforgettable. There he stood, with me, in front of the new cathedral, this pallid, skinny youth, with the first dark down showing on his upper lip, in his shabby pepper-and-salt suit, threadbare at the elbows and collar, with his eyes glued to some architectural detail, analysing the style, criticising or praising the work, disapproving of the material – all this with such thoroughness and such expert knowledge as though he were the builder and would have to pay for every shortcoming out of his own pocket. Then he would get out his drawing pad and the pencil would fly over the paper. This way, and no other way, was the manner of solving this problem, he would say. I had to compare his idea with the actual work, had to approve or disapprove, and all this with a passion as though both our lives depended on it.

Here, he could give full vent to his mania for changing everything, because a city always has good buildings and bad. He could never walk through the streets without being provoked by what he saw. Usually he carried around in his head, at the same time, half a dozen different building projects, and sometimes I could not help feeling that all the buildings of the town were lined up in his brain like a giant panorama. But as soon as he had selected one detail, he concentrated on this with all his energy. I remember one day when the old building of the Upper Austria and Salzburg Bank on the central square was demolished. With feverish impatience he followed the rebuilding. He was terribly worried lest the new building should not fit into its new surroundings. When, in the middle of it, he had to leave for Vienna he asked me to give him periodical reports on the progress of the work. In his letter of 21 July 1908 he writes, 'As soon as the bank is completed, please send me a picture postcard.' As there was no picture postcard available, I got out of it by procuring a photograph of the new building and sending it to him. Incidentally, the building met with his approval.

There were a lot of such houses in which he took a constant interest. He dragged me along wherever there was a building going up. He felt responsible for everything that was being built. But even more than with these concrete examples was he taken up with the vast schemes that he himself originated. Here his mania for change knew no limit. At first I watched these goings-on with some misgiving and wondered why he so obstinately occupied himself with plans which, I thought, would never come to anything. But the more remote the realisation of a project was, the more did he steep himself in it. To him these projects were in every detail as actual as though they were already executed and the whole town rebuilt according to his design. I often got confused and could not distinguish whether he was talking about a building that existed or one that was to be created. But to him it did not make any difference; the actual construction was only a matter of secondary importance.

Nowhere is his unshakeable consistency more evident. What the fifteen-year-old planned, the fifty-year-old carried out, often, as for instance in the case of the new bridge over the Danube, as faithfully as though only a few weeks, instead of decades, lay between planning and execution. The plan existed; then came influence and power and the plan became reality. This happened with uncanny regularity, as though the fifteen-year-old had taken it for granted that one day he would possess the necessary power and means. This is just too much for me to take in. I cannot conceive that such a thing is possible. One is tempted to use the word 'miracle', because there is no rational explanation for it.

Indeed, the plans which that unknown boy had drawn up for the rebuilding of his home town Linz, are identical to the last detail with the town planning scheme which was inaugurated after 1938. I am almost afraid of giving, in the following pages, my account of these early plans, lest my veracity should be suspected. And yet every single syllable of what I am going to recount is true.

On my eighteenth birthday, 3 August 1906, my friend presented me with a sketch of a villa. Similar to that planned for Stefanie, it was in his favourite

Renaissance style. By good luck, I have preserved the sketches. They show an imposing, palazzo-like building, whose frontage is broken up by a built-in tower. The ground plan reveals a well-thought-out arrangement of rooms, which are pleasantly grouped around the music room. The spiral staircase, a delicate architectural problem, is shown in a separate drawing, and so is the entrance hall, with its heavy beamed ceiling. The entrance is outlined with a few brisk strokes in a separate sketch. Adolf and I also selected a fitting site for my birthday present; it was to stand on the Bauernberg. When, later, I met Hitler in Bayreuth, I took good care not to remind him of this imaginary house. He would have been capable of actually giving me a villa on the Bauernberg, which presumably would have been finer than the original idea, which was very much in the taste of the epoch.

More impressive still are two sketches, still in my possession, samples of his numerous designs for a new concert hall in Linz. The old theatre was inadequate in every respect, and some art lovers in Linz had founded a society to promote the construction of a modern theatre. Adolf immediately joined this society and took part in a competition for ideas. He worked for months on his plans and drafts and was seriously convinced that his suggestions would be accepted. His anger was beyond measure when the society smashed all his hopes by giving up the idea of a new building and, instead, had the old one renovated. I refer to his biting remarks in a letter he sent me on 17 August 1908. 'It seems they intend to patch up the old junk-heap once more.'

Full of fury, he said that what he would like to do best would be to wrap up his manual of architecture and send it off to the address of this 'Theatre-Rebuilding Society Committee for the Execution of the Project for the Rebuilding of the Theatre'. How well did this monster title express his rage!

My two sketches, on either side of one sheet, date from that period. One side shows the auditorium. Columns break up the walls and the boxes are placed in between them. The balustrade is adorned by various statues. A mighty, domed ceiling covers the hall. On the back of this bold project, Adolf explained to me the acoustic conditions of the intended building, in which I, as a musician, was particularly interested. It clearly shows how the sound waves, rising from the orchestra, are reflected from the ceiling in such a way as to be – so to speak – poured over the audience below. Adolf took a great interest in acoustic problems. I remember, for instance, his suggestion to remodel the Volksgarten hall, whose bad acoustics always annoyed us, by structural alterations to the ceiling.

And now for the rebuilding of Linz. Here his ideas were legion, yet he did not change them indiscriminately, and indeed held fast to his decisions once they were taken, and that is why I remember so much about them. Every time we passed one spot or another, all his plans were ready immediately.

The wonderfully compact main square was a constant delight to Adolf, and his only regret was that the two houses nearest to the Danube disturbed the free vista of the river and the range of hills beyond. On his plans, the two houses were pushed apart sufficiently to allow a free view onto the new, widened bridge without, however, substantially altering the former aspect or the square, a solution which, later, he actually carried out. The municipal hall, which stood on the square, he thought unworthy of a rising town like Linz. He visualised a new, stately municipal hall, to be built in a modern style, far removed from that neo-Gothic style which at that time was the vogue for municipal halls, in Vienna and Munich for instance. In a different way, Hitler proceeded in the remodelling of the old castle, an ugly, box-like pile which overlooked the old city. He had discovered an old print by Merian depicting the castle as it was before the great fire. Its original appearance should be restored and the castle turned into a museum.

Another building which never failed to arouse his enthusiasm was the museum, built in 1892. We often stood and looked at the marble frieze which was 110 metres long and reproduced scenes from the history of the country in relief. He never got tired of gazing at it. He extended the museum beyond the adjoining convent garden and enlarged the frieze to 220 metres to make it, as he asserted, the biggest relief frieze on the continent. The new cathedral, then in course of reconstruction, occupied him constantly. The Gothic revival was, in his opinion, a hopeless enterprise, and he was angry that the Linzers could not stand up to the Viennese. For the height of the Linz spire was limited to 134 metres out of respect for the 138-metre high Stefansdom in Vienna. Adolf was greatly pleased with the new corporation of masons which had been founded in connection with the building of the cathedral, as he hoped this would result in the training of a number of capable masons for the town. The railway station was too near the town and, with its network of tracks, impeded the traffic as well as the town's development. Here, Adolf found an ingenious solution which was far ahead of his time. He removed the station out of town into the open country and ran the tracks underground across the town. The space gained by the demolition of the old station was designated for an extension of the public park. Reading this, one must not forget that the year was 1907, and it was an unknown youth of eighteen, without training or qualifications, who propounded these projects which revolutionised town planning, and which proved how capable he was, even then, of brushing aside existing ideas.

In a similar way, Hitler also reconstructed the surroundings of Linz. An interesting idea dominated his plans for the rebuilding of Wildberg castle. Its original state was to be restored and it was to be developed as a kind of open-air museum with a permanent population – quite a new idea. Certain types of artisans and workmen were to be attracted to the place. Their trades had to be partly in the medieval tradition, but should also partly serve modern purposes, a tourist industry, for instance. These inhabitants of the castle were to dress in ancient fashion. The traditions of the old guilds should rule, and a *Meistersinger* school was to be established. This 'island where the centuries had stood still' (these were his very words) would become a place of pilgrimage for all those who wanted to study life as it was lived in a medieval stronghold. Improving upon Dinkelsbühl and Rothenburg, Wildberg would not only show architecture but real life. Visitors would have to pay a toll at the gates, and so contribute to the upkeep of the local inhabitants. Adolf gave much thought to the choice of suitable artisans and I remember that we discussed the subject at great length. After all, I was just about to take my master's examination and was, therefore, entitled to have my say.

Quite a different project, of absolutely modern design, was the tower on the Lichtenberg. A mountain railway should run up to the peak, where a comfortable hotel would stand . The whole would be dominated by a tower 300 metres high, a steel construction which kept him very busy. The gilded eagle on top of the Stefansdom in Vienna would be visible on clear days through a telescope from the highest platform of the tower. I think I remember seeing a sketch of this project.

The boldest project, however, which put all the others in the shade, was the building of a grandiose bridge which would span the Danube at a great height. For this purpose he planned the construction of a high-level road. This would start at the Gugl, then still an ugly sandpit, which could be filled in with the town's refuse and rubbish, and provide the space for a new park. From there, in a broad sweep, the new road would lead up to the Stadtwald. (Incidentally, the city engineers went thus far some time ago, without knowing Hitler's plans. The road which has meanwhile been built, corresponds exactly to Hitler's projects.)

The Kaiser Franz Josef Warte in the Jägermayerwald – it is still standing

– was to be demolished and replaced by a proud monument. In a hall of fame there would be assembled the portrait busts of all the great men who had deserved well of the province of Upper Austria; from the top of the hall one would have a magnificent view over a vast expanse of country; and the whole edifice was to be crowned by a statue of Siegfried, raising aloft his sword Nothung. Valhalla, the Hall of Liberation at Kehlheim and the Hermann Monument in the Teutoburger Wald were obvious models. From this spot the bridge would sweep in one arch to the steep slope of the opposite bank. Adolf got his inspiration for this from the legend of a daring horseman who, pursued by his enemies, is said to have jumped from this point into the appalling depths below, to swim across the Danube and reach the other side. My imagination boggled at the dimensions of this bridge. The span of the arch was calculated to be more than 500 metres. The summit was 90 metres above the level of the river. I much regret that no sketches of this really unique project survive. This bridge across the deep valley, my friend declared, would give Linz an edifice without rival in the whole world. When we stood on one bank of the river, or the other, Adolf would explain to me all the details of the scheme.

These bold, far-reaching plans made a strange impression on me, as I still clearly remember. Although I saw in the whole thing nothing but a figment of the imagination, I could, nevertheless, not resist its peculiar fascination. What exercised my friend's mind and was hastily jotted down on scraps of paper, was more than nebulous fanaticism; these apparently absurd conceptions contained something compelling and convincing – a sort of superior logic. Each idea had its natural sequel in another, and the whole was a clear and rational chain of thought. Purely romantic conceptions, such as the 'Medieval Revival of Wildberg Castle' obviously betrayed Richard Wagner's paternity. They were linked to extremely modern technical devices, such as the replacement of level crossings by underground railway tracks. This was no unbridled wallowing in sheer fantasy, but a well-disciplined, almost systematic process. This 'architecture set to music' attracted me, perhaps, just because it seemed fully feasible – although we two impoverished devils had no possibility of realising these plans. But this did not disturb my friend in the least. His belief, that one day he would carry out all his tremendous projects, was unshakeable. Money was of no importance – it was only a matter of time, of living long enough.

This absolute faith was too much for my rational way of thinking. What was our future? I might become, at best, a well-known conductor. And Adolf? A gifted painter or draughtsman, perhaps a famous architect. But how far distant were these professional goals from that standing and reputation, those riches and power necessary for the rebuilding of an entire city. And who knows whether my friend, with his incredible flights of fancy and impulsive temperament, would stop at the rebuilding of Linz, for he was incapable of keeping his hands off anything within reach. Consequently I had grave doubts and occasionally I dared to remind him of the undeniable fact that all our worldly possessions put together did not amount to more than a few crowns – hardly enough to buy drawing paper. Usually Adolf brushed my objections impatiently aside, and I still remember his grim expression and disdainful gestures on such occasions. He took it for granted that one day the plans would be executed with the greatest of exactitude, and prepared for this moment accordingly. Even the most fantastic idea was thought out in the greatest detail. How was the material for the bridge to be transported across the Danube? Should it be stone or steel? How were the foundations for the end abutments to be laid? Would the rock stand the weight? These questions were, in part, irrelevant for the expert, in part, however, very much to the point. Adolf lived so much in his vision of the future Linz that he adapted his day-to-day habits to it; for instance, we would visit the hall of fame, the memorial temple or our medieval open-air museum.

One day when I interrupted the bold flow of his ideas for the national monument and asked him soberly how he proposed to finance this project, his first reply was a brusque, 'Oh, to hell with the money!' But apparently my query had disturbed him. And he did what other people do who want to get rich quickly – he bought a lottery ticket. And yet there was a difference between the way Adolf bought a lottery ticket and the way other people did. For other people only hope, or rather dream, of getting first prize, but Adolf was sure he had won from the moment of buying the ticket and had only forgotten to collect the money. His only possible worry was how to spend this not inconsiderable sum to the best advantage.

It was typical of him that he often mingled his most fantastic ideas with the coolest calculations, and the same thing happened with the purchase of the lottery ticket. Whilst he was already, in his imagination, spending his winnings, he carefully studied the lottery conditions and worked out our chance with the greatest precision. Adolf invited me to go shares with him in this venture. He was quite systematic about it. The price of the ticket was ten crowns, of which I had to find five. He stipulated, however, that these five crowns should not be given to me by my parents, but I had to earn them myself. At that time I earned some pocket-money and also got occasional tips from the customers. Adolf insisted on knowing exactly where these five crowns came from, and when he was satisfied that my contribution was really my own, we went together to the office of the state lottery to buy the ticket. It took him a long time to make up his mind, and I still do not know what considerations prompted his choice. As he was absolutely sceptical about occultism and more than rational in these matters, his behaviour remained a mystery to me. But in the end he found his winner. 'Here it is!' he said, and put the ticket carefully away in the little black notebook in which he wrote his poems.

The time that elapsed before the draw was for me the happiest period of our friendship. Love and enthusiasm, great thoughts, lofty ideas, all that we had already. The only thing that was lacking was money. Now we had that, too. What more could we want?

Although the first prize represented a lot of money, my friend was by no means tempted to spend it thoughtlessly – on the contrary. He went about it in the most calculating and economical way. It would have been senseless to invest the whole sum in one of the projects, say the rebuilding of the museum, for this would only have been a small part within the framework of the great town-planning scheme. It was more reasonable to use the money for our own benefit, to help us to a standing in public life which would enable us to progress further towards our ultimate aims.

It would have been too expensive to build a villa for ourselves; it would have swallowed up so much of our fortune that we would have moved into this splendour quite penniless. Adolf suggested a compromise: we should rent a flat, he said, and adapt it to our purpose. After long and careful examination of the various possibilities, we selected the second floor of 2 Kirchengasse in Urfahr, for this house was in a quite exceptional position. Near the bank of the Danube, it had a view over the pleasant, green fields which culminated in the Pöstlingberg. We crept into the house secretly, looked at the view from the staircase window, and Adolf made a sketch of the ground plan.

Then we moved in, so to speak. The larger wing of the flat should be for my friend, the smaller one was reserved for me. Adolf arranged the rooms so that his study was as far removed as possible from mine, so that he, at his drawing board, would not be disturbed by my practising.

My friend also saw to the furnishing of the rooms, drawing each single piece of furniture to scale on the ground plan. The furniture was of most beautiful and superior quality, made by the town's leading craftsmen, by no means cheap, mass-produced stuff. Even the decorations for the walls of every single room were designed by Adolf. I was only allowed to have a say about the curtains and draperies, and I had to show him how I suggested dealing with the rooms he had given me. He was certainly pleased with the self-assured manner in which I cooperated with the arrangement of the flat. We had no doubt that the first prize was ours. Adolf's own faith had bewitched me into believing as he did. I, too, expected to move into 2 Kirchengasse very soon.

Although simplicity was the keynote of our home, it was nevertheless imbued with a refined, personal taste. Adolf proposed to make our home the centre of a circle of art lovers. I would provide the musical entertainment. He would recite something, or read aloud, or expound his latest work. We would make regular trips to Vienna to attend lectures and concerts, and go to the theatre. (I realised then that Vienna played an important part in my friend's world of ideas. Strange that he had opted for the Kirchengasse in Urfahr.)

Winning the first prize would not alter our mode of life. We would remain simple people, wearing clothes of good quality, but certainly not ostentatious. With regard to our dress, Adolf had a delicious idea which delighted me immeasurably. We should both dress in exactly the same way, he suggested, so that people would take us for brothers. I believe that, for me, this idea alone made it worthwhile to win the lottery. It shows how our mere theatre acquaintanceship had ripened into a deep, close-knit friendship.

Of course, I would have to leave my parents' home and give up my trade. My musical studies would leave no time for such things for, as our studies progressed, our understanding for artistic experiences would increase and engross us completely.

Adolf thought of everything which was necessary, even the running of the household, as the day of the draw was approaching. A refined lady should preside over our home and run it. It had to be an elderly lady, to rule out any expectations or intentions which might interfere with our artistic vocation. We also agreed on the staff that this big household would need. Thus, everything was prepared. This image remained with me for a long time to come: an elderly lady, with greying hair but incredibly distinguished, standing in the brilliantly lit hall, welcoming on behalf of her two young, gifted gentlemen of seventeen and eighteen years respectively, the guests who formed their circle of select, lofty-minded friends.

During the summer months we were to travel. The first and foremost destination was Bayreuth, where we were to enjoy the perfect performances of the great master's music dramas. After Bayreuth, we were to visit famous cities, magnificent cathedrals, palaces and castles, but also industrial centres, shipyards and ports. 'It shall be the whole of Germany,' said Adolf. This was one of his favourite sayings.

The day of the draw arrived. Adolf came rushing wildly round to the workshop with the list of results. I have rarely heard him rage so madly as then. First he fumed over the state lottery, this officially organised exploitation of human credulity, this open fraud at the expense of docile citizens. Then his fury turned against the state itself, this patchwork of ten or twelve, or God knows how many nations, this monster built up by Habsburg marriages. Could one expect other than that two impoverished devils should be cheated out of their last couple of crowns?

Never did it occur to Adolf to reproach himself for having taken it for granted that the first prize belonged to him by right, and this in spite of the fact that he had brooded for hours over the conditions of the lottery, and calculated exactly how small our chances were in view of the number of tickets in existence and the number of prizes offered. I could find no explanation for this contradiction in his character, but there it was. For the first time he had been deserted by his willpower, which always seemed to move matters that concerned him in the desired direction. This he could not bear, for it was worse than the loss of the money and having to give up the flat and the lady housekeeper receiving our guests with distinguished nonchalance.

It seemed to Adolf more reasonable to rely upon himself and build his own future, rather than trust government institutions like lotteries. This would spare him from such setbacks. Thus, after a short period of utter depression, he returned to his earlier projects.

One of his favourite plans was the replacement of the bridge which linked Linz and Urfahr. We used to cross the bridge daily, and Adolf was particularly fond of this walk. When the floods of May 1868 destroyed five supports of the old wooden bridge, it was decided to build an iron bridge, which was completed in 1872. This rather ugly bridge was far too narrow for the traffic, although in those days there were no motor cars, and it was always overcrowded to a frightening degree.

Adolf liked to listen to the cursing drivers who, with wild oaths and much cracking of their whips, would try to make way for themselves. Although generally he showed little interest in the thing at hand and preferred to take the long view for his projects, he suggested here a provisional solution to remedy the existing state of affairs. Without altering the bridge itself, to either side should be added a footpath, two metres wide, which would carry the pedestrian traffic and thus relieve the roadway.

Naturally, nobody in Linz listened to the suggestions of this young dreamer, who could not even produce decent school reports. All the more enthusiastically did Adolf now occupy himself with the complete rebuilding of the bridge. The ugly iron structure must be demolished. The new bridge must be so proportioned as to give the visitor who approached the Danube from the main square the impression of seeing not a bridge, but a broad, impressive street. Mighty statues would underline the artistic aspect of the whole.

It is greatly to be regretted that, so far as I know, none of the numerous sketches which Hitler then made for the new bridge has been preserved, for it would be very interesting to compare these sketches with the plans which, thirty years later, Adolf Hitler prepared for this bridge and ordered to be executed. We owe it to his impatience to see the new Linz built that, in spite of the outbreak of war in 1939, that structure, the central project of his Linz town plan, was completed.

# Chapter 11

# 'In That Hour It Began . . .'

It was the most impressive hour I ever lived through with my friend. So unforgettable is it that even the most trivial things – the clothes Adolf wore that evening, the weather – are still present in my mind as though the experience were exempt from the passing of time. Far from the bright lights of the city, on the solitary heights of the Freinberg mountain, I saw the whole wonder of the firmament as if it were newly created, and the breath of the eternal stirred me as never before. When I look back, the thing which has remained with me the most stark and clear in my friendship with Adolf Hitler is neither his speeches nor his political ideas, but that single hour on the Freinberg. It was then that his future life was decided. Of course, out of respect for his mother he would maintain the pretence of a planned artistic career, for even aiming to be a painter was a more concrete goal than saying 'I am going to be a politician.' The decision to become a politician was seized in that hour on the heights above the city of Linz. Perhaps the word 'decision' is not quite accurate, for it was not a voluntary act but rather a visionary recognition of the road that had to be followed and which lay beyond his own will.

Adolf stood outside my house in his black overcoat, his dark hat pulled down over his face. It was a cold, unpleasant November evening. He waved to me impatiently. I was just cleaning myself up from the workshop and getting ready to go to the theatre. *Rienzi* was being performed that night. We had never seen this Wagner opera and looked forward to it with great excitement. In order to secure our place by the pillars in the promenade we had to be early. Adolf whistled to hurry me up.

He had told me something about this opera. Richard Wagner began it at Dresden in 1838 and worked on it during a stay by the Baltic. It was interesting that he should compose a work about Rome in the Middle Ages when he was learning about the north. He completed *Rienzi* in Paris and, when first performed in Dresden two years later, it made his name as a composer of opera even though it lacked the uniqueness of his later works.

After *Rienzi*, Wagner concentrated his attentions on the north and found in the gods of Germanic mythology his special realm. *Rienzi*, although set in the year 1347, was saturated with the spirit and rhythm of the revolution which swept across German soil ten years later.

Now we were in the theatre, burning with enthusiasm, and living breathlessly through Rienzi's rise to be tribune of the people of Rome, and his subsequent downfall. When at last it was over, it was past midnight. My friend, his hands thrust into his coat pockets, silent and withdrawn, strode through the streets and towards the outskirts. Usually after an artistic experience that had moved him he would start talking straight away, sharply criticising the performance, but after *Rienzi* he remained quiet a long while. This surprised me, and I asked him what he thought of it. He threw me a strange, almost hostile glance. 'Shut up!' he said brusquely.

The cold damp mist lay oppressively over the narrow streets. Our solitary steps resounded on the pavement. Adolf took the road that led up to the Freinberg. Without speaking a word, he strode forward. He looked almost sinister, and paler than ever. His turned-up collar increased this impression.

I wanted to ask him, 'Where are you going?', but his pallid face looked so forbidding that I suppressed the question. As if propelled by an invisible force, Adolf climbed up to the summit of the Freinberg, and only now did I realise that we were no longer in solitude and darkness, for the stars shone brilliantly above us.

Adolf stood in front of me and now he gripped both my hands and held them tight. He had never made such a gesture before. I felt from the grasp of his hands how deeply moved he was. His eyes were feverish with excitement. The words did not come smoothly from his mouth as they usually did, but rather erupted, hoarse and raucous. From his voice I could tell even more how much this experience had shaken him.

Gradually his speech loosened and the words flowed more freely. Never before and never again have I heard Adolf Hitler speak as he did in that hour, as we stood there alone under the stars, as though we were the only creatures in the world.

I cannot repeat every word that my friend uttered. I was struck by something strange, which I had never noticed before, even when he had talked to me in moments of the greatest excitement. It was as if a second ego spoke from within him, and moved him as much as it did me. It was not at all a case of a speaker being carried away by his own words. On the contrary, I rather felt as though he himself listened with astonishment and emotion to what burst forth from him with elementary force. I will not attempt to interpret this phenomenon, but it was a state of complete ecstasy and rapture, in which he transferred the character of Rienzi, without even mentioning him as a model or example with visionary power, to the plane of his own ambitions. But it was more than a cheap adaptation; the impact of the opera was rather a sheer external impulse which compelled him to speak. Like flood waters breaking their dykes, his words burst forth from him. He conjured up in grandiose, inspiring pictures his own future and that of his people.

Hitherto I had been convinced that my friend wanted to become an artist, a painter or perhaps an architect. This was now no longer the case. Now he aspired to something higher, which I could not yet fully grasp. It rather surprised me, as I thought that the vocation of the artist was for him the highest, most desirable goal. But now he was talking of a mandate which, one day, he would receive from the people, to lead them out of servitude to the heights of freedom.

It was a young man whose name then meant nothing who spoke to me in that strange hour. He spoke of a special mission which one day would be entrusted to him and I, his only listener, could hardly understand what he meant. Many years had to pass before I realised the significance of this enraptured hour for my friend.

His words were followed by silence. We descended into the town. The clock struck three. We parted in front of my house. Adolf shook hands with me, and I was astonished to see that he did not go in the direction of his home, but turned again towards the mountains. 'Where are you going now?' I asked him surprised. He replied briefly, 'I want to be alone.'

In the following weeks and months he never again mentioned this hour on the Freinberg. At first it struck me as odd and I could find no explanation for his strange behaviour, for I could not believe that he had forgotten it altogether. Indeed he never did forget it, as I discovered thirty-three years later. But he kept silent about it because he wanted to keep that hour entirely to himself. That I could understand, and I respected his silence. After all, it was his hour, not mine. I had played only the modest role of a sympathetic friend.

In 1939, shortly before war broke out, when for the first time I visited Bayreuth as the guest of the Reich Chancellor, I thought I would please my host by reminding him of that nocturnal hour on the Freinberg, and so I told Adolf Hitler what I remembered of it, assuming that the enormous multitude of impressions and events which had filled these past decades would have pushed into the background the experience of a seventeen-year-old youth. But after a few words, I sensed that he recalled that hour vividly and had retained all its details in his memory. He was visibly pleased that my account confirmed his own recollections. I was also present when Adolf Hitler retold this sequel to the performance of *Rienzi* in Linz to Frau Wagner, at whose home we were both guests. Thus my own memory was doubly confirmed. The words with which Hitler concluded his story to Frau Wagner are also unforgettable for me. He said solemnly, 'In that hour it began.'

# Chapter 12

# Adolf Leaves for Vienna

I had been noticing for a long time that Adolf, whether he was talking about art, politics or his own future, was no longer satisfied with friendly and familiar, though bourgeois Linz, and cast his eyes more and more frequently towards Vienna. The Austrian capital, still a resplendent imperial city and the metropolis of a state of 45 million people, promised him fulfillment of all his hopes for the future. At the time of which I speak, the summer of 1907, Adolf knew Vienna from a visit he had paid it in the previous year. In May and June 1906, he had stayed there long enough to grow enthusiastic about everything that had especially attracted him – the Hof Museum, the Hof Opera, the Burg Theatre, the magnificent buildings on the Ring – but not long enough to observe the distress and misery which were concealed by the magnificent façade of the city. This deceptive picture, largely produced by his artistic imagination, held a powerful attraction for him. In his thought he was no longer in Linz but already in Vienna, and his incredible capacity for ignoring the reality in front of him, and for accepting as real what existed only in his imagination, now came into full play.

I have to correct here a small error which Adolf Hitler made in *Mein Kampf* in regard to his first stay in Vienna. He is wrong when he says that he was not yet sixteen years old, for actually he had just had his seventeenth birthday. For the rest, his account corresponds entirely with my own recollection.

I well remember the enthusiasm with which my friend spoke of his impressions of Vienna. Details of his account, however, escape my memory. It is all the more fortunate that the postcards which he wrote to me on this first visit are still preserved. There are, altogether, four postcards which, apart from their biographical interest, are important graphological documents, for they are the earliest substantial examples of Adolf Hitler's handwriting still existing. It is a strangely mature, rather flowing hand, which one would hardly connect with a youth of barely eighteen, whilst the incorrect spelling not only bears witness to patchy schooling, but also to a certain indifference in such matters. All the picture postcards he sent me were, significantly enough, of buildings. A different kind of young man of his age would certainly have chosen a different kind of picture postcard for his friend.

The first of these cards, dated 7 May 1906, is a masterpiece of the postcard production of the period and must have cost him a pretty penny – it opens out into a kind of triptych, with a full view of the Karlsplatz, with the Karlskirche in the centre. The text is:

> In sending you this postcard I have to apologise for not having written sooner. Well, I have safely arrived and am going around everywhere. Tomorrow I am going to the opera *Tristan* and the day after *Die fliegende Holländer* etc. Although I find everything very beautiful, I am longing for Linz. Tonight Stadt Theatre.
> Greetings from your friend
> *Adolf Hitler.*

On the picture side of the card, the Conservatoire is expressly marked, probably the reason for his choice of this particular view, for he was already playing with the idea that one day we would study together in Vienna, and never missed an opportunity of reminding me of this possibility in the most alluring form. On the lower margin of the picture he added, 'Greetings to your esteemed parents.'

I would like to mention that the words 'Although I find everything very beautiful I am longing for Linz' do not refer to Linz but to Stefanie, for whom his love was all the greater the further from her he was. It certainly satisfied his impetuous longing for her that he, a lonely stranger in this heartless metropolis, could write these words, which only the friend who shared his secrets would understand.

On the same day, Adolf sent me a second postcard, which depicts the stage of the Hof Opera. Presumably this particularly successful photograph, which shows a part of the decor, had appealed to him. On it he wrote:

> The interior of the edifice is not very stirring. If the exterior is mighty majesty, which gives the building the seriousness of an artistic monument, the inside, though commanding admiration, does not impress one with its dignity. Only when the mighty sound waves flow through the hall and when the whispering of the wind gives way to the terrible roaring of the sound waves, then one feels the grandeur and forgets the gold and velvet with which the interior is overloaded.
> *Adolf H.*

On the front of the card there is again added: 'Greetings to your esteemed parents.' Adolf is completely in his element here. The friend is forgotten, even Stefanie is forgotten; no greeting, not even a hint, so overwhelmed is he by his recent experience. His clumsy style clearly reveals that his power of expression is not sufficient to do justice to the depth of his feelings. But even his poor style, which sounds like the ecstatic stammering of an enthusiast, reveals the magnitude of his experience. After all, it had been the greatest dream of our boyhood in Linz to see, one day, a perfect production at the Vienna Opera House instead of the performances in our provincial theatre, which left so much to be desired. Certainly Adolf, with his glowing description, aimed at my own art-loving heart. For what could make Vienna more attractive to me than the enthusiastic echo of such artistic impressions?

On the very next day, 8 May 1906, he wrote again; it is rather surprising that he wrote three times in the space of two days. His motive becomes clear from the contents of the postcard, which shows the exterior of the Vienna Opera House. He writes:

> I am really longing for my dear Linz and Urfar [*sic*]. Want or must see Benkieser again. What might he be doing, so I am arriving on Thursday on the 3.55 in Linz. If you have time and permission, meet me. Greetings to your esteemed parents!
> Your friend,
> *Adolf Hitler.*

The word 'Urfar', misspelt in a hurry, is underlined, although Adolf's mother was still living in the Humboldtstrasse, and not in Urfahr, and of course that remark referred to Stefanie, as did the agreed codeword, Benkieser. The phrase 'want or must see Bekieser' is typical of Adolf's style and character. Also significant are the words, 'If you have time and permission, meet me.' Although it was a matter of urgency for him, he respects my duty of obedience to my parents, nor does he omit to greet them on this card.

Unfortunately I cannot verify whether Adolf really returned to Linz the following Thursday, or if this indication was only intended to satisfy his unappeasable longing for Stefanie. However, his remark in *Mein Kampf* that his first sojourn in Vienna lasted only a fortnight is incorrect. Actually, he stayed there about four weeks, as is evidenced by the postcard of 6 June 1906. This card, which shows the Franzensring and the parliament building, is on conventional lines: 'To you and to your esteemed parents, I send herewith best wishes for the holidays and kind regards. Respectfully, Adolf Hitler.'

With this memory of his first day in Vienna transfigured by his yearning for Stefanie, Adolf entered the critical summer of 1907. What he suffered in those weeks was in many respects similar to the grave crisis of two years earlier when, after much heart-searching, he had finally settled his accounts with the school and made an end of it. Outwardly, this seeking for a new path showed itself in dangerous fits of depression. I knew only too well those moods of his, which were in sharp contrast to his ecstatic dedication and activity, and realised that I could not help him. At such times he was inaccessible, uncommunicative and distant. It might happen that we did not meet at all for a day or two. If I tried to see him at home, his mother would receive me with great surprise. 'Adolf has gone out,' she would say, 'He must be looking for you.' Actually Adolf would wander around aimlessly and alone for days and nights in the fields and forests surrounding the town. When I met him at last, he was obviously glad to have me with him, but when I asked him what was wrong, his only answer would be, 'Leave me alone', or a brusque, 'I don't know myself.' And if I insisted, he would understand my sympathy, and then say in a milder tone, 'Never mind, Gustl, but not even you can help me.'

This state lasted several weeks. One fine summer evening, however, when we were strolling beside the Danube, the tension began to ease. Adolf reverted to his old, familiar tone. I remember this moment exactly. As usual, we had been to see Stefanie pass by arm-in-arm with her mother. Adolf was still under her spell. Even though he saw her at this time almost every day, these meetings never became something commonplace for him. Whilst Stefanie had probably long since become bored by the silent, but strictly conventional adulation of the pale, thin youth, my friend lost himself increasingly in his wishful dreams the more he saw her. Yet he was past those romantic ideas of elopement or suicide. He explained to me in eloquent words his state of mind: the vision of the beloved one pursued him day and night; he was unable to work or even to think clearly and he feared he would go mad if this state of affairs went on much longer, though he saw no way of altering the situation, for which Stefanie was not to blame, either. 'There is only one thing to be done,' he cried, 'I must go away – far away from Stefanie.'

On our way home he explained his decision in greater detail. His relationship with Stefanie would become more bearable for him once he was living at a distance and could not meet her every day. It did not occur to him that in this way he might lose Stefanie altogether – so deeply convinced was he that he had won her for ever. The true situation was different. Adolf, perhaps, already realised that, if he wanted to win Stefanie, he would have to speak to her or take some such decisive step – it is probable that even he began to find the exchange of glances on the Landstrasse a little childish. Nevertheless he felt instinctively that it would abruptly destroy his life's dream if he actually made Stefanie's acquaintance. Indeed, as he said to me, 'If I introduce myself to Stefanie and her mother, I will have to tell her at once what I am, what I have and what I want. My statement would bring our relations abruptly to an end.' This awareness, and the simultaneous realisation that he had to put his relationship with Stefanie on a firm basis to avoid ridicule, were for him the horns of a dilemma, from which he saw only one way out – flight. He started at once to expound his plan to the last detail. I received precise instructions what to tell Stefanie if she asked, full of astonishment, what had become of my friend. (She never did.) Adolf himself realised that, if he wanted to marry her, he would have to offer her a secure existence.

But this unsolved and, for a person of my friend's nature, insoluble problem of his relationship with Stefanie was only one of the many reasons which prompted him to quit Linz, although it was the most personal and therefore decisive. Another reason was that he was anxious to escape the atmosphere that prevailed at home. The idea that he, a young man of eighteen, should continue to be kept by his mother had become unbearable to him. It was a painful dilemma which, as I could see for myself, made him almost physically ill. On the one hand, he loved his mother above everything: she was the only person on earth to whom he felt really close, and she reciprocated his feeling to some extent, although she was deeply disturbed by her son's unusual nature, however proud she was at times of him. 'He is different from us,' she used to say.

On the other hand, she felt it to be her duty to carry out the wishes of her late husband, and to prevail on Adolf to embark on a safe career. But what was 'safe', in view of the peculiar character of her son? He had failed at school and ignored all his mother's wishes and suggestions. A painter – that was what he had said he wanted to become. This could not seem very satisfactory to his mother for, simple soul that she was, anything connected with art and artists appeared to her frivolous and insecure. Adolf tried to change her mind by telling her of his intention to study at the Academy. That sounded better; after all, the Academy, of which Adolf spoke with increasing enthusiasm, was really a kind of school, where his mother thought he might make up for what he had missed in the Realschule.

When listening to these domestic discussions, I was always surprised by the sympathetic understanding and patience with which Adolf tried to convince his mother of his artistic vocation. Contrary to his habit, he never became cross or violent on these occasions. Often, Frau Klara would also unburden herself to me, for she saw in me too an artistically gifted young man with high aims. Having a better understanding of musical matters than of her son's dabbling in drawing and painting, she frequently found my opinions more convincing than his, and Adolf was very grateful for my support. But, in Frau Klara's eyes there was one important difference between Adolf and me: I had learnt an honest trade, finished my apprenticeship and passed my journeyman's examination. I would always have a safe haven to shelter in, whereas Adolf was just steering into the unknown. This vision tormented his mother unceasingly. Nevertheless, he succeeded in convincing her that it was essential for him to go to the Academy to study painting. I still remember distinctly how pleased he was over it. 'Now mother will not raise any more objections,' he told me one day, 'I will definitely go to Vienna at the beginning of September.' Adolf had also settled with his mother the financial side of the plan. His living expenses and the Academy fees were to be paid out of the small legacy left him by his father and now administered by his guardian. Adolf hoped that, with great economy, he would be able to manage on this for a year. What would happen afterwards remained to be seen, he said. Perhaps he would earn something by the sale of some drawings and pictures.

The main opponent of this plan was his brother-in-law Raubal who, with his revenue official's limited horizon, was incapable of understanding Adolf's thoughts. That was rubbish, he said; it was high time that Adolf learned something decent. Although Raubal, after some violent altercations with Adolf, in which he always came off worst, avoided any further argument with him, he tried all the harder to influence Frau Klara. Adolf found out most of this from 'the kid', the pet name he used for his eleven-year-old sister. When Paula told him that Raubal had been to see his mother, Adolf would fall into a rage. 'This Pharisee is ruining my home for me,' he once remarked to me in a fury. Apparently, Raubal had also got in touch with Adolf's guardian, for one day the worthy peasant Mayrhofer, who would have liked best to have made a baker out of Adolf and had already found an apprenticeship for him, came from Leonding to see Frau Klara. Adolf was afraid that his guardian might induce her to hold back the legacy. This would have put a stop to his moving to Vienna. But the plan did not get so far, though for some time the decision was very much in doubt. By the end of this tough struggle, everybody was against Adolf – even, as happens in tenement buildings, the other tenants. Frau Klara listened to this more or less well-meant chatter and became completely confused by it all.

Often, when Adolf had his fits of depression and was wandering through the woods, I used to sit with her in her little kitchen, listening sympathetically to her laments, trying hard to comfort the wretched woman without being unfair to my friend, and at the same time helping him where I could. I could easily put myself in Adolf's shoes. It would have been simple enough for him, with his great energy, just to pack up and go, if consideration for his mother had not prevented him. He had come to hate the petit-bourgeois world in which he had to live. He could hardly bear to return to that narrow world after lonely hours spent in the open. He was always in a ferment of rage, hard and intractable. I had a lot to put up with in those weeks. But the secret of Stefanie, which we shared, bound us inseparably together. The sweet magic which she, the unattainable, radiated, calmed the stormy waves. So, as his mother was so easily influenced, the matter remained undecided, although Adolf had long since made up his mind.

On the other hand, Vienna was calling. That city had a thousand possibilities for an eager young man like Adolf, opportunities which might lead to the most sublime heights or to the most sombre depths. A city magnificent and at the same time cruel, promising everything and denying everything – that was Vienna. She demanded the highest stake from everyone who pledged himself to her. And that is what Adolf wanted.

No doubt, Adolf had his father's example before him. What would he have become if he had not gone to Vienna? A poor, haggard cobbler somewhere in the poverty-stricken Waldviertel. And see what Vienna made of this poor, orphaned, cobbler's boy!

Ever since his first visit in the spring of 1906, these rather vague ideas had assumed concrete form in Adolf's mind. He who had dedicated his life to art, could develop his talents only in Vienna, for in that city were concentrated its most perfect achievements in every field. During his first short stay there he had already been to the Hof Opera and seen *Die fliegende Holländer*, *Tristan* and *Lohengrin*. By these standards, the performances in the Linz Landestheater appeared provincial and inadequate. In Vienna, the Burg Theatre, with its classic productions, awaited the young man. There was also the Vienna Philharmonic Orchestra which, with justification, was

126

then considered the best in the world. The museums with their immeasurable treasures, the picture galleries and the Hof Library provided endless possibilities for study and self-improvement.

Linz had little more to offer Adolf. What rebuilding had to be done in this city he had already done, mentally, and no more large, tempting problems were left for him to solve. And I was always there to report any further alterations to the town, such as the new Bank of Upper Austria and Salzburg building on the main square, or the projected new theatre. But he wanted to look at grander things – the magnificent buildings of the centre of Vienna, the vast, truly imperial layout of the Ringstrasse – rather than the humble little Landstrasse in Linz. Moreover his growing interest in politics found no outlet in conservative Linz, where political life ran in well-defined grooves. Simply nothing happened that might have had any political interest for a young man; there was no tension, no conflict, no unrest. It was a great adventure to move from this absolute calm into the centre of the storm. All the energies of the Habsburg state were concentrated in Vienna. Thirty nations struggled for their national existence and independence, and thus created an atmosphere like that of a volcano. How the young heart would rejoice at throwing itself unrestrainedly into this struggle.

At long last the great moment arrived. Adolf, beaming with delight, came to see me at the workshop, where we were very busy at that time. 'I'm leaving tomorrow,' he said briefly. He asked me to accompany him to the station, as he did not want his mother to come. I knew how painful it would have been for Adolf to take leave of his mother in front of other people. He disliked nothing more than showing his feelings in public. I promised him to come and help him with his luggage.

Next day I took time off and went to the Blütengasse to collect my friend. Adolf had prepared everything. I took his suitcase, which was rather heavy with books he did not want to leave behind, and hurried away to avoid being present at the farewells. Yet I could not avoid them entirely. His mother was crying and little Paula, whom Adolf had never bothered with much, was sobbing in a heart-rending manner. When Adolf caught up with me on the stairs and helped me with the suitcase, I saw that his eyes too were wet. We took the tram to the railway station, chatting about trivialities, as often happens when one wants to hide one's feelings. It moved me deeply to say goodbye to Adolf, and I felt miserable going home alone. It was a good thing that there was so much work waiting for me at the workshop.

Unfortunately, our correspondence of that period is lost. I only remember that for several weeks I had no news at all from him. And it was during those days that I felt most deeply how much he meant to me. Other young people of my age did not interest me, as I knew in advance that they would only turn out to be disappointing, with few other interests than their own shallow and superficial doings. Adolf was much more serious and mature than most people of his age. His horizon was wide and his passionate interest in everything had carried me along with it. Now I felt very lonely and miserable, and to find some comfort I went to the Blütengasse to see Frau Klara. Talking to somebody so fond of Adolf would certainly make me feel better.

I thought that Adolf would already have written to his mother, for after all it was a fortnight since he had left, and I would get his address and write to him, according to instructions, of all that had transpired meanwhile. Actually, not much had happened, but for Adolf every detail was important. I had seen Stefanie at the Schmiedtoreck and indeed she had been surprised to see me there alone, for that much she knew about us, that in this 'affair' I played only a secondary role. The chief protagonist was missing. That seemed strange to her. What could it mean? Though Adolf was only a silent admirer, he was more persistent and tenacious than all the others. She did not want to lose this faithful adorer. Her enquiring glance caught me so unexpectedly that I was almost tempted to address her. But Stefanie was not alone, being, as usual, accompanied by her mother, and moreover my friend had given me strict instructions to wait until Stefanie herself asked me. Surely, as soon as she realised that he had gone for good she would take the opportunity of running over the bridge alone to entreat me impetuously to tell her what had become of my friend. Perhaps he had had an accident, or he was ill again as he was that time two years ago, or perhaps even dead. Unthinkable! Anyhow, though that conversation had not yet taken place, I had enough material to fill four pages of a letter. But what on earth had happened to Adolf? Not a line from him. Frau Klara opened the door to me and greeted me warmly, and I could see that she had been longing for me to come. 'Have you heard from Adolf?' she asked me, still at the door. So he had not written to his mother either, and this made me feel anxious. Something out of the ordinary must have happened. Perhaps things had not gone according to plan in Vienna.

Frau Klara offered me a chair. I saw how much good it did her to be able to unburden herself. Ah, the old lament, which I had come to know by heart! But I listened patiently. 'If only he had studied properly at the Realschule he would almost be ready to matriculate. But he won't listen to anybody.' And she added, 'He's as pig-headed as his father. Why this crazy journey to Vienna? Instead of holding on to his little legacy, it's just being frittered away. And after that? Nothing will come of his painting. And story writing doesn't earn anything either. And I can't help him – I've got Paula to look after. You know yourself what a sickly child she is but, just the same, she must get a decent education. Adolf doesn't give it a thought, he goes his way, just as if he were alone in the world. I shall not live to see him making an independent position for himself . . .'

Frau Klara seemed more careworn than ever. Her face was deeply lined. Her eyes were lifeless, her voice sounded tired and resigned. I had the impression that, now that Adolf was no longer there, she had let herself go, and she looked older and more ailing than ever. She certainly had concealed her condition from her son to make the parting easier for him. Or perhaps it was Adolf's impulsive nature that kept up her vitality. Now, on her own, she seemed to me an old, sick woman.

I forget, unfortunately, what happened during the course of the following weeks. Adolf had briefly informed me of his address. He was living in the 6th District at 29 Stumpergasse, Staircase II, second floor, door No. 17, in the flat of a woman with the curious name of Zakreys. That was all he wrote. But I guessed that there was more behind this obstinate silence, for I knew that Adolf's silences usually meant that he was too proud to talk.

I quote therefore from his own description in *Mein Kampf* of his second sojourn in Vienna, which by general consent is entirely truthful:

I had gone to Vienna with the intention of taking the entrance examination for the Academy. I had set out, armed with a thick wad of drawings, convinced that it would be child's play to pass. At the Realschule I had been by far the best in my class at drawing, and since then my ability had developed quite extraordinarily, so I was quite satisfied with myself and this made me hope, proudly and happily, for the best . . .

So here I was for the second time in the beautiful city, waiting impatiently but hopefully for the results of the entrance examination. I was so sure of success that the news of my rejection hit me like a bolt from the blue. Yet that was what happened. When I went to see the rector and asked to know the reasons why I had not been admitted to the General Painting School of the Academy, I was told by this gentleman that the drawings I had submitted showed clearly that I had no aptitude for painting, my ability seemed rather to lie in the field of architecture, and I should not go to the Painting School, but rather to the Academy's School of Architecture. That I had never been to an architectural school, nor received any training in architecture, seemed to him hard to believe.

Defeated, I left the monumental building on the Schiller Platz for the first time in my young life at variance with myself, for what I had been told about my ability seemed to me to disclose in a flash the discord from which I had long suffered without, hitherto, clearly realising the whys and wherefores of it.

In a few days I knew inwardly that I would become an architect. Yet this was an incredibly difficult path, for what I had missed out of obstinacy at the Realschule now took its bitter revenge. Admission to the School of Architecture was dependent on attending a technical school for building, and entrance to the latter required one to have matriculated from a secondary school. I did not meet any of these conditions and, as far as could be foreseen therefore, the fulfillment of my dream to become an artist was impossible.

He had been refused by the Academy; he had failed even before he had got a footing in Vienna. Nothing more terrible could have happened to him. But he was too proud to talk about it, and so he concealed from me what had occurred. He concealed it from his mother too. When later we met again, he had to some extent already lived down this hard verdict. He did not mention it at all. I respected his silence and did not ask him any questions because I suspected that something had gone wrong with his plans. Not until the next year, when we were lodging together in Vienna, did all these circumstances gradually become clear to me.

Adolf's talent for architecture was so obvious that it would have justified an exception – how many less talented students were to be found at the Academy! This decision was therefore as biased and bureaucratic as it was unjust. Yet Adolf's reaction to this humiliation was typical. He made no attempt to obtain exceptional treatment or to humiliate himself in front of people who did not understand him. There was neither revolt nor rebellion, instead came a radical withdrawal into himself, an obstinate resolve to cope alone with adversity, an embittered 'now, more than ever!' which he flung at the gentlemen of the Schiller Platz just as, two years earlier, he had settled his account with his school teachers. Whatever disappointments life brought him, they were but a spur for him to brave all obstacles and to continue on the path on which he had embarked.

In *Mein Kampf* he wrote: 'As the goddess of misery took me in her arms and so often threatened to break me, the will to resist grew, and in the end the will triumphed.'

# Chapter 13

# His Mother's Death

I remember that Adolf's mother had to undergo a serious operation at the beginning of 1907. She was then in the hospital of the Sisters of Mercy in the Herrenstrasse, and he visited her there daily. The surgeon in charge of her case was a Dr Urban. I forget what her illness was, but it was probably cancer of the breast. Although Frau Klara recovered sufficiently to run her household again, she remained very weak and ailing, and every now and again she had to take to her bed. Yet a few weeks after Adolf had left for Vienna she seemed to be better, for I met her by chance on the Promenade where, at that time, a street market used to be held, peasant women coming in from the country to sell eggs, butter and vegetables. 'Adolf is all right,' she told me contentedly, 'If only I knew what on earth he is studying! Unfortunately, he does not mention that at all. However, I imagine that he is very busy.'

That was good news which pleased me too, for Adolf had not written to me about his activities in Vienna. Our correspondence was mainly concerned with Benkieser – otherwise Stefanie. But his mother must not be told of that, of course. I asked Frau Klara how she was. Not at all well, she said; she had a lot of bad pain, and very often could not sleep at night. But she warned me not to write to Adolf about it, for perhaps she would soon be better. When we parted she asked me to come to see her again soon.

We were then very busy in the workshop, indeed business had never before been as good as in that year, and orders came in regularly and often. Yet in spite of this heavy work, I devoted every moment of my leisure to my musical training. I played the viola both in the Music Society and the great Symphony Orchestra. So the weeks passed, and it was late in November when at last I found time to visit Frau Hitler. I was shocked when I saw her. How wilted and worn was her kind, gentle face. She was lying in bed and stretched out her pale, thin hand to me. Little Paula pushed a chair up beside her. She started at once to talk about Adolf and was happy about the hopeful tone of his letters. I asked her if she had informed him of her illness and offered to do so for her in case writing was too great an effort. But she refused hastily. If her condition did not improve, she said, she would have to send for Adolf from Vienna. She was sorry she had to tear him away from his hard work – but what else could she do? The little one had to go to school every day, Angela had enough worries of her own (she was expecting a second baby), and she could not rely on her son-in-law Raubal at all. Since she had taken Adolf's side and supported him in his decision to go to Vienna, Raubal had been angry with her and now never showed up; he had even prevented his wife Angela from looking after her. So there was nothing left but to go to the hospital as the doctor had advised, she said. The Hitler's family doctor was the very popular Dr Bloch, known in the town as the 'poor people's doctor', an excellent physician and a man of great kindness who sacrificed himself for his patients. If Dr Bloch had advised Frau Hitler to go to Spital hospital, her condition must be grave. I was wondering whether it was not, after all, my duty to inform Adolf. Frau Klara had said how awful it was for her that Adolf was so far away. I never realised as clearly as on that visit how devoted she was to her son. She thought and planned for his welfare with all the strength that was left to her. In the end, she promised me that she would tell Adolf of her condition.

When I took leave of her that evening, I was very dissatisfied with myself. Was there no way of helping the poor woman? I knew how devoted Adolf was to his mother; something had to be done. If his mother really needed help, little Paula was too clumsy and too frightened to be of any use. When I got home I talked to my mother. She offered at once to look after Frau Hitler even though she was a complete stranger, but this was vetoed by my father who, with his exaggerated ideas of correct behaviour, thought it was bad manners to offer one's help without being asked. A few days later I went again to see Frau Klara. I found her up, busy in the kitchen. She felt somewhat better and she was already regretting that she had told Adolf about her illness. I stayed with her a long time that evening. She was more talkative than usual and, quite contrary to her habit, she began to tell me about her life. Some of it I understood, and a lot I guessed at, though much was left unsaid; nevertheless, the story of a life of suffering was disclosed to a young man then in the full hopes of his nineteen years.

But in the workshop time was pressing, and my father was a strict boss. Even concerning my artistic ambitions he used to say: work first – then music. And with a special performance coming on, there was one orchestral rehearsal after another. Sometimes I literally did not know how to cram everything in. Then one morning, as I was energetically filling a mattress,

Adolf suddenly appeared in the room. He looked terrible. His face was so pale as to be almost transparent, his eyes were dull and his voice hoarse. I felt that a storm of suffering must be hidden behind his icy demeanour. He gave me the impression that he was fighting for life against a hostile fate.

There was hardly a greeting, no question about Stefanie, nothing about what he had been doing in Vienna. 'Incurable, the doctor says' – this was all he could utter. I was shocked by the unequivocal diagnosis. Probably Dr Bloch had told him of his mother's condition. Perhaps he had called in another doctor for consultation and could not reconcile himself to this cruel verdict.

His eyes blazed, his temper flared up. 'Incurable – what do they mean by that?' he screamed. 'Not that the malady is incurable, but that the doctors aren't capable of curing it. My mother isn't even old. Forty-seven isn't an age where you give up hope. But as soon as the doctors can't do anything, they call it incurable.'

I was familiar with my friend's habit of turning everything he came across into a problem. But never had he spoken with such bitterness, with such passion as now. Suddenly it seemed to me as though Adolf, pale, excited, shaken to the core, stood there arguing and bargaining with Death, who remorselessly claimed its victim.

I asked Adolf if I could help. He did not hear me – he was too busy with this settling of accounts. Then he interrupted himself and declared in a sober, matter-of-fact voice: 'I shall stay in Linz and keep house for my mother.' 'Can you do that?' I asked. 'One can do anything when one has to', and he said no more.

I went with him as far as the street. Now, I thought, he would certainly ask after Stefanie; perhaps he had not liked to mention her in the workshop. I would have been glad if he had, because I had carried out my instructions faithfully and could tell him a good deal, even though the expected conversation had not taken place. I also hoped that Adolf, in his deep spiritual affliction, would find comfort in the thought of Stefanie. And it certainly was so. Stefanie meant more to him in those dark weeks than ever before. But he stifled any mention of her, so deeply was he engrossed in his preoccupation for his mother.

I cannot recollect exactly when Adolf returned from Vienna. It was perhaps late in November, but possibly even December. But the weeks that follow remain indelibly in my memory; they were, in a certain sense, the most beautiful, the most intimate weeks of our friendship. How deeply these days impressed me can be gathered from the mere fact that from no other period of our association do so many details stand out in my memory. He was as though transformed. So far I had been certain that I knew him thoroughly and in all his aspects. After all, we had lived closely together for more than three years in an exclusive friendship that did not permit of any secrets. Yet in those weeks it seemed to me that my friend had become a different person.

Gone were the problems and ideas which used to agitate him so much, gone all thought of politics. Even his artistic interests were hardly noticeable. He was nothing but his mother's faithful and helpful son.

I had not taken Adolf very seriously when he said that he would now take over the household in the Blütengasse, for I knew Adolf's low opinion of such monotonous chores, necessary though they were. And so I was sceptical as to his good intentions and imagined that they would not exceed a few well-meant gestures. But I was profoundly mistaken. I did not understand that side of Adolf sufficiently, and had not realised that his unbounded love for his mother would enable him to carry out this unaccustomed domestic work so efficiently that she could not praise him enough for it. Thus one day on my arrival at the Blütengasse I found Adolf kneeling on the floor. He was wearing a blue apron and scrubbing out the kitchen, which had not been cleaned for a long time. I was really immensely surprised and I must have shown it, for Frau Klara smiled in spite of her pain and said to me: 'There, you see, Adolf can do anything.' Then I noticed that Adolf had changed the furniture around. His mother's bed now stood in the kitchen because that was heated during the day. The kitchen cupboard had been moved into the living room, and in its place was the couch, on which Adolf slept, so that he could be near her during the night as well. Paula slept in the living room.

I could not refrain from asking how he managed the cooking. 'As soon as I've finished the scrubbing, you can see for yourself,' said Adolf. But before I did, Frau Klara told me that every morning she discussed the dinner with Adolf. He always chose her favourite dishes and prepared them so well that she herself could not have done better. She enjoyed her food immensely, she insisted, and she had never eaten with such good appetite as since Adolf had returned.

I looked at Frau Klara, who had sat up in bed. The fervour of her words had coloured her usually pale cheeks. The pleasure of having her son back and his devotion to her had transfigured the serious, worn face. But behind this mother's joy were the unmistakable signs of suffering. The deep lines, the drawn mouth and the sunken eyes showed how right the doctor had been.

To be sure, I should have known that my friend would not fail, even in this out-of-the-ordinary task, for whatever he did, he did thoroughly. Seeing the seriousness with which he carried out the running of the household, I suppressed a chaffing remark although Adolf, who was always so punctilious about his neat dress, certainly looked comical in his old clothes with the apron tied around him. Nor did I utter a word of appreciation, so touched was I by his changed attitude, knowing how much self-restraint this work was costing him.

Frau Klara's condition was changeable. Her son's presence improved her general state and cheered her up. Sometimes she would even get up in the afternoon and sit in the armchair. Adolf anticipated her every wish and took the most tender care of her. I had never before seen in him such loving tenderness. I did not trust my own eyes and ears. Not a cross word, not an impatient remark, no violent insistence on having his own way. He forgot himself entirely in those weeks and lived only for his mother. Although Adolf, according to Frau Klara, had inherited many of his father's traits, I realised then how much his nature resembled his mother's. Certainly this was partly due to the fact that he had spent the previous four years of his life alone with her. But over and above that there was a peculiar spiritual harmony between mother and son which I have never since come across. All that separated them was pushed into the background. Adolf never mentioned the disappointment which he had suffered in Vienna. For the time being, cares for the future no longer seemed to exist. An atmosphere of relaxed, almost serene contentment surrounded the dying woman.

Adolf, too, seemed to have forgotten everything that had preoccupied him. Only once, after I had said goodbye to Frau Klara, did he come to the door with me and ask me if I had seen Stefanie. But this question was now put in a different tone. It no longer expressed the impatience of the impetuous lover, but the secret anxiety of a young man who feared that fate would now deprive him of the last thing that made life worth living. I gathered from his hasty question how much this girl meant to him in those grave days, more perhaps than if she had actually been as close to him as he would have wished. I reassured him: I often met Stefanie going over the bridge with her mother and everything seemed unaltered.

December was cold and bleak. For days on end, a damp heavy mist hung over the Danube. The sun shone rarely and, when it did, appeared so feebly as to give no warmth at all. His mother's condition deteriorated visibly and Adolf asked me to come only every other day. As often as I entered the kitchen Frau Klara greeted me by lifting her hand a little and stretching it out towards me, and a faint smile would pass over her face, now distorted with pain. I remember a small but significant incident. Going through Paula's exercise books, Adolf had noticed that she was not getting on in school as well as her mother expected. Adolf took her by the hand and led her to their mother's bed and there made her swear always to be a diligent and well-behaved pupil. Perhaps Adolf wanted to show his mother by this little scene that he had meanwhile realised his own faults. If he had stayed on at the Realschule until matriculation he would have avoided the disaster in Vienna. No doubt this decisive event which had, as he said later, for the first time put him at variance with himself, was at the back of his mind during those terrible days and added to his depression.

When I returned to the Blütengasse two days later and knocked softly on the door, Adolf opened it immediately, came out into the corridor and closed the door behind him. He told me that his mother was not at all well and was in terrible pain. Even more than his words, his emotion made me realise the seriousness of the situation. I thought it better to leave and Adolf agreed with me. We shook hands silently and I departed.

Christmas was approaching. Snow had fallen at last and the town had assumed a festive garb. But it did not feel like Christmas. I walked across the Danube bridge to Urfahr. I learned from the people in the house that Frau Klara had already received extreme unction. I wanted to make my visit as short as possible. I knocked, and Paula opened the door. I entered hesitantly. Frau Klara was sitting up in bed. Adolf had his arm around her shoulders to support her as the terrible pain was less severe when she was sitting up.

I remained standing by the door. Adolf signed to me to go. As I was opening the door, Frau Klara waved to me with her outstretched hand. I shall never forget the words which the dying woman then uttered in a whisper. 'Gustl', she said – usually she called me Herr Kubizek, but in that hour she used the name by which Adolf always called me – 'go on being a good friend to my son when I'm no longer here. He has no one else.' With tears in my eyes I promised, and then I went. This was the evening of 20 December.

The next day Adolf came to see us at home. He looked worn out and we could tell from his distraught face what had happened. His mother had died in the early hours of the morning, he said. It was her last wish to be buried at the side of her husband in Leonding. Adolf could hardly speak, so deeply shaken was he by the loss of his mother.

My parents expressed their sympathy, but my mother realised that the best thing was to turn to practical matters straight away. Arrangements had to be made for the funeral. Adolf had already seen the undertakers and the funeral was fixed for 23 December at nine o'clock. But there was much else to be seen to. The removal of the body to Leonding had to be arranged, the necessary documents procured and the funeral announcements printed. All this helped Adolf to get over his emotional shock, and he calmly made the necessary preparations.

On 23 December 1907, I went with my mother to the house of mourning. The weather had changed: it was thawing and the streets were covered in slush. The day was damp and misty, and one could hardly see the river. We entered the apartment to take leave of the deceased with flowers, as was customary. Frau Klara was laid out on her bed. Her waxen face was transfigured. I felt that death had come to her as a relief from terrible pain. Little Paula was sobbing, but Adolf restrained himself. Yet a glance at his face was sufficient to know how he had suffered in those hours. Not only had he now lost both his parents, but with his mother he had lost the only creature on earth on whom he had concentrated his love and who had loved him in return.

My mother and I went down into the street. The priest came. The body had been laid in the coffin, which was brought down to the hall. The priest blessed the deceased and then the small cortège moved off. Adolf followed the coffin. He wore a long, black overcoat, black gloves and carried in his hand, as was customary, a black top hat. The dark clothing made his white face seem even paler. He looked stern and composed. On his left, also in black, was his brother-in-law Raubal, and between them the eleven-year-old Paula. Angela, who was well advanced in pregnancy, followed the mourners in a closed carriage. The whole funeral made a wretched impression on me. In addition to my mother and myself, there were only a few tenants of No. 9 Blütengasse, and a few neighbours and acquaintances from their former home in the Humboldtstrasse. My mother, too, felt how miserable this cortège was, but in the kindness of her heart she immediately defended those who had stayed away. Tomorrow was Christmas, she said, and it was quite impossible for many women, with the best will in the world, to get away.

At the church door the coffin was taken from the hearse and carried inside. After the mass, the second blessing took place. As the body was to be taken to Leonding, the funeral cortège then went through the Urfahr main thoroughfare. The church bells were ringing as it approached. Instinctively I raised my eyes to the windows of the house where Stefanie lived. Perhaps my ardent wish that she should not desert my friend in this, his gravest hour, had called her. I can still see how the window opened, a young girl appeared, and Stefanie looked down interestedly at the little procession passing beneath. I glanced at Adolf; his face remained unchanged, but I did not doubt that he, too, had seen Stefanie. He told me later that this was so, and confessed how much in that painful hour the sight of his beloved had comforted him. Was it by intention or chance that Stefanie came to the window at that moment? Perhaps it was just that she had heard the church bells and wondered why they were ringing so early in the morning. Adolf, of course, was convinced that she wanted to show him her sympathy.

In the Hauptstrasse a second closed carriage was waiting, which Adolf and Paula entered while the procession broke up. Raubal joined his wife. Then the hearse and two carriages started off to Leonding for the interment.

On the following morning, 24 December, Adolf came to my house. He looked worn out, as though any minute he might collapse. He seemed to be desperate, quite empty, with no spark of life in him. As he felt how worried my mother was about him, he explained that he had not slept for days. My mother asked him where he was going to spend Christmas Eve. He said that the Raubals had invited him and his sister. Paula had already left, but he had not made up his mind yet whether he would go or not. My mother exhorted him to help make Christmas a peaceful occasion, now that all the members of the family had suffered the same loss. Adolf listened to her in silence. But when we were alone he said to me brusquely, 'I'm not going to Raubal's.'

'Where else will you go?' I asked him impatiently, 'After all, it's Christmas Eve.' I wanted to ask him to join us. But he did not even let me finish, and shut me up quite energetically, in spite of his sorrow. Suddenly he pulled himself together and his eyes became bright. 'Perhaps I shall go to Stefanie,' he said.

This answer was doubly characteristic of my friend: firstly, because he was capable of forgetting completely in such moments that his relationship with Stefanie was nothing but wishful thinking, a beautiful illusion; and secondly, because even when he realised this he would, after sober reflection, prefer to stick to his wishful thinking rather than unbosom himself with real people.

Later he confessed to me that he had really been determined to go to Stefanie, although he knew very well that such a sudden visit, without a previous appointment, without even having been introduced to her, and moreover on Christmas Eve, was contrary to good manners and social convention and would probably have meant the end of his relationship with her. He told me that on his way, however, he had seen Richard, Stefanie's brother, who was spending his Christmas holiday in Linz. This unexpected meeting had made him give up the idea, for it would have been painful for him if Richard, as was inevitable, had been present at the interview. I did not ask any more questions; it really did not matter whether Adolf was deceiving himself with this pretext, or whether he only offered it to me as an excuse for his behaviour. Certainly when I saw Stefanie at the window the sympathy which showed on her face was undoubtedly genuine. However, I very much doubt if she recognised Adolf at all in his funeral attire and in these peculiar circumstances. But of course I did not express this doubt to him, because I knew that it would only have robbed my friend of his last hope.

I can well imagine what Adolf's Christmas Eve in the year 1907 was really like. That he did not want to go to Raubal I could understand. I could also understand that he did not want to disturb our quiet little family celebration, to which I had invited him. The serene harmony of our home would have made him feel his loneliness even more. Compared with Adolf, I considered myself fortune's favourite, for I had everything he had lost: a father who provided for me, a mother who loved me and a quiet home which welcomed me into its peace.

But he? Where should he have gone that Christmas Eve? He had no acquaintances, no friends, nobody who would have received him with open arms. For him the world was hostile and empty. So he went – to Stefanie. That is to say – to his dream.

All he ever told me of that Christmas Eve was that he had wandered around for hours. Only towards morning had he returned home and gone to sleep. What he thought, felt and suffered I never knew.

# Chapter 14

# 'Come with Me, Gustl!'

Adolf had often said these words jestingly when speaking of his intention of going to live in Vienna. But later on, when he realised how impressed I was by his remarks, the idea grew in his mind that we would go there together, he to attend the Academy of Arts and I the Conservatoire. With his magnificent imagination he produced such a colourful picture of this life, so clear and so detailed, that I often did not know if it was just wishful thinking or reality. For me, such fantasies had a more practical aspect. To be sure, I had learned my trade well and satisfied my father as well as our customers by my efforts. But the hours in the dusty workshop had impaired my health and our doctor, my secret ally, advised emphatically against my continuing to work as an upholsterer. This meant for me that I would try to make my beloved music my profession, a desire which assumed a more and more concrete shape, although the obstacles were many. I had learned all that was to be learned in Linz. My teachers also encouraged me in my decision to devote my life to music, but this meant my going to live in Vienna. Thus the 'come with me, Gustl' which my friend had at first uttered so light-heartedly took on the character of a firm invitation and a definite goal. Nevertheless I feel that without Adolf's determined intervention, my unadventurous nature would not have allowed me to change my profession and go to live in Vienna.

Yet my friend certainly thought primarily of himself. He had a horror of going alone, because this, his third journey to Vienna, was a quite different proposition from his earlier visits. Then, he still had his mother and, though he was away, his home still existed. He was not then taking a step into the unknown, for the knowledge that his mother was waiting to welcome him with open arms at any time and in any circumstances gave a firm and reliable substance to his insecure life. His home was a quiet centre round which his stormy existence revolved. Now he had lost it. Going to Vienna would be the last and final decision from which there was no turning back – a jump into the dark. During the months he had spent there last autumn, he had not succeeded in making any friends; perhaps he had no desire to do so. Relatives of his mother lived there with whom he had formerly had some contact and, unless I am mistaken, he had even stayed with them during his first visit. He never went to see them again and did not even mention them. It was quite understandable that he should have avoided his relatives, because he was afraid that they might question him about his work and livelihood. They would certainly have discovered then that the Academy had rejected him, and he would have suffered starvation and misery rather than have appeared to be in need of help. Nothing was therefore more natural than that he should take me with him, as I was not only his friend, but also the only person with whom he shared the secret of his great love. Since his mother's death, Adolf's 'come with me Gustl' had begun to sound more like a friendly entreaty.

After New Year's Day 1908, I went with Adolf to visit the grave of his parents. It was a fine winter day, cold and clear, which has forever remained in my memory. Snow covered all the familiar landmarks. Adolf knew every inch of our route, as for years this had been his way to school.

He was very composed, a change that surprised me for I knew that his mother's death had shaken him deeply, and had even caused him physical suffering that had brought him near to collapse from exhaustion. My mother had invited him to share our meals during Christmas, in order that he might recover his strength and leave for a while the empty, cold house in which everything reminded him of his mother. He had come, but had sat silent and serious at our table. It was not yet time to talk to him of future plans.

Now, as he walked solemnly by my side, looking much older than I, much more mature and manly, he was still deeply immersed in his own affairs. Yet I was surprised how clearly and detachedly he spoke of them, almost as if it were of someone else's business. Angela had let him know that Paula could now live with them. Her husband had agreed to that, but had refused to receive Adolf into the family since he, Adolf, had behaved disrespectfully to him. Thus he was relieved of his greatest worry, for the child at least had a secure home. He himself had never intended to seek asylum with the Raubals. He had expressed his gratitude to Angela and had informed her that all his parents' furniture would go to Paula. The funeral expenses were paid out of his mother's estate. Incidentally Angela had given birth to a baby girl the day before, who was also to be christened Angela.* His guardian, he added, the mayor of Leonding, had promised to

---

* The future Geli Raubal, Hitler's paramour in the 1920s. [Ed.]

settle the affairs connected with the inheritance and also to help him to apply for an orphan's pension.

All this sounded very sober and sensible. Afterwards, he began to talk of Stefanie. He was determined, he said, to bring the present state of affairs to an end. At the next opportunity, he would introduce himself to Stefanie and her mother, as this had not been possible during the Christmas holidays. It was high time, he said, to bring matters to a head.

We were walking through the snow-covered village. There was a small one-storeyed house, No. 61, which had once belonged to Adolf's father: the big beehive, of which his father had been so proud, was still there, but now it was owned by strangers. Next to it was the cemetery. His father's grave, in which his mother had now been buried, was near the eastern wall, and the fresh little mound was covered with snow. Adolf stood in front of it with a stern, set face. He looked hard and severe, and there were no tears in his eyes. His thoughts were with his beloved mother. I stood by his side and prayed.

On our way back, Adolf said that he would probably stay in Linz throughout the month of January until the home was finally disposed of and the estate settled. He foresaw, he said, some heated arguments with his guardian. Certainly his guardian wanted to do his best for Adolf, but what use was this to him if the 'best' was nothing more than an apprenticeship to a master baker in Leonding?

Old Josef Mayrhofer, Hitler's guardian, died in 1956 at Leonding. Naturally he was often asked about his experiences with the young Hitler, and his impressions of him. In his simple, disinterested manner, he replied to all questioners – first the enemies, then the friends, and then again the enemies of his ward – and his replies were always the same, irrespective of his questioner's opinions.

One day in January 1908, he would say, the Hitler-Adi, grown tall, with dark down on his upper lip and a deep voice, almost a grown man, came to see him to discuss the question of his inheritance. But his first sentence was: 'I am going to Vienna again.' All attempts to dissuade him failed – a stubborn fellow, like his father, the old Hitler.

Josef Mayrhofer retained possession of the documents relating to these discussions. The application for an orphan's pension for himself and his sister which Adolf made at his guardian's request, reads as follows:

To the Respected Imperial and Royal Finance Administration.
The respectfully undersigned herewith request the kind

allocation of the orphan's pension due to them. Both of these applicants, after the death of their mother, widow of an Imperial and Royal customs official, on 21 December 1907, are now without either parent, are minors and are incapable of earning their own living. The guardian of both applicants – Adolf Hitler, born 20 April 1889 at Braunau am Inn, and Paula Hitler, born 21 January 1898 at Fischlham bei Lambach, Upper Austria – is Herr Josef Mayrhofer of Leonding near Linz. Both applicants are domiciled in Linz.

Repeating respectfully their request
*Adolf Hitler  Paula Hitler*,
Urfahr, 10 February 1908

Incidentally, Adolf obviously signed the application for his sister Paula, for the surname 'Hitler' in both signatures shows the same downward-sloping tendency which was so characteristic of his signature in later years. Beside, he made a mistake in the date of birth of his sister, who was born in 1896.

According to the legislation then in force regarding state officials, orphans under 24 years of age, with no means of their own, were entitled to claim an orphan's pension amounting to one half the widow's pension which their mother had been receiving. Frau Hitler had received a pension of 100 crowns monthly since her husband's death: therefore, Adolf and Paula were entitled jointly to a total of 50 crowns monthly, and so Adolf's share was 25 crowns monthly. This was not enough for him to live on, of course – for example, he had to pay 10 crowns monthly to Frau Zakreys for his room.

The application was granted, and the first payment made on 12 February 1908, when Adolf was already in Vienna. Incidentally, three years later he renounced his share in favour of Paula although he could have continued to claim it until he reached the age of 24 in April 1913. The document of renunciation was also retained by his guardian at Leonding.

The document concerning the inheritance which Adolf signed in the presence of his guardian before he left for Vienna also mentioned his share in his father's estate, amounting to about 700 crowns. It is possible that he had already spent part of this money during his previous stay in Vienna, but in view of his very economical way of life – the only large item in his budget was books – he was left with enough to tide him over at least the beginning of his new sojourn there. As regards our joint future, Adolf was more fortunate than I, not only because he had some capital and a fixed monthly income, however small – a matter which I still had to arrange with my parents – but also because, having prevailed over his guardian, he was free to make his own decisions, whereas my decisions were subject to my parents' confirmation. For me, moreover, moving to Vienna meant giving up the trade I had learned, whereas Adolf could continue to lead there more or less his previous life. Al these circumstances made it increasingly difficult for me to come to a decision. Adolf could not understand this for some time although from the beginning he had taken the lead in this whole difficult affair. As far back as the beginning of our friendship, when I could still only visualise my future in the dusty upholsterer's workshop, though nearly a year younger than I Adolf had made it abundantly clear to me that I ought to become a musician. Having put this idea into my head, he never gave up his efforts to persuade me. He comforted me when I despaired, he bolstered up my self-confidence when I was in danger of losing it, he praised, he criticised, he was occasionally rude and violent and railed at me furiously, but he never lost sight of the goal which he had set for me. And if sometimes we had such furious rows that I believed it was the end of everything, we would enthusiastically renew our friendship after a concert or performance in which I had taken part.

By God, nobody on earth, not even my mother who loved me so much and knew me so well was as capable of bringing my secret aspirations into the open and making them come true as my friend, although he had never had any systematic musical training.

In the winter of 1907, when work in our business was slackening and I had more time to myself, I took lessons in harmonics from the conductor of the Linz Theatre. My studies were as thorough as they were successful, and filled me with enthusiasm. Unfortunately, there was no scope in Linz for studying the other subjects of musical theory, such as counterpoint, orchestration and the history of music, nor was there a seminary for training in conducting and composition, much less any stimulus for free composition. This sort of training was only available at the Vienna Conservatoire; besides, there I would have the opportunity of hearing first-class performances of operas and concerts.

Though I had made up my mind to go to Vienna, unlike my friend I lacked the necessary determination to carry through my decision against all odds. But Adolf had already prepared the ground. Without my knowledge he had succeeded in convincing my mother of my musical vocation, for what mother does not like to hear a brilliant career prophesied for her son as a conductor, especially when she is so devoted to music herself? And there was also her justifiable anxiety about my health, as my lungs could no longer stand the perpetual dust in the workshop. So my mother, who had grown fond of Adolf just as Frau Klara had become fond of me, was won over and everything now depended on my father's consent. Not that he openly opposed my wish. My father was in every respect the opposite of Adolf's father, as he had been described to me by my friend. He was always quiet, and apparently took no interest in what was going on around him. All his thoughts were devoted to the business which he had created out of nothing, had successfully steered through grave crises and had now built up into a reputable, prosperous enterprise. He regarded my musical tastes as idle dilettantism, as he could not believe that it was possible to build a secure existence on more or less useless fiddling and strumming. To the last, he could not understand that I, knowing poverty and distress, was willing to renounce security in favour of a vague future. How often did I hear him say 'A bird in the hand is worth two in the bush', or bitterly, 'What was the use of all my drudgery?'

I was working harder than ever in the workshop, as I did not want it said that I was neglecting my trade for the sake of my musical studies. My father saw in my industry a sign that I wanted to remain in the trade and take over his business one day. My mother knew how devoted my father was to his work and so kept silent in order not to upset him. So, at the time when my musical future depended absolutely on attending the Vienna Conservatoire, things seemed to have reached a deadlock within our domestic circle. I worked feverishly in the workshop, and said nothing. My mother also said nothing and my father, thinking that I had finally abandoned my plan, did the same.

At this juncture Adolf came to see us. At one glance he realised what the situation was and intervened immediately. To begin with, he brought me up to date with his own affairs. During his stay in Vienna, he had made detailed enquiries about the study of music and now he gave me exact information on the subject, telling me, in his tempting way, how much he had enjoyed attending operas and concerts. My mother's imagination was also fired by these vivid descriptions, and so a decision became more and more imperative. It was, however, essential that Adolf himself should convince my father.

A difficult enterprise! What use was the most brilliant eloquence if the old master-upholsterer had no regard for anything connected with art? He was quite fond of Adolf but, after all, he only saw in him a young man who had failed at school and thought too highly of himself to learn a trade.

My father had tolerated our friendship, but actually would have preferred a more sound companion for me. Adolf was, therefore, in a decidedly unfavourable position and it is astonishing that nevertheless he managed to win over my father to our plan in so comparatively short a time. I would have understood it if there had been a violent clash of opinions – in that case Adolf would have been in his element and able to play all the trumps which he held. But that was not the case. I cannot recollect that any argument in the usual sense took place at all. Adolf treated the whole matter as of no great importance and, in particular, implied that the decision rested with my father alone. He accepted the fact that my father only half gave his consent, suggesting a temporary solution: as the current scholastic year at the Conservatoire had already started in the previous autumn, I should go to Vienna for a trial period only to look a round for a while. If the facilities for training came up to my expectations, I could then make a final decision, but failing this, I could return home and enter my father's business. Adolf, who hated compromise and with whom it was usually all or nothing was, surprisingly enough, agreeable to this course. I was blissfully happy as never before in my life, for now I had achieved my purpose without upsetting my father, and my mother shared my joy.

At the beginning of February, Adolf returned to Vienna. His address remained the same, he told me when he left, as he had paid rent in advance to Frau Zakreys, and I should write to him in good time announcing my arrival. I helped him carry his luggage to the station, four cases altogether unless I am mistaken, every one of them very heavy. I asked him what they contained, and he answered 'all my belongings'. They were almost entirely books.

At the station Adolf once again spoke of Stefanie. Unfortunately he had had no opportunity to talk to her, he said, for he had never met her unaccompanied. What he had to tell Stefanie was for her ears only. 'Perhaps I shall write to her,' he added in conclusion. But I thought that this idea, expressed by Adolf for the first time, was merely a sign of embarrassment or at the most a cheap consolation. My friend entered the train and, standing at the window, shook me by the hand. As the train moved off, he called out to me, 'Follow me soon, Gustl'.

My good mother had already started preparing my clothes and linen for my journey to great, unknown Vienna. In the end, even my father wanted to contribute something – he made me a big wooden box which was reinforced with strong iron bands. I put into it my music, and my mother filed the remaining space with clothes and shoes.

In the meantime, a postcard arrived from Adolf dated 18 February 1907 showing a view of the armour collection at the Vienna Museum of the History of Art. 'Dear Friend,' it began – and this form of address proved how much our relationship had deepened since his mother's death. 'Dear Friend, am anxiously expecting news of your arrival. Write soon so that I can prepare everything for your festive welcome. The whole of Vienna is awaiting you, therefore come soon. I will, of course, come and meet you.' On the back of the postcard he wrote: 'Now the weather here is improving. I hope you will have better weather too. Well, as I said before, at first you will stay with me. Later we shall see. One can get a piano here in the so-called Dorotheum for as little as 50 to 60 florins. Well, many regards to you and your esteemed parents, from your friend, Adolf Hitler.' Then a postscript. 'Beg you again, come soon.'

Adolf had addressed the card as usual to 'Gustav' Kubizek. He spelt this sometimes 'Gustav', at others 'Gustaph'. He heartily disliked my first name, August, and always called me 'Gustl'. which was closer to Gustav than August. He would probably have preferred it if I had formally changed my forename. He even addressed me as Gustav when he wrote to me on my saint's day, the feast of St Augustine, 28 August. Under my name there is the abbreviation 'Stud.', and I remember that he liked to refer to me as 'Stud. Mus.'

This postcard, unlike the previous ones, is much more cheerful. Typical of Adolf's mood is the humour permeating it. 'The whole of Vienna is waiting for you,' he says, and he intends to prepare 'a festive welcome'. All this indicates that, after the dark and depressing days which he had spent in Linz following his mother's death, he was feeling relaxed and free in Vienna, however uncertain the future might be. Nevertheless, he must have been very lonely. The 'anxiously' in the first sentence of his card was no doubt meant seriously, and the fact that he repeats 'come soon' even in the form 'beg you again, come soon' proves how much he was looking forward to my arrival. Even the information as to the cheap piano was intended to encourage me to come without delay. He may have feared secretly that my vacillating father would change his mind at the last moment.

The day of my departure, 22 February 1907, arrived. In the morning I went to the Carmelite church with my mother. I felt how painful my departure was for her, although she stuck tenaciously to her resolve. Yet I also remember a typical remark which my father made when he saw my mother weeping. 'I can't understand why you are so depressed, mother,' he said, 'We haven't asked Gustl to go, he wanted to leave himself.' My mother, in her grief at my parting, concentrated on my creature comforts, giving me a nice piece of roast pork, and the dripping, which was for spreading on my bread, was put into a special container. She baked me some buns, gave me a large chunk of cheese, a jar of jam and a bottle of coffee. My brown canvas bag was full to overflowing with food.

So, off I went to the station after my last dinner at home, well provided for in every respect. My parents saw me off. My father shook my hand and said, 'Always do the right thing.' But my mother, with tears in her eyes, kissed me and, as the train started, made the sign of the cross on my forehead. For a long time I felt her tender fingers there as they traced the cross.

# Chapter 15

# No. 29 Stumpergasse

My first impression on arriving in Vienna was one of noisy and excited confusion. I stood there, holding my heavy case, so bewildered that I did not know which way to turn. All these people! And this noise and tumult! This was terrible. I was almost inclined to turn tail and go straight home again. But the crowds, thrusting and complaining, were jostling me through the barrier where the ticket inspectors and police stood, till I found myself in the station hall looking round for my friend. I shall always remember this first welcome in Vienna. While I stood there, still overwhelmed by all the shouting and hustling, recognisable from a mile away as a country bumpkin, Adolf behaved as a perfectly acclimatised city dweller. In his dark, good-quality overcoat, dark hat and the walking stick with the ivory handle, he appeared almost elegant. He was obviously delighted to see me and greeted me warmly, kissing me on the cheek lightly, as was then the custom.

The first problem was the transport of my bag for, thanks to my mother's presents, this weighed very heavily. As I was looking around for a porter, Adolf grabbed one of the handles and I took the other. We crossed the Mariahilfe Strasse – people everywhere coming and going about their affairs, and such a terrible noise that one could not hear oneself speak – but how thrilling were the electric arc-lights that made the station yard as bright as day.

I still remember how glad I was when Adolf soon led me down a side street, the Stumpergasse. Here it was quiet and dark. Adolf stopped in front of a fairly new-looking house on the right side, No. 29. As far as I could see, it was a very fine house, most imposing and distinguished looking, perhaps too distinguished for such youngsters as we were, I thought. But Adolf went straight through the entrance and crossed a small courtyard. The house on the far side of this courtyard was much humbler. We went up a dark staircase to the second floor. There were several doors opening on this floor – ours was No. 17.

Adolf unlocked the door. An unpleasant smell of paraffin greeted me and ever since for me this smell has been connected with the memory of that apartment. We seemed to be in a kitchen, but the landlady was not about. Adolf opened a second door. In the small room that he occupied, a miserable paraffin lamp was burning.

I looked around me. The first thing that struck me were the sketches that lay around on the table, on the bed, everywhere. Adolf cleared the table, spread a piece of newspaper on it and fetched a bottle of milk from the window. Then he brought sausage and bread. But I can still see his white, earnest face as I pushed all these things aside and opened the bag. Cold roast pork, stuffed buns and other lovely things to eat. All he said was, 'Yes, that's what it is to have a mother!' We ate like kings. Everything tasted of home.

After all the commotion, I began to collect myself. Then came the inevitable questions about Stefanie. When I had to confess that I had not been for the evening stroll on the Landstrasse for some considerable time, Adolf told me that I ought to have gone for his sake. Before I could reply there was a knock on the door. A little old woman, withered and altogether of a rather comic appearance, slipped inside.

Adolf rose and introduced me in his most formal manner: 'My friend Gustav Kubizek of Linz, a music student.' 'Pleased to meet you, pleased to meet you,' the old woman repeated several times, and announced her own name: Maria Zakreys. From the sing-song tone and peculiar accent, I realised that Frau Zakreys was not a real Viennese. Or rather, she was a Viennese, perhaps even a typical one, but she had not first seen the light of day in Hernals or Lerchenfeld, but rather in Stanislau or Neutitschein. I never asked and never found out – after all, it made no difference. In any case, Frau Zakreys was the only person in this city of millions with whom Adolf and I ever had any dealings.

Tired as I was this first evening, I remember that Adolf showed me around the city. How could a person who had just come to Vienna got to bed without having seen the opera house? So I was dragged to the opera house. The performance was not yet over. I admired the entrance hall, the magnificent staircase, the marble balustrade, the deep, soft carpets and the gilded decorations on the ceiling. Once away from the humble abode in the Stumpergasse, I felt as though I had been transported to another planet, so overwhelming was the impression.

Now it was I who insisted on seeing the Stefansdom. We turned in the Kärntnerstrasse. But the evening mist was so thick that the spire was lost to view. I could just make out the heavy, dark mass of the nave stretching up into the grey monotony of the mist, almost unearthly, as though not built by human hands. In order to show me something else special, Adolf took me to the Maria am Gestade church which, compared with the overpowering bulk of the Stefansdom, seemed to me like a delicate Gothic chapel.

When we got home we each had to pay the grumpy janitor whom we had woken up a *Sperrsechserl* [a penny for unlocking] to open the big door of the house. Frau Zakreys had made me up a primitive bed on the floor of Adolf's room. Although midnight was long past Adolf kept talking excitedly. But I stopped listening – it was just too much for me. The moving farewell from my home, my mother's sad face, the journey, the arrival, the noise, the clamour, the Vienna of the Stumpergasse, the Vienna of the Opera House – worn out, I fell asleep.

Of course, I could not stay at Frau Zakreys's. Anyhow, it was impossible to put a grand piano in the little room. So the next morning, when Adolf finally got up, we set out to look for a room. As I wanted to stay as near as possible to my friend we wandered at first along the nearby streets. Once more I saw this alluring city, Vienna, from the 'other side'. Gloomy court-yards, narrow, ill-lit tenements and stairs, ever more and more stairs. Adolf paid Frau Zakreys ten crowns, and that was what I reckoned to pay. But the rooms we were shown at that price were mostly so small and wretched that it would have been impossible to get a grand piano in them, and when we did find a room that would have been big enough, the landlady would not hear of having a lodger who would be practising the piano in it.

I was very depressed and low-spirited, full of homesickness. What kind of a big city was this Vienna? Full of indifferent, unsympathetic people – it must be awful to live here. I walked with Adolf, despairing and miserable, along the Zollergasse. Once more we saw a notice 'room to let'. We rang the bell and the door was opened by a neatly dressed maid who showed us into an elegantly furnished room containing magnificent twin beds. 'Madame is coming immediately,' said the maid, curtsied and vanished. We both knew at once that it was too stylish for us. Then 'madame' appeared in a doorway, very much a lady, not so young, but very elegant.

She wore a silk dressing gown and slippers trimmed with fur. She greeted us smilingly, inspected Adolf, then me, and asked us to sit down. My friend asked which room was to let. 'This one,' she answered, and pointed to the two beds. Adolf shook his head and said curtly, 'Then one of the beds must come out, because my friend must have room for a piano.' The lady was obviously disappointed that it was I and not Adolf who wanted a room, and asked whether Adolf already had lodgings. When he answered in the affirmative she suggested that I, together with the piano I needed, should move into his room and he should take this one. While she was suggesting this to Adolf with some animation, through a sudden movement the belt which kept the dressing gown together came undone. 'Oh, excuse me, gentlemen,' the lady exclaimed, and immediately re-fastened the dressing gown. But that second had sufficed to show us that under her silk covering she wore nothing but a brief pair of knickers.

Adolf turned as red as a peony, gripped my arm and said, 'Come Gustl!'. I do not remember how we got out of the house. All I remember is Adolf's furious exclamation as we arrived back in the street. 'What a Frau Potiphar!' Apparently such experiences were also part of Vienna.

Adolf must have realised how hard it was for me to find my way around in this bewildering city, and on our way home he suggested that we should room together. He would speak to Frau Zakreys; perhaps she would fix something up in her own house. In the end he succeeded in persuading her to move into his little room and let us take over the somewhat bigger room that she occupied. We agreed on a rent of twenty crowns monthly. She had nothing against my practising the piano, so this was an excellent solution for me.

The next morning, while Adolf was still asleep, I went to register at the Conservatoire. I produced my references from the Linz Music School and was examined immediately. First came an oral examination, then I had to sing something at sight and to round off followed a test in harmony. All went well and I was asked to go to the administration office. Director Kaiser – and for me he really was the Emperor – congratulated me and told me about the curriculum. He advised me to register as an extra-mural student at the university and to attend lectures in the history of music. Then he introduced me to the conductor Gustav Gutheil, with whom I should study, amongst other things, the practical side of conducting. In addition to this, I was accepted as a viola player in the Conservatoire orchestra. All this was quite straightforward and soon, in spite of the initial bewilderment, I felt on firm ground. As so often happened in my life, I found help and consolation in music; even more, it now became my whole life. I had finally escaped from the dusty upholsterer's workshop and could devote myself entirely to my art.

In the nearby Liniengasse I discovered a piano store called Feigl and inspected the instruments for hire. They were not particularly good ones, of course, but I did finally find a grand piano that was fairly good and I hired it for ten crowns monthly. When Adolf came home in the evening – I did not yet know how he spent his days – he was astonished to see the grand piano. For that comparatively small room an upright model would have been more suitable. But how was I to become a conductor without a grand piano! Admittedly it was not as easy as I thought.

Adolf immediately took a hand to try out the best place to put it. He agreed that to get enough light, the piano had to stand near the window. After much experiment the contents of the room – two beds, a night-chest, a wardrobe, a washstand, a table and two chairs – were distributed to the best advantage. In spite of this, the instrument took up the whole space of the right hand window. The table was pushed into the other window enclosure. The space between the beds and the piano, as well as that between the beds and the table, was hardly more than one foot wide. And for Adolf, room to stride up and down was every bit as important as playing the piano was for me. At once he tried it out. From the door to the curve of the piano – three steps! That was enough, because three steps one way and three steps the other made six, even though Adolf in his continual pacing up and down had to turn so often that it became almost a case of moving around his own axis.

The bare, sooty rear side of the house in front was all we could see from our room. Only if you stood very close to the free window and looked sharply upwards would you see a narrow slice of the firmament, but even this modest bit of sky was generally hidden by smoke, dust or fog. On exceptionally lucky days the sun would shine through. To be sure it shone hardly at all on our house, much less in our room, but on the rear of the house facing us streaks of sunshine were to be seen for a couple of hours, and this had to compensate us for the sun that we so sorely missed.

I told Adolf that I had got through the entrance examination at the Conservatoire quite well and was glad that I was now firmly settled down to my studies. Adolf remarked baldly, 'I had no idea I had such a clever friend.' This did not sound very flattering, but I was used to such remarks from him. Apparently he was at a very critical period, was very irritable, and shut me up brusquely when I began to talk about my studies. He finally reconciled himself to the piano. He could practise a bit too, he remarked. I said I was willing to teach him – but here again I had put my foot in it. In ill-temper he snarled at me, 'You can keep your scales and such rubbish, I'll get on by myself.' The he calmed down again and said, in a conciliatory tone, 'Why should I become a musician, Gustl? After all, I have you!'

Our circumstances were modest in the extreme. I certainly could not do much with the monthly allowance my father made me. Regularly at the beginning of each month Adolf received a certain sum from his guardian. I do not know how much this was, perhaps only the twenty-five crowns orphan's pension, of which he had to pay out ten immediately to Frau Zakreys; perhaps it was more, if his guardian was paying out capital in instalments from whatever his parents may have left. Perhaps relatives helped to support him, for instance, the hump-backed Aunt Johanna, but I do not know. I know only that even then Adolf often went hungry, although he would not admit this to me.

What did Adolf have for an ordinary day's meals? A bottle of milk, a loaf of bread, some butter. For lunch he often bought a piece of poppy-seed cake or nut cake to add to it. That is what he made do with. Every fortnight my mother sent a food parcel, and then we feasted. But in money matters Adolf was very precise. I never knew how much, or rather, how little, money he had. Doubtless he was secretly ashamed of it. Occasionally anger got the better of him and he would shout with fury, 'Isn't this a dog's life?' Nevertheless he was happy and contented when we could go once more to the opera, or listen to a concert, or read an interesting book.

For a long time I could not find out where he ate his lunch. Any enquiries about it would be dismissed crossly – these were not subjects one discussed. As I had some spare time in the afternoon, sometimes I used to come home directly after lunch, but I never found Adolf at home. Perhaps he was sitting in the soup kitchen in the Liniengasse where I sometimes had my midday meal. No, he was not there. I went to the Auge Gottes [a municipal low-cost dining hall]. Neither was he there. When I asked him in the evening why he never came to the soup kitchen, he made a long speech about the contemptible institution of these soup kitchens which only symbolised the segregation of the social classes.

As an extra-mural student of the university I was permitted to eat in the canteen – it was still the old canteen, for the new one erected by the German Schulverein did not then exist – and I could also procure cheap meal tickets for Adolf, and finally he consented to come with me. I knew how much he liked sweets so, as well as the main dish, I got some cakes.

I thought he would enjoy this because you could see from his face how hungry he was, but as he sulkily gulped it down, he hissed at me venomously, 'I don't understand how you can enjoy anything amongst such people!' Of course, there used to gather in the canteen students from all the nations of the realm, together with several Jewish students. That was reason enough to stop him going there. But, to tell the truth, in spite of all his determination, he let hunger get the better of him. He squeezed himself in next to me in the canteen, turned his back on the rest and greedily wolfed down his favourite nut cake. Many a time, in my political indifference, I was secretly amused to see him swinging between anti-semitism and his passion for nut cake. For days on end he could live on milk and bread and butter only. I was certainly not spoilt, but this was beyond me.

We did not make any acquaintances. Adolf would never have permitted me time for anybody but himself. More than ever did he regard our friendship as one that excluded any other relationship. Once, as a result of pure chance, he treated me to a very explicit reproof in this respect. Harmony was my hobby-horse. In Linz I had shone at it, and here I got on swimmingly. One day Professor Boschetti called me to the office and asked me whether I would like to do some coaching in the subject. Then he introduced me to my future pupils: the two daughters of a brewer in Kolomea, the daughter of a landowner in Radautz, and also the daughter of a businessman in Spalato.

I was most depressed by the startling difference between the good class boarding house in which these young ladies lived and our wretched hole that always stank of paraffin. Usually, at the end of the lesson, I partook of a tea so substantial that it served me for supper as well. When there was added to the group the daughter of a cloth manufacturer from Jägerndorf in Silesia and the daughter of a magistrate in Agram, my half-dozen pupils together represented every corner of the widespread Habsburg Empire.

And then the unexpected happened. One of them, the girl from Silesia, found she could not get on with some written homework, and came round to me in the Stumpergasse to ask for my help. Our good old landlady raised her eyebrows when she saw the pretty young girl. But that was all right, I was indeed only concerned with the musical example which she had not understood, and I explained it to her. As she copied it down quickly, Adolf came in. I introduced him to my pupil, 'My friend from Linz, Adolf Hitler.' Adolf said nothing. But hardly had the girl got outside than he went for me wildly – for since his unfortunate experience with Stefanie he was now a woman hater. Was our room, already spoilt by that monster, that grand piano, to become the rendezvous for this crew of musical women? he asked me furiously.

I had a job to convince him that the girl was not suffering from the pangs of love, but from examination pains. The result was a detailed speech about the senselessness of women studying. Like blows the words fell on me, as though I were the cloth manufacturer or the brewer who had sent his daughter to the Conservatoire. Adolf got himself more and more involved in a general criticism of social conditions. I cowered silently on the piano stool while he, enraged, strode the three steps along and the three steps back and hurled his indignation in the bitterest terms, first against the door, and then against the piano.

Altogether, in these early days in Vienna, I had the impression that Adolf had become unbalanced. He would fly into a temper at the slightest thing. There were days when nothing I could do seemed right to him, and he made our life together very hard to bear. But I had known Adolf now for over three years. I had gone through terrible days with him after the wreck of his scholastic career, and also after his mother's death. I did not know what this present mood of deep depression was due to, but I thought that sooner or later it would improve.

He was at odds with the world. Wherever he looked, he saw injustice, hate and enmity. Nothing was free from his criticism, nothing found favour in his eyes. Only music was able to cheer him up a little as, for instance, when we went on Sundays to the performances of sacred music in the Burgkapelle. Here one could hear at no expense soloists from the Vienna Opera House and the Vienna Boys' Choir. Adolf was particularly fond of the latter and he told me again and again how grateful he was for that early musical training he had received at Lambach. But in other ways at that time to remember his childhood was particularly painful to him.

All this time he was ceaselessly busy. I had no idea what a student at the Academy of Arts was supposed to do – in any case, the subjects must be exceedingly varied. One day he would be sitting for hours over books, then again he would sit writing till the small hours, or another day would see the piano, the table, his bed and mine, and even the floor, completely covered with designs. He would stand, staring down tensely at his work. move stealthily on tiptoe amongst the drawings, improve something here, correct something there, muttering to himself all the time and underlining his rapid words with violent gestures. Woe betide me if I disturbed him on these occasions. I had great respect for this difficult and detailed work, and said I liked what I saw of it.

When, getting impatient, I opened the piano, he would shuffle the sheets quickly together, put them in a cupboard, grab up a book and make off to the Schönbrunn. He had found a quiet bench there amongst the lawns and trees where no one ever disturbed him. Whatever progress he made with his studies in the open air was accomplished on this seat. I, too, was fond of this quiet spot, where one could forget one lived in a metropolis. Often in later years I visited this lonely bench.

It seemed that a student in architecture could spend much more time in the open air and work more independently than could a Conservatoire student. On one occasion when he had once more written all hours of the night – the ugly, smoky little paraffin lamp had nearly burnt out and I was still awake – I asked him bluntly what was going to be the end of all this work. Instead of answering, he handed me a couple of hastily scribbled sheets. Astounded I read:

> Holy mountain in the background, before it the mighty sacrificial block surrounded by huge oaks: two powerful warriors hold firmly by the horns the black bull which is to be sacrificed and press the beast's mighty head against the hollow in the sacrificial block. Behind them, erect in light coloured robes, stands the priest. He holds the sword with which he will slaughter the bull. All around, solemn, bearded men, leaning on their shields, their lances ready, are watching the ceremony intently.

I could not see any connection between this extraordinary description and the study of architecture, so I asked what it was supposed to be. 'A play,' replied Adolf. Then, in stirring words, he described the action to me. Unfortunately, I have long since forgotten it. I remember only that it was set in the Bavarian mountains at the time of the bringing of Christianity to those parts. The men who lived on the mountains did not want to accept the new faith. On the contrary, they had bound themselves by oath to kill the Christian missionaries. On this was based the conflict of the drama.

I would have liked to have asked Adolf whether his studies in the Academy left him so much free time that he could write dramas, too, but I knew how sensitive he was about everything appertaining to his chosen profession. I could appreciate his attitude, because certainly he had struggled hard enough to get his chance to study. I suppose that is what made him so touchy in this respect, but nevertheless there seemed to me something not quite right about it all.

His mood worried me more and more as the days went by. I had never known him torment himself in this way before, far from it. In my opinion, he possessed rather too much than too little self-confidence. But now things seemed to have changed round. He wallowed deeper and deeper in self-criticism. Yet it only needed the lightest touch – as when one flicks on the light and everything becomes brilliantly clear – for his self-accusation to become an accusation against the times, against the whole world. Choking with his catalogue of hates, he would pour his fury over everything, against mankind in general who did not understand him, who did not appreciate him and by whom he was persecuted. I see him before me, striding up and down the small space in boundless anger, shaken to his very depths. I sat at the piano with my fingers motionless on the keyboard and listened to him, upset by his hymn of hate, and yet worried about him, for his ranting at the bare walls was heard only by me, and perhaps by Frau Zakreys working in the kitchen, who would be worrying whether the crazed young man would be able to pay his next month's rent. But those at whom these burning words were directed, they did not hear him at all. So of what use was all the great display?

Suddenly, in the middle of this hate-ridden harangue in which he challenged a whole epoch, one sentence revealed to me how deep was the abyss on whose edge he was tottering. 'I shall give up Stefanie.' These were the most terrible words he could utter, for Stefanie was the only creature on God's earth whom he excepted from this infamous inhumanity – a being who, made radiant by his glowing love, gave his tormented existence sense and purpose. His father dead, his mother dead, his only sister still a child, what was there left to him? He had no family, no home; only his love, only Stefanie in the midst of all his sufferings and catastrophes had remained steadfastly by his side – admittedly only in his imagination. Until now this imagination had been strong enough to be a help to him, but in the spiritual convulsion through which he was now passing, apparently even this obstinately-held conviction had broken down. 'I thought you were going to write to her?' I interposed, meaning to help him by this suggestion.

He brushed my remark away with an impatient gesture (it was only forty years later that I learned he really had written to her then), and then came the words that I had never before heard him utter: 'It's mad to wait for her. Certainly mama has already picked out the man for Stefanie to marry. Love? They won't worry about that. A good match, that's all that matters. And I'm a poor match, at least in the eyes of mama.' Then came a furious reckoning with 'mama', with everybody who belonged to these fine circles who, through cleverly arranged marriages among themselves, continued to enjoy their unmerited social privileges.

I gave up the attempt to practise the piano and went to bed whilst Adolf absorbed himself in his books. I still remember how shocked I was then. If Adolf could no longer cling to the thought of Stefanie, whatever would become of him?

My feelings were divided: on the one hand, I was glad that he was finally released from this hopeless love for Stefanie, and on the other hand I knew that Stefanie was his only ideal, the only thing that kept him going and gave his life an aim.

The next day, for a trifling reason, there was a bitter row between us. I had to practise. Adolf wanted to read. As it was raining he could not go off to Schönbrunn. 'This eternal strumming', he shouted at me, 'one's never free from it.'

'It's quite simple,' I answered, and getting up, took my timetable out of my music case and with a drawing pin fixed it to the cupboard door. Now he could see exactly when I was out, when not, and just when my hours for practising were. 'And now hang your timetable under it,' I added. Timetable! He did not need any such thing. He kept his timetable in his head. That was good enough for him and it had to be good enough for me. I shrugged my shoulders doubtfully. His work was anything but systematic. He worked practically only at night: in the morning he slept.

I had quickly settled into the life of the Conservatoire, and my teachers were satisfied with my work – more than satisfied, as was shown by their offering me the extra coaching. Naturally I was proud of it, and certainly a bit conceited. Music is perhaps the one art where a lack of formal education does not seem to matter so much. So, pleased with myself and contented, I set off happily every morning for the Conservatoire. But just this sureness of purpose, this certainty of success, awoke in Adolf the most bitter comparisons, although he never mentioned it.

So now, the sight of the timetable stuck on the wall, which must have seemed to him like an officially accredited guarantee for my future, brought about an explosion.

'This Academy', he screamed, 'is a lot of of-fashioned fossilised civil servants, bureaucrats, devoid of understanding, stupid lumps of officials. The whole Academy ought to be blown up!' His face was livid, the mouth quite small, the lips almost white. But the eyes glittered. There was something sinister about them, as if all the hate of which he was capable lay in those glowing eyes! I was just going to point out that those men of the Academy on whom he so lightly passed judgement in his measureless hatred were, after all, his teachers and professors, from whom he could certainly learn something, but he forestalled me: 'They rejected me, they threw me out, they turned me down.'

I was shocked. So that was it. Adolf did not go to the Academy at all. Now I could understand a great deal that had puzzled me about him. I felt his hard luck deeply, and asked him whether he had told his mother that the

Academy had not accepted him. 'What are you thinking of?' he replied, 'How could I burden my dying mother with this worry?'

I could not help but agree. For a while we were both silent. Perhaps Adolf was thinking of his mother. Then I tried to give the conversation a practical turn. 'And what now?' I asked him.

'What now, what now,' he repeated irritably, 'Are you starting too – what now?' He must have asked himself this question a hundred times and more, because he had certainly not discussed it with anyone else. 'What now?' he mocked my anxious enquiry again, and instead of answering, sat himself down at the table and surrounded himself with his books. 'What now?'

He adjusted the lamp, took up a book, opened it and began to read. I made to take the timetable down from the cupboard door. He raised his head, saw it and said calmly, 'Never mind.'

# Chapter 16

# Adolf Rebuilds Vienna

We often saw the old Emperor, dressed in his gala uniform, when he rode in his carriage from Schönbrunn through the Mariahilfe Strasse to the Hofburg. On such occasions Adolf did not make much ado about it, neither did he refer to it later, for he was not interested in the Emperor as a person but only in the state which he represented, the Austro-Hungarian monarchy.

All my recollections of life in Vienna are sharpened by contrast, and thus are more clearly etched in my memory. Indeed, in the course of the turbulent year 1908, there took place two political events which agitated the people.

On the one hand was the Emperor's diamond jubilee. Franz Josef had ascended the throne in 1848, and in all the years since there had been long periods of peace. Since 1866, forty-two years previously, Austria had not been involved in a war, and only rarely did one come across a veteran who could describe Königgratz or Custozza at first hand. Therefore the people rather saw the Kaiser as the champion of peace, and the preparations for the celebrations were proceeding with great enthusiasm.

On the other hand, there was the annexation of Bosnia, decreed in connection with the jubilee, a matter which caused heated arguments amongst the citizens. This extension of the external power of the country only revealed its weakness within, and soon all the signs were of war. In fact, the events which took place in 1914 might easily have happened then, six years earlier. It was no mere coincidence that the 1914–18 war actually had its origins in Sarajevo.

The people of Vienna, among whom we two unknown youngsters were living, were at that time torn between loyalty to the old Emperor and anxiety about the threatened war. Everywhere we noticed a deep chasm between the social classes. There was the vast mass of the lower classes who often had too little to eat and merely existed in miserable dwellings without light or sun. In view of our standard of living, we unhesitatingly included ourselves in this category. It was not necessary for us to go out to study the mass misery of the city – it was brought into our own home. Our own damp and crumbling walls, bug-infested furniture and the unpleasant odour of paraffin were typical of the surroundings in which hundreds of thousands of people in this city lived. When we went with empty stomachs into the centre of the city, we saw the splendid mansions of the nobility with garishly attired servants in front, and the sumptuous hotels in which Vienna's rich society – the old nobility, the captains of industry, landowners and magnates – held their lavish parties: poverty, need, hunger on the one side, and reckless enjoyment of life, sensuality and prodigal luxury on the other.

I was too homesick to draw any political inferences from these contrasts. But Adolf, homeless, rejected by the Academy, without any chance of changing his miserable position, developed during this period an ever-growing sense of rebellion. The obvious social injustice which caused him almost physical suffering also aroused in him a demoniacal hatred of that unearned wealth, presumptuous and arrogant, which we saw around us. Only by violently protesting against this state of affairs was he able to bear his own 'dog's life'. To be sure, it was largely his own fault that he was in this position, but this he would never admit. Even more than from hunger, he suffered from the lack of cleanliness, as he was almost pathologically sensitive about anything concerning the body. At all costs, he would keep his linen and clothing clean. No one, meeting this carefully dressed young man in the street would have thought that he went hungry every day, and lived in a hopelessly bug-infested back room in the 6th District. It was more the lack of cleanliness in the surroundings in which he was forced to live than the lack of food which provoked his inner protests against the prevailing social conditions. The old imperial city, with its atmosphere of false glamour and spurious romance, and its now evident inner decay, was the ground on which his social and political opinions grew. All that he later became was born of this dying imperial Vienna. Although he wrote later, 'The name of this city of lotus-eaters represents for me five years of misery and distress,' this statement shows only the negative side of his experience in Vienna. The positive side was that his constant revolt against the existing social order produced his political philosophy, to which little was added in later years.

In spite of this sympathetic interest in the poverty of the masses, he never sought direct contact with the inhabitants of the imperial city. He profoundly disliked the typical Viennese. To begin with, he could not stand their soft, though melodious, accent, and he ever preferred the clumsy

German spoken by Frau Zakreys. Above all, he hated the subservience and dumb indifference of the Viennese, their eternal muddling-through, their reckless improvidence. His own character was just the opposite. As far as I can remember, Adolf was always very reserved, simply because he disliked any physical contact with people, but within him everything was in a ferment and urged him on to radical and total solutions. How sarcastic he was about the Viennese partiality to wine, and how he despised them for it. Only once did we go to the Prater pleasure gardens, and this only out of curiosity. He could not understand why people wasted their precious time with such nonsense. When he heard people laughing uproariously at some side-show, he would shake his head, full of indignation at so much stupidity, and ask me angrily if I could understand it. In his opinion, they must have been laughing at themselves, which he could well understand. In addition, he was disgusted at the medley of Viennese, Czechs, Magyars, Slovaks, Romanians, Croats, Italians and God knows what else which surged through the Prater. To him, the Prater was nothing but a Viennese Babel. There was here a strange contradiction which always struck me: all his thoughts and ambitions were directed towards the problem of how to help the masses, the simple, decent but under-privileged people with whom he identified himself – they were ever-present in his thoughts – but in actual fact he always avoided any contact with people. The motley crowd in the Prater was practically repugnant to him. However much he felt for the little man, he always kept him at the greatest possible distance.

On the other hand, the arrogance of the ruling classes was equally alien to him, and he understood even less the apathy and resignation which in those years was gaining a hold on the leading intellectuals. The knowledge that the end of the Habsburg state was inevitable had bred, especially among the traditional upholders of the monarchy, a kind of fatalism which accepted whatever might befall, with the typically Viennese 'there's nothing one can do about it'. This bitter-sweet tone of resignation also prevailed amongst Vienna's poets, for instance Rilke, Hofmannsthal, Wildgans – names which never reached us, not because we had no appreciation of the words of a poet, but because the mood which prompted the work of those poets was foreign to us. We had come from the country and were nearer to nature than were the city folk. In addition, we were of a different generation from those weary and resigned people. Whilst the hopeless social conditions and their apparent inevitability produced in the older generation nothing but apathy and complete indifference, they forced the younger generation into radical opposition and violent criticism. And Adolf, too, felt the need to criticise and counter-attack. He did not know what resignation meant. He who resigned, he thought, lost his right to live. But he dissociated himself from his contemporaries, who were at that time very arrogant and turbulent, and went his own way, refusing to join any of the then existing political parties. Although he always felt a sense of responsibility for everything that happened, he was always a lonely and solitary man, determined to rely upon himself, and so to reach his goal.

One other thing should be mentioned – Adolf's visits to the typical working-class district of Meidling. Although he never told me exactly why he went there, I knew he wanted to study personally the housing and living conditions of the workers' families. He was not interested in any individual: he only wanted to know the ways of the class as a whole. Therefore he made no acquaintances in Meidling, his aim being to study a cross-section of the community quite impersonally.

However much he avoided close contact with people, he had nevertheless grown fond of Vienna as a city; he could have lived quite happily without the people, but never without the city. Small wonder then that the few people whom he later came to know in Vienna thought of him as a lone wolf and eccentric, and regarded as pretence or arrogance his refined speech, his distinguished manners and elegant bearing, which belied his obvious poverty. In fact, the young Hitler made no friends in Vienna.

All the more enthusiastic was he about what people had built in Vienna. Think only of the Ringstrasse! When he saw it for the first time, with its fabulous buildings, it seemed to him the realisation of his boldest artistic dreams, and it took him a long time to digest this overwhelming impression. Only gradually did he find his way about this magnificent exhibition of modern architecture. I often had to accompany him on his strolls along the Ring. Then he would describe to me at some length this or that building, pointing out certain details, or he would explain to me its origins. He would spend literally hours in front of it, forgetting not only the time but all that went on around him. I could not understand the reason for these long drawn out and complicated inspections – after all, he had seen everything before, and already knew more about it than most of the inhabitants of the city. When I occasionally became impatient, he shouted at me rudely, asking whether I was his real friend or not; if I were, I should share his interests. Then he continued with his dissertation. At home he would draw for me ground plans and sectional plans, or enlarge upon some interesting detail. He borrowed books on the origin of various buildings, the Hof Opera, the parliament, the Burg Theatre, the Karlskirche, the Hof Museums, the City Hall. He brought home more and more books, among them a general handbook of architecture. He showed me the various architectural styles, and particularly pointed out to me that some of the details on the buildings of the Ringstrasse demonstrated the excellent workmanship of local craftsmen.

When he wished to study a certain building, the external appearance alone did not satisfy him. I was always astonished how well informed he was about side doors, staircases and even back doors and little-known means of access. He approached a building from all sides; he hated nothing more than splendid and ostentatious façades intended to conceal some fault in the layout. Beautiful façades were always suspect. Plaster, he thought, was an inferior material that no architect should use. He was never deceived, and often was able to show me that some construction which aimed at mere visual effect was just bluff. Thus the Ringstrasse became for him an object by which he could measure his architectural knowledge, and demonstrate his opinions.

At that time also, his first schemes for the replanning of large squares emerged. I distinctly remember his expositions. For instance, he regarded the Heldenplatz, between Hofburg and Volksgarten, as an almost ideal spot for mass meetings, not only because the semi-circle of the adjacent buildings lent itself in a unique way to holding the assembled multitude, but also because every individual in the crowd would receive a great monumental impression whichever way he looked. I thought these observations were the idle play of an overheated imagination, but nevertheless I always had to take part in such experiments. The Schwarzenbergplatz was also very much beloved by Adolf. We sometimes went there during an interval at the Hof Opera in order to admire in the darkness the fantastically illuminated fountains. That was a spectacle after our own hearts. Incessantly the foaming water rose, coloured red, yellow and blue in turn by the various spotlights. Colour and movement combined to produce an incredible abundance of light effects, casting an unreal and unearthly spell over the whole square.

To be sure, Adolf, influenced by the Ringstrasse architecture, was also interested in great projects during his time in Vienna – concert halls, theatres, museums, palaces, exhibitions – but gradually his style of planning changed. In the first place these monumental buildings were, in a certain sense, so perfect that even he, with his unbridled will to build, could find no room for change or improvement. Linz had been quite different in this respect. With the exception of the massive pile of the old castle, he had been completely dissatisfied with every building he had seen in Linz. Small wonder, therefore, that he planned a new and more dignified successor to the old City Hall of Linz which was rather narrow and, squeezed in amongst the houses of the main square, was not very imposing, and that in the end, during our strolls through the town, he rebuilt the whole city. Vienna was different, not only because it was difficult for him to conceive as a unit the enormous dimensions of the city, but also because with growing political understanding, he became increasingly aware of the necessity for healthy and suitable housing for the masses of the population. In Linz it had never been a matter of great concern to him how these people, who would be affected by his great building projects, would react to them. In Vienna, however, he began to build for people. What he explained to me in long, nocturnal discussions, what he drew and planned, was no longer building for building's sake, as it had been in Linz, but conscientious planning which took into account the needs and requirements of the occupiers. In Linz, it was still purely architectural building: in Vienna, social building. That is how one could describe his progress. This was also due to the merely external factor that Adolf had been fairly comfortable in Linz, especially in the pleasant apartment in Urfahr. Now, in contrast, in the gloomy sunless back room off the Stumpergasse in Vienna, he felt every morning when he awoke, looking at the bare walls and depressing view, that building was not, as he had thought hitherto, mostly a matter of show and prestige, but rather a problem of public health, of how to remove the masses from their miserable hovels.

'Near the palaces of the Ringstrasse lingered thousands of unemployed, and below this *via triumphalis* of old Austria dwelt in the twilight and mud of the canals the homeless.' With these words in *Mein Kampf* Hitler announced that change in his attitude which led him from the respectful admiration of great imperial architecture to a contemplation of social misery. 'I still shudder even today when I think of those pitiful shanties, crowded *pensions* and massed living quarters, of this dark picture of despair, filth and anger.'

Adolf had told me that during the past winter when he was still alone in Vienna, he had often been to warmed public rooms in order to save on fuel, of which his inadequate stove consumed large quantities without giving much heat. There, one could sit in a warmed room without payment, and there were plenty of newspapers available. I suppose that Adolf, in his conversations with the people who frequented these places, gained his first depressing insight into the scandalous housing conditions of the metropolis.

In our hunt for lodgings which, so to speak, heralded my entry into Vienna, I had had a foretaste of the misery, distress and filth that awaited us. Through dark, foul-smelling backyards, up and down stairs, through sordid and filthy hallways, past doors behind which adults and children huddled together in a small and sunless room, the human beings decayed and miserable as their surroundings – this impression has remained unforgettably with me, just as the reverse side of the medal, that in the one house which might have come up to our sanitary and aesthetic standards, we met that acme of viciousness which, in the person of the seductive 'Frau Potiphar', seemed to us more repulsive than the wretchedness of the poor people. There followed those nocturnal hours in which Adolf, striding up and down between door and piano, explained to me in powerful words the causes of these squalid housing conditions.

He started with the house in which we ourselves were living. On an area which was essentially enough for an ordinary garden, there were tightly packed three buildings, each in the others' way and robbing each other of light, air and elbow room.

And why? Because the man who bought the ground wanted to make as large a profit as possible. Therefore he had to build as compactly as possible and as high as possible, because the more of these box-like compartments he could pile one on top of the other, the more income he received. The tenant in his turn has to get from his apartment as much value as he can, and therefore sub-lets some of the rooms, usually the best ones: take, for example, our good Frau Zakreys. And the sub-tenants crowd together in order to have a room available for a lodger. So each one wants to make a profit out of the other, and the result is that all except the landlord do not have enough living space. The basement flats are also a scandal, getting neither light, sun nor air. If this is unbearable for grown-ups, for children it is deadly.

Adolf's lecture ended in a furious attack on the real estate speculators and the exploiting landlords. One term which I heard for the first time on that occasion still rings in my ears: these 'professional landlords' who make a living from the awful housing condition of the masses. The poor tenant usually never meets his landlord, as the latter does not live in these tenements he owns – God forbid! – but somewhere in the suburbs, in Hietzing or Grinzing, in a luxurious villa where he enjoys an abundance of that of which he deprives others.

Another day Adolf made his observations from the tenant's angle. What were such a poor devil's minimum needs for a decent home? Light – the houses must be detached. There must be gardens, playing grounds for the children. Air – the sky must be visible: something green, a modest piece of nature. But look at our back building, he said. The sun shines only on the roof. The air – of that we would rather not speak. The water – there is one single tap outside on the landing, to which eight families have to come with their pails and jugs. The whole floor has one highly insanitary lavatory in common, and it is almost necessary to take one's turn in a queue. And on top of all that, the bugs!

When, during the weeks that followed – I had learned in the meantime that he had been rejected by the Academy – I asked Adolf occasionally where he was during the day, he answered: 'I am working on the solution of the housing problem in Vienna, and I am doing certain research for this purpose: I therefore have to go around a lot.'

During that period he would often pore over his plans and drawings throughout the night. but he never spoke about it, nor did I ask him any more questions. But suddenly, I think it was towards the end of March, he said: 'I shall be away for three days.'

He returned on the fourth day, dead tired. Goodness knows where he had been, where he had slept and how hungry he had been. From his scanty reports I gathered that he had approached Vienna from some outlying point, perhaps from Stockerau or the Marchfeld, to gain an idea of the land available for the purpose of relieving the city's congestion. He worked all night again, and then, at long last, showed me the project. In the first place, some simple ground plans, workers' flats with the minimum requirements: kitchen, living room, separate bedrooms for parents and children, water laid on in the kitchen and lavatory and, at that time an unheard of innovation, a bath. Then Adolf showed me his plans for various types of houses, neatly sketched in Indian ink. I remember them so clearly because for weeks these sketches were hanging on our walls, and Adolf returned to the subject repeatedly. In our airless and sunless sub-tenants' existence, I realised more sharply the contrast between our own surroundings and Adolf's attractive light and airy houses. For, as my glance wandered away from these pretty sketches, it fell on the crumbling, badly distempered wall which still showed traces of our nightly bug hunt. This vivid contrast has printed indelibly on my memory the vast and grandiose plans of my friend.

'The tenements will be demolished.' With this pithy pronouncement, Adolf began his work. I should have been surprised had it been otherwise as, in everything he planned, he went all out and detested half measures and compromise – life itself would bring these. But his task was to solve the problem radically – that is to say, from the roots. Private speculation in land would be forbidden. Areas along both banks of the Danube would be added to the open spaces resulting from the demolition of the working-class districts, and wide roads would be laid across the whole. The vast building area would be provided with a network of railway lines. Instead of big railway stations, there would be suitably scattered over the whole territory and connected with the town centre, a series of small local stations which would cater for specified districts and offer favourable speedy communication between home and place of work. The motor car at that time had not been envisaged as an important means of transport. The streets of Vienna were still dominated by the horse-drawn fiacre. The bicycle was only slowly becoming a cheap and practical means of travel. Only the railways were, in those days, able to provide transport for the masses.

Adolf's design was by no means concerned with the one-family or owner-occupier type of house as is being built today, nor was he interested in 'settlement'. His idea was still based on the old type of tenement house, carved up into fractions. Thus came into being as his smallest unit the four-family house, a two-storeyed, well-proportioned structure, containing two flats on the ground floor and two on the first floor. This basic unit was the prevailing type. Where conditions required, from four to eight of these units were to be combined to form housing blocks for eight to sixteen families, but these blocks too remained 'near the ground', that is to say, they still consisted of two storeys only, and were surrounded by gardens, playing grounds and groups of trees. The sixteen-family house was the limit.

Having designed the types of house necessary to relieve the congestion in the town, my friend could now turn his attention to the problem itself. On a big map of the town, which was too large for the table and had to be spread out on the piano, Adolf laid out the network of railways and roads. Industrial centres were marked, residential districts suitably located. I was always in his way when he was engaged on this vast planning job. There was not a square foot of space in the room not used for this task. If Adolf had not pursued his course with such grim determination, I would have regarded the whole thing as an interesting but idle pastime. Actually I was so depressed by our own bad housing that I became almost as fanatical as my friend, and that is no doubt the reason why so many details have remained in my memory.

In his way, Adolf thought of everything. I still remember that he was preoccupied with the problem of whether inns would be necessary or not in this new Vienna. Adolf was as radically opposed to alcohol as he was to nicotine. If one neither smoked nor drank, why should one go to an inn? In any case, he found for this new Vienna a solution which was as radical as it was bold: a new popular drink. On one occasion in Linz I had to redecorate some rooms in the office building of the firm Franck, who manufactured a coffee substitute. Adolf came to see me there. The firm provided the workers with an excellent iced beverage which cost only one heller a glass. Adolf liked this drink so much that he mentioned it again and again. If one could provide every household, he said, with this cheap and wholesome beverage, or with similar non-alcoholic drinks, one could do without the inns. When I remonstrated that the Viennese, from my knowledge of them, would be most unlikely to give up their wine, he replied brusquely, 'You won't be asked!' as much as to say, in other words, 'Nor will the Viennese either.'

Adolf was particularly critical of those countries, and Austria was one of them, which had established a tobacco monopoly. In this way, he argued, the state ruined the health of its own subjects. Therefore all tobacco factories must be closed and the import of tobacco, cigars and cigarettes forbidden, but he did not find a substitute for tobacco as a companion to his 'people's drink'.

Altogether, the nearer Adolf came in his imagination to the realisation of his projects, the more utopian the whole business became. As long as it was only a matter of the basic principles of his planning, everything was quite reasonable, but when he thought out the details of its execution, Adolf juggled with ideas which seemed to me completely nebulous. Having to pay ten of my father's hard-earned crowns for a half-share in a bug-ridden room, I had the fullest sympathy with the idea that in his new Vienna there should be no landlords and tenants. The ground was to be owned by the state, and the houses were not to be private property but administered by a sort of housing co-operative. One would pay no rent, but instead a contribution to the building costs of the house, or a kind of housing tax. So far I could follow him, but when I asked him timidly, 'Yes, but in this way you cannot finance such an expensive building project. Who is going to pay for it?' I provoked his most violent opposition. Furiously, Adolf flung replies at me of which I understood little. Besides, I can hardly remember details of these explanations which consisted almost entirely of abstract conceptions. But what remains in my memory are certain regularly recurring expressions which, the less they actually meant, the more they impressed me.

The principal problems of the whole project were to be solved, as Adolf put it, 'in the storm of the revolution'. It was the first time that, in our wretched dwelling, this ponderous phrase was uttered. I do not know if Adolf picked it up from his copious reading. At any rate, at the moment when his flight of ideas would come to a standstill, the bold words 'storm of the revolution' would crop up regularly and give a new fillip to his thoughts, though he never paused to explain it. It could mean, I found out, either everything or nothing. For Adolf it was everything, but for me nothing until he, with his hypnotic eloquence had convinced me too that it needed a tremendous revolutionary storm to break out over the tired old earth to bring about all that which had long since been ready in his thoughts and plans, just as a mild rain in late summer brings the mushrooms springing up everywhere.

Another ever-recurring expression was the 'German ideal state', which together with the conception of 'the Reich' was the dominating factor in his thinking, This 'ideal state' was in its basic principles both national and social, social above all in respect of the poverty of the masses of the working class. More and more thoroughly, Adolf worked on the idea of a state which would give its due to the social requirements of our times, but the idea remained vague and was largely determined by his reading. Thus he chose the term 'ideal state' – most likely he had read it in one of his many books – and left it to the future to develop its details, for the time being only sketched in general outline, but of course with 'the Reich' as its final aim.

Also in connection with his bold building projects, Adolf first adopted a third expression which had already become a familiar formula in that period: 'social reform'. This expression too embraced much that was still swirling around in his brain in a very unformed state. But the eager study of political literature and visits to the parliament, to which he dragged me, gradually lent the expression 'social reform' a concrete meaning.

One day when the storm of the revolution broke and the ideal state was born, the long overdue social reform would become reality. This would be the moment to tear down the tenements of the 'professional landlords' and to begin with the building of his model houses in the beautiful meadows behind the Nussdorf.

I have dwelt so long on these plans of my friend because I regard them as typical of the development of his character and his ideas during his sojourn in Vienna. To be sure, I realised from the beginning that my friend would not remain indifferent to the misery of the masses of the metropolis, for I knew that he did not close his eyes to anything and that it was quite contrary to his nature to ignore any important phenomenon. I would never have believed that these experiences in the suburbs of Vienna would have stirred up his whole personality so enormously, for I had always thought of my friend as basically an artist, and would have understood if he had grown indignant at the sight of the masses who appeared to be hopelessly perishing in their misery, yet remained aloof from all this, so as not to be dragged down into the abyss by the city's inexorable fate. I reckoned with his susceptibility, his aestheticism, his constant fear of physical contact with strangers – he shook hands only rarely and then only with a few people – and I thought this would be sufficient to keep him at a distance from the masses. This was only true of personal contacts, but with his whole overflowing heart he stood then in the ranks of the under-privileged. It was not sympathy in the ordinary sense which he felt for the disinherited. That would not have been sufficient. He not only suffered with them, he lived for them and devoted all his thoughts to the salvation of those people from distress and poverty. No doubt, this ardent desire for a total reorganisation of life was his personal response to his own fate, which had led him, step by step, into misery. Only by his noble and grandiose work, which was intended 'for everybody' and appealed 'to all' did he find again his inner equilibrium. The weeks of dark visions and grave depressions were past; he was again full of hope and courage.

For the time being, however, good old Maria Zakreys was the only person who occupied herself with these plans. To be exact, she really did not occupy herself with them, for she had given it up as a bad job to try to bring order into this mess of plans, drawings and sketches. She was satisfied as long as the two students from Linz paid their rent regularly.

As far as Linz was concerned, Adolf only thought to transform it into a fine, attractive town whose distinguished buildings should raise it from its low, provincial standing, but Vienna he wanted to transform into a modern residential city in which distinction and prestige did not matter – this he left to imperial Vienna. What mattered was that the uprooted masses, who had become estranged from their own soil and their own people, should again settle down on firm ground.

The old imperial city changed, on the drawing board of a nineteen-year-old youth who lived in a dark back room of the Mariahilfe suburb, into a spacious, sunlit and exuberant city consisting of four-, eight- and sixteen-family houses.

Chapter 17

# Solitary Reading and Study

There can be no doubt that Adolf was, at that time, convinced that he was destined to become an architect. How he would ever find his way into practice, even with this thorough private study, unable as he was to produce any testimonials and diplomas, this never caused him any worry. We hardly ever spoke about it, for my friend was absolutely sure that by the time he had concluded his studies, circumstances would have changed (either peacefully or with violence, as a consequence of his 'storm of the revolution') to such an extent that formal qualifications would no longer matter, but only actual ability.

> That at that time I should serve my love for architecture with some fanaticism was natural. Along with music it seemed to me to be queen of the arts. Under such circumstances to busy myself with it was not 'work' but the greatest contentment. I could read or sketch late into the night and I never got tired. This strengthened my belief that my beautiful dream of the future, even though it might take years, would eventually become reality. I was almost convinced that one day I would make my name as an architect.

This is what he wrote in *Mein Kampf*.

Thus did Adolf see his future clearly before him. Back in Linz he had already defeated what he called his school's biased, unjust and idiotic treatment of him by throwing himself heart and soul into the study of a subject of his own choosing, so he had no difficulty in doing the same here in Vienna, where a similar situation confronted him. He cursed the old-fashioned, fossilised bureaucracy of the Academy where there was no understanding for true artistry. He spoke of the trip-wires which had been cunningly laid – I remember his very words – for the sole purpose of ruining his career. But he would show these incompetent, senile fools that he could go ahead without them. From his salvoes of abuse of the Academy, I gained the impression that these teachers, by rejecting the young man, had involuntarily engendered in him more eagerness and energy than their teaching would ever have done.

But my friend had to face another problem: what was he to live on during his years of study? Many years would pass before he could make himself a position as an architect. Personally, I doubted if, indeed, anything would ever come of my friend's private studies. Admittedly he studied with incredible industry and a determination which one would have thought beyond the strength of his undernourished and weakened body. But his pursuits were not directed towards any practical goal. On the contrary, every now and again he got lost in vast plans and speculations. Drawing a comparison with my musical studies, which were progressing absolutely according to plan, I could only conclude that Adolf was casting his net far too wide and dragging in everything that had only the remotest connection with architecture, and he did it, moreover, with the greatest thoroughness and precision. How could all that ever lead to any conclusion – not to mention the fact that more and more new ideas assailed him and distracted him from his professional training.

The contrast between his boundless, unsystematic labours and my precisely regulated studies at the Conservatoire did nothing to help our friendship, if only because our respective work at home necessarily led to friction. When, on top of this, Professor Boschetti sent me some private pupils, our disagreements became sharper. Now one could see, he said, that bad luck was pursuing him, there was a great conspiracy against him – he had no possibility of earning any money.

One evening – I suppose it was after a pupil of mine had been in for a lesson – I seized the opportunity to try and persuade him to look around for some remunerative work. Of course, if one is lucky, one can give lessons to young ladies, he began. I told him that, without my taking the initiative, Professor Boschetti had sent me these pupils – it was a pity that they had to be taught harmonics rather than architecture. Incidentally, I went on more firmly, if I were as gifted as he was, I would have long since looked around for some part-time job.

He listened with interest, almost as though the whole thing did not refer to him at all, and then I let him have it. Drawing, for instance, that was something he really could do, as even his teachers had admitted. What about looking for a job with a newspaper or in a publishing firm? Perhaps he could illustrate books, or do sketches for newspapers. He answered evasively that he was glad I credited him with such skill, but anyhow this kind of newspaper illustration was best left to the photographers, for not even the best artist could be as quick as a photographer.

Then what about a job as a drama critic, I continued? This was a job which he was actually doing, because after every visit to the theatre he came home to me with a very severe and radical, yet interesting and comprehensive view. Why should I remain the only inhabitant of Vienna ever to hear his opinions? He should try to get in touch with an influential paper, but he would have to take care not to show too much bias. What did I mean by that, he wanted to know. The Italian, Russian and French operas, too, had their right to exist I replied. One had to accept foreign composers as well, for art has no national frontiers. We started a heated argument, as whenever music was the topic under discussion I stood my ground, for I did not speak for myself alone, but felt that I was the representative of the institute whose pupil I was.

Although I fully shared Adolf's enthusiasm for Richard Wagner, I could, nevertheless, not bring myself to reject all the rest. But he struck uncompromisingly to his point. I still remember well that, in my excitement, I flung at Adolf the words from the final chorus of Beethoven's Ninth Symphony, *'Seid umschlungen, Millionen, diesen Kuss der ganzen Welt'* ('Become entwined you millions in this the whole world's embrace'). The work of the artist must belong to the whole world. So there was trouble even before he took the job of an opera critic, remarked Adolf, and so this plan was also buried.

Adolf wrote a great deal during this period. I had discovered that it was mainly plays, dramas actually. He took the plots from Germanic mythology or German history, but hardly any of these plays were really finished. Nevertheless, it might have been possible to make some money out of them. Adolf showed me some of his drafts, and I was struck by the fact that he attributed much importance to magnificent staging. Except for the drama about the coming of Christianity, I cannot remember any one of these plays, only that they all required an enormous production. Wagner had accustomed us to the idea of pretentious productions, but Adolf's ideas dwarfed anything devised by the master. I knew a thing or two about operatic production and was not slow to utter my doubts. With his settings ranging through heaven and hell, I explained to him, no producer would accept any one of his plays. He should be much more modest in all that concerned his scenery. Altogether it would be best for him not to write operas at all, but rather simple plays, comedies perhaps, which were popular with the public. The most profitable thing would be to write some unpretentious comedy. Unpretentious? This was all that was needed to make him furious. So this attempt, too, ended in failure.

Gradually I came to realise that all my efforts were wasted. Even if I had managed to persuade Adolf to submit his drawings or his literary work to a newspaper editor or publisher, he would soon have quarrelled with his employer, for he could never tolerate any interference with his work, and it would presumably make no difference that he was getting paid for it. He simply could not bear taking orders from people, for he received enough orders from himself.

Later, when we had already parted, Adolf found in Vienna a very characteristic solution for this problem which enabled him to make a modest living and still remain his own master. As his talent was best suited to drawing works of architecture rather than the human figure, he made most accurate and neat sketches of famous Vienna buildings, such as the Karlskirche, the parliament, the Maria am Gestade church and similar subjects, coloured them and sold them whenever he could.

In *Mein Kampf* he expressed it thus: 'I worked at that time (he means 1909 and 1910) on my own account as a sketch artist and water-colour painter. It was hardly enough to live on but was good for my chosen profession.' In other words, he preferred to starve rather than give up his independence.

Having no expert knowledge, I cannot give any opinion on the special studies Adolf was then pursuing. Moreover, I was too busy myself to get any real idea of his work. What I noticed, however, was that he surrounded himself increasingly with technical books. I recall especially a big history of architecture because he loved to choose one of its pictures at random, cover the caption and tell me what it was, Chartres Cathedral, for instance, or the Palazzo Pitti in Florence. His memory was prodigious: it never failed him and was, of course, a great advantage in his work.

He worked tirelessly on his drawings. I had the impression that he had already learnt, in Linz, the basic principles of draughtsmanship, though only from books. I do not remember Adolf ever having tried to apply in practice what he had learnt, or ever attending classes in architectural drawing. He never showed any desire to mix with people who shared his own professional interests, or to discuss with them common problems. Rather than meet people with specialised knowledge, he would sit alone on his bench in the Schönbrunn Park, in the vicinity of the Gloriette, holding imaginary conversations with himself about the subject matter of his books. This extraordinary habit of studying a certain subject and penetrating very deeply into its very essence, whilst anxiously avoiding any contact with its practical application, this peculiar self-sufficiency, reminded me of Adolf's relationship with Stefanie. His boundless love of architecture, his passionate interest in building, remained fundamentally a mere intellectual pastime. Just as he used to rush to the Landstrasse to see Stefanie when he needed some tangible confirmation of his feelings, so he would escape from the overpowering effects of his theoretical studies into the Ringstrasse, and recover his inner equilibrium among its splendours.

As time went on, I came to understand my friend's one-sided preference for the Ringstrasse, although to my mind the impact of such buildings as the Stefansdom, or the Belvedere – older and more original in their style – was stronger and more convincing. But Adolf altogether disliked the Baroque, as it was too ornate for his taste. The Ringstrasse buildings had been constructed after the demolition of the city's fortifications, that is to say, in the second half of the past century, and were anything but uniform in style. Instead, almost every style was represented. The parliament was in the Classical, or rather pseudo-Hellenic style, the City Hall neo-Gothic and the Burg Theatre, an object of Adolf's special admiration, late Renaissance. Yet they had one thing in common which was specially attractive for my friend – their ostentation. The real motive for his increasing preoccupation with these buildings, his use of the Ringstrasse as his professional training ground, was the fact that these buildings of the preceding generation enabled him to study without difficulty the history of their construction, to re-draw their plans, so to speak, by his own effort, and to recall the life and achievements of the great architects of that epoch – Theophil Hansen, Semper, Hasenauer, Siccardsburg and van der Nüll.

I discovered with apprehension that new ideas, experiences and projects disorganised my friend's professional studies. As long as these new interests had some connection with architecture, they just became part of his general education, but there was much that was diametrically opposed to his professional plans and, moreover, politics gained an increasingly firm hold on him. I asked Adolf occasionally what connection there was between the remote problems which we encountered during our visits to parliament and his professional preparation. He would answer, 'You can build only when you have first created the political conditions for it.' Sometimes his answers were rather rude. Thus I remember him once answering my question how he proposed to solve a certain problem, 'Even if I found the solution to this problem I wouldn't tell it to you because you wouldn't understand it.' But although he was often brusque, moody, unreliable and far from conciliatory,

I could never be angry with him because these unpleasant sides of his character were overshadowed by the pure fire of an exalted soul.

I stopped asking him questions about his profession. It was much better for me to go quietly my own way and show him my own ideas of how to reach one's goal. After all, I had not even reached the lower classes of the Realschule and had only been to a council school, but just the same I was now a student at the Conservatoire, as good as any boy who had matriculated. My friend's studies took just the opposite course to mine. Whilst training for a profession normally grows more and more specialised in the course of time, Adolf's studies became more general, more diffuse, more abstract and remote from anything practical. The more tenaciously he repeated his own slogan 'I want to become an architect', the more nebulous did this goal become in reality. It was the typical attitude of a young man, who would actually be hindered by a profession, in reaching what he feels is his true vocation.

In *Mein Kampf* he wrote:

> Since my early youth I tried to read in the right way and was supported in the best way possible by memory and understanding. And looked at like that, my time in Vienna was especially fruitful and valuable ... I read endlessly and as a basis. Whatever time I had left over after working was devoted to study. I am convinced today that in general, creative ideas appear initially in youth, in so much as they make themselves available at all. I distinguish between the wisdom of age, which is only valid as the result of experiences on a broad basis, and the inexhaustible fruitfulness of youth, where ideas have not been thought through because of the fullness of their number. They are the building material for future plans from which the wiser, older man takes the stones, hews the blocks and then sets about constructing the building, providing that the so-called wisdom of the old man and the fruitfulness of the youth have not been suffocated.

So, for my friend it was books, always books. I could not imagine Adolf without books. He stacked them in piles around him. He had to have with him at his side the book he was currently working through. Even if he did not happen to be reading it just them, it had to be around. Whenever he went out, there would usually be a book under his arm. This was often a problem, for he would rather abandon nature and the open sky than the book.

179

Books were his whole world. In Linz, in order to procure the books he wanted, he had subscribed to three libraries. In Vienna he used the Hof Library so industriously that I asked him once in all seriousness whether he intended to read the whole library, which of course earned me some rude remarks. One day he took me to the library and showed me the big reading room. I was almost overwhelmed by these enormous masses of books, and I asked him how he managed to get what he wanted. He began to explain to me the use of the catalogue, which confused me even more.

Hardly anything would disturb him when he was reading, but sometimes he disturbed himself, for as soon as he opened a book he started talking about it, and I had to listen patiently whether I was interested in the subject or not. Every now and then, in Linz even more frequently than in Vienna, he would thrust a book into my hands and demand that I, as his friend, should read it. It did not matter so much to him that I should widen my own horizons as that he should have somebody with whom he could discuss the book, even though that somebody was only a listener.

As to the way one should a read a book he devoted three pages to the subject in *Mein Kampf*:

> I know people who 'read' endlessly, book after book, but whom I would not grace with the adjective 'well-read'. It is true that they have an enormous amount of 'knowledge', but their brain does not know how to distribute and classify it into the various materials.

In this respect my friend was undoubtedly far superior to the average reader. Reading began for him when he selected the book. Adolf had an especial feel for poets and authors who had something of value to say to him. He never read books simply to pass the time; it was a deadly earnest occupation. I got that impression more than once. What an upset if I did not take his reading seriously enough and played the piano while he was studying.

It was interesting the way Adolf selected a book. The most important thing was the contents page. Then he went through the book, not from first page to last but just extracting the essence. Once he had done that he had carefully ordered and categorised it in his memory. I often wondered if there could be any more room left in his head but it almost seemed that the more material he absorbed the better his memory became. It seemed a marvel – there really was room in his brain for an entire library.

As I have mentioned before, outstanding among his books were the

German heroic legends. Whatever his mood or external circumstances, he would always come back to them and read them again although he already knew them by heart. The volume which he had in Vienna was, I believe, *Gotter- und Heldensagen, Germanisch-Deutscher Sagenschatz* – 'Legends of Gods and Heroes: The Treasures of Germanic-German Mythology'.

In Linz, Adolf had started to read the classics. Of Goethe's *Faust* he once remarked that it contained more than the human mind could grasp. Once we saw the rarely performed second part at the Burg Theatre, with Josef Kainz in the title role. Adolf was very moved and spoke of it for a long time. It is natural that, of Schiller's works, *Wilhelm Tell* affected him most deeply. On the other hand, strange to relate, he did not like *Die Räuber* very much. He was profoundly impressed by Dante's *Divine Comedy* although, to my mind, he was much too young when he read it. I know that he was interested in Herder, and we saw together Lessing's *Minna von Barhelm*. He liked Stifter partly I suppose because he encountered in his writing the familiar picture of his native landscape, whilst Rosegger struck him, as he once put it, as 'too popular'.

Every now and then he would choose books which were then in vogue, but in order to form a judgment of those who read them, rather than of the books themselves. Ganghofer meant nothing to him, whilst he greatly praised Otto Ernst, with whose works he was familiar. Of modern plays we saw Frank Wedekind's *Frühlings Erwachen* and *Der Meister von Palmyra* by Wilbrandt. Adolf read Ibsen's plays in Vienna without being very much impressed by them.

As for philosophical works, he always had his Schopenhauer by him, later Nietzsche too, yet I knew little about these, for he regarded these philosophers as, so to speak, his personal affair – private property which he would not share with anybody. This reticence was possibly due also to the fact that we shared a love of music and this provided us with common ground more rewarding than that of philosophy which for me was rather a remote subject.

In conclusion I should like to stress the same point with regard to my friend's reading that I have mentioned before in describing his professional studies: he read prodigiously and, with the help of his extraordinary memory, stored up an amount of knowledge which was far above the standard of a twenty-year-old – but he avoided any factual discussion about it.

When he urged me to read a certain book, he knew in advance that I would never be his equal in any argument, and it is even possible that he selected the books which he recommended me to read with this thought in mind. He was not interested in 'another opinion', nor in any discussion of the book.

His attitude to books was the same as his attitude to the world in general. He absorbed with fervour everything he could lay his hands on, but he took great care to keep at a safe distance from anything that might put him to the test.

He was a seeker, certainly, but even in his books he found only what suited him. One day when I asked him if he really intended to complete his studies by the aid of books alone, he looked at me, surprised, and barked: 'Of course, *you* need teachers, I can see that. But for me they are superfluous.' In the further course of this conversation he called me an 'intellectual scrounger' and a 'parasite at other people's tables'. I never felt, and particularly not in those days when we were lodging together in Vienna, that he was seeking anything concrete in his piles of books, such as principles and ideas for his own conduct; on the contrary, he was only looking for confirmation of those principles and ideas he already had. For this reason his reading, except perhaps in German mythology, was not a mater of edification, but a sort of check-up on himself.

I remember him in Vienna expounding his many problems and usually winding up with a reference to some book, 'You see, the man who wrote this is of exactly the same opinion as I am.'

# Chapter 18

# Nights at the Opera

The high spots of our friendship were our visits together to the Hof Opera, and memories of my friend are inseparably connected with these wonderful experiences. The theatre in Linz saw the beginning of our youthful friendship, and this was re-affirmed whenever we visited the foremost opera house in Europe. As we grew older, the contrasts between us made themselves increasingly noticeable and the difference in our family backgrounds, our professional aspirations and our attitude to public and political life separated us more and more. Yet our fervent enthusiasm for everything that was beautiful and noble, which found its highest artistic expression in the performances of the Vienna opera, linked us ever more closely. In Linz our relationship had been smooth and harmonious, but in Vienna the conflicts and tensions grew, largely due to our lodging together in a single room. It was fortunate that at the same time the influence of our common artistic experiences fortified our friendship.

True to tradition, we humble, poverty-stricken students had to fight hard for the chance of seeing these performances. It is true that in theory there existed cheap tickets for the promenade which, in Vienna as in Linz, used to be our aim, but we never got one, not even through the Conservatoire. So we had to pay the full price – two crowns – a lot of money when one thinks that Adolf, after having paid his rent, was left with fifteen crowns for the whole month. Moreover, although we paid the full price we had to fight hard to get even these tickets, the sale of which started only one hour before the performance began.

Having finally secured the ticket, there started a rush towards the promenade which was fortunately not far from the box office. It was below the imperial box and one could hear excellently. Women were not admitted to the promenade which pleased Adolf hugely, but on the other hand it had the disadvantage of being split up into two halves by a brass railing, one for civilians, one for the military. These young lieutenants who, according to my friend, came to the opera less for the sake of the music than for social reasons, paid only ten hellers for their tickets whilst we poor students were fleeced twenty times that amount. This always made Adolf very wild. Looking at these elegant lieutenants who, ceaselessly yawning, could hardly wait for the interval to display themselves in the foyer as though they had just come out of their box, he said that among the visitors to the promenade artistic understanding varied in inverse proportion to the price of the tickets. Moreover the military half of the promenade was never full, whilst in the civilian half students, young employees and artisans trod on each other's toes.

One disadvantage was that the promenade was usually the haunt of the claque, and this often spoilt our pleasure. The usual procedure was very simple: a singer who wanted to be applauded at a certain point would hire a claque for the evening. Its leader would buy their tickets for his men and in addition pay them a sum of money. There existed professional claqueurs who worked at a fixed rate. So it would often happen that at a most unsuitable moment, roars of applause would break out all around us. This made us boil over with indignation. I remember once, during *Tannhäuser*, we silenced a group of claqueurs by our hissing. One of them, who continued to shout 'Bravo!' even though the orchestra was still playing, was punched in the side by Adolf. On leaving the theatre, we found the leader of the claque waiting for us with a policeman. Adolf was questioned on the spot and defended himself so brilliantly that the policeman let him go, but he was in time to catch up with the claqueur in question in the street and give him a sound box on the ears.

As nobody was admitted to the promenade in hat and coat, we left them behind when we went to the opera so as to save the cloakroom fee. To be sure, it was often bitterly cold coming out of the heated theatre into the night. But what did that matter after *Lohengrin* or *Tristan*?

What was most annoying for us was that we had to be home by ten o'clock at the latest if we wanted to save the *Sperrsechserl*. It took us, according to Adolf's precise calculations, at least fifteen minutes to walk home from the opera, and so we had to leave there at a quarter to ten. The consequence was that Adolf never succeeded in hearing the end of those operas which finished later and I had to play for him on the piano what he had missed.

Richard Wagner's musical dramas were still the object of our undivided love and enthusiasm. For Adolf, nothing could compete with the great mystical world that the master conjured up for us. Thus, for instance, when I wanted to see some magnificent Verdi production in the Hof Opera, he would bully me until I gave up my Verdi and went with him to the Volksoper in Währing, where they were doing Wagner. He preferred a mediocre Wagner performance a hundred times to a first-class Verdi. I thought differently, but what was the use? I had to yield, as usual, for when it was a question of a Wagner performance, Adolf would tolerate no opposition. No doubt he had heard of a much better performance of the work in question – I do not remember whether it was *Lohengrin* or *Tristan* – at the Hof Opera, but this was not the point at issue. Listening to Wagner meant to him not a simple visit to the theatre but the opportunity of being transported into that extraordinary state which Wagner's music produced in him, that trance, that escape into the mystical dream world which he needed in order to sustain the enormous tension of his turbulent nature.

The standard of the cast and orchestra at the Volksoper was remarkably high and much superior to anything we had been accustomed to in Linz. Another advantage was that one could get a cheap seat there without having to spend a long time in the queue for the box office. What displeased us was the cold, modernistic style of the building, and the dull unimaginative interior of the theatre, which was matched by the lack of glamour in its productions. Adolf used to call this theatre 'the people's soup kitchen'.

Our theatre-going in Linz had given us the grounding for the full enjoyment in Vienna of the immortal master's work. We were thoroughly familiar with his operas, without having been spoilt, and consequently the Hof Opera, and even the modest theatre in Währing, seemed to create anew for us Richard Wagner's world.

Of course, we knew by heart *Lohengrin*, Adolf's favourite opera – I believe he saw it ten times during our time together in Vienna – and the same is true of the *Meistersinger*. Just as other people quote their Goethe or Schiller, we would quote Wagner, preferably the *Meistersinger*. We know, of course, that Wagner intended to immortalise his friend Franz Liszt in the figure of Hans Sachs, and to attack his bitter enemy, Hanslick, in the person of Beckmesser. Adolf often quoted from the third scene of the second act:

> And still I don't succeed
> I feel it and yet I cannot understand it
> I cannot retain it nor forget it
> And if I grasp it I cannot measure it.

In this my friend saw the unique, eternal formula with which Richard Wagner castigated the want of comprehension of his contemporaries and which, so to speak, applied to his own fate, for his father, his family, his teachers, although they had certainly 'felt' that there was something outstanding about him, for the love of God could not understand it. And when people had, at long last, grasped what they wanted, they still remained incapable of 'measuring' the extent of his will. These lines were for him a daily exhortation, a never-failing comfort which helped him as did the picture of the great master himself before which he stood in his darker hours.

We studied with libretto and score those works of Wagner that we had not seen in Linz. So Wagnerian Vienna found us well prepared and, naturally enough, we entered at once the ranks of his worshippers, and wherever we could we acclaimed the work of the master of Bayreuth with fervent enthusiasm.

What had been for us the height of artistic experience in Linz was reduced to the level of poor, well-intentioned provincial performances after we had seen the perfect Wagner interpretations by Gustav Mahler at the Vienna Hof Opera. But Adolf would not have been Adolf if he had contented himself with regretful memories. He loved Linz, which he always thought of as his home town, even though both parents were dead and there was only one human being left there to whom he was passionately devoted: Stefanie, who still did not know what she meant to the pale youth who had stood and waited for her day after day at the Schmiedtoreck. The cultural life of Linz had to be brought to a level commensurate with that of Vienna; with savage determination Adolf set to work.

On leaving Linz he had put great hopes in the Theatre Rebuilding Society, of which he had become an enthusiastic member, but these worthies who had got together to give Linz a new, dignified theatre were apparently making no headway. Nothing was ever heard of it and Adolf's impatience grew. So he started working on his own. He took pleasure in applying to his own home town that style of monumental architecture with which he had become familiar in imperial Vienna.

He had already removed from the central area of the town the railway station with its ugly workshops, smoke-stained sheds and cumbersome railway tracks, and transferred it to the outskirts. This enabled him to enlarge the park, add a zoo, a palm house and, of course, an illuminated fountain. It was in the centre of this well-tended park that the new Linz opera house should be erected, smaller in size than the Vienna Hof Opera but its equal in technical equipment. The old theatre was to become a playhouse and be put under the same direction as the opera. In this way my friend got over the deplorable conditions of his home town and all the greater was the enjoyment he derived from Vienna's artistic attractions.

We saw almost all Richard Wagner's works. *Die fliegende Holländer,* *Lohengrin, Tannhäuser, Tristan und Isolde* and *Die Meistersinger* have remained unforgettable to me, as has also *Der Ring der Niebelungen* and even *Parsifal.* Occasionally of course Adolf saw other operas as well, but they never meant as much to him as Wagner's. In Linz we had already seen a surprisingly good *Figaro,* which had filled Adolf with delight. I still remember his saying, on our way home, that the Linz theatre should in future concentrate on operas which, like *Figaro,* were within its scope. A production of *Die Zauberflöte,* on the other hand, was a complete failure, and Weber's *Freischütz* was so bad that Adolf never wanted to see it again, but in Vienna. of course, everything was different. We saw perfect performances, not only of Mozart operas, but also of Beethhoven's *Fidelio.* Italian opera never attracted Adolf, although Italian composers like Donizetti, Rossini, Bellini and especially Verdi and Puccini, who was then still very modern, were highly appreciated in Vienna and played to full houses.

The Verdi operas we saw together were *Un Ballo in Maschera, Il Trovatore, Rigoletto* and *La Traviata,* but *Aida* was the only one which he liked at all. For him, the plots of Italian operas laid too much emphasis upon theatrical effect. He objected to trickery, knavery and deception as the basic elements of a dramatic situation. He said to me once, 'What would these Italians do if they had no daggers?' He found Verdi's music too unpretentious, relying too much on melody. How rich and varied by comparison was Wagner's range! One day when we heard an organ-grinder playing *La donna é mobile,* Adolf said, 'There's your Verdi!' When I replied that no composer was safe from such debasement of his works, he barked at me furiously, 'Can you imagine the Grail story on a barrel organ?'.

Neither Gounod, whose *Margarete* he regarded as vulgar, nor Tchaikovsky, nor Smetana, met with his approval. No doubt he was handicapped here by his obsessions with German mythology. He rejected my contention that music should appeal to all races and nations. For him nothing counted but Germany ways, German feeling and German thought. He accepted none but the German masters. How often did he tell me that he was proud to belong to a people who had produced such masters.

Time and again we came back to Richard Wagner. In the course of my professional training I obtained new, substantial insight into the compositional creativity of the master, and with it grew my understanding, my penetration of his music. Adolf took a lively interest in this development of my musical conception. His devotion to, and veneration of, Wagner took almost the form of a religion.

When he listened to Wagner's music he was a changed man: his violence left him, he became quiet, yielding and tractable. His gaze lost its restlessness; his own destiny, however heavily it may have weighed upon him, became unimportant. He no longer felt lonely and outlawed, misjudged by society. As if intoxicated by some hypnotic agent, he slipped into a state of ecstasy, and willingly let himself be carried away into that mystical universe which was more real to him than the actual workaday world. From the stale, musty prison of his back room, he was transported into the blissful regions of Germanic antiquity, that ideal world which was the lofty goal for all his endeavours.

Thirty years later, when he met me again in Linz, his friend whom he had last seen as a student of the Vienna Conservatoire, he was convinced that I had become an important conductor, but when I appeared before him as a humble municipal employee, Hitler, by then Reich Chancellor, alluded to the possibility of my assuming the direction of an orchestra.

I declined with thanks. I no longer felt up to the task. When he realised that he could not help his friend with this generous offer, he recalled our common experiences at the Linz theatre and the Vienna Hof Opera, which had elevated our friendship from the commonplace to the sacred sphere of his own world, and invited me to come to Bayreuth.

I should never have thought that those outstanding artistic experiences of my Vienna student days could still be surpassed. And yet this was the case, for what I experienced in Bayreuth as the guest of the friend of my youth was the culmination of everything that Richard Wagner had ever meant in my life.

# Chapter 19

# Adolf Writes an Opera

Soon our life together showed its drawbacks because of the different subjects that Adolf and I were studying. In the morning, when I was at the Conservatoire, my friend was still asleep, and in the afternoon when Adolf wanted to work, my practising disturbed him. This led to frequent friction.

Conservatoire, fiddlesticks! What did he have his books for? He wanted to prove to me that, even without the Conservatoire, he could equal my achievements in the musical field. For it was not the professor's wisdom that counted, he said, but genius.

This ambition led him to a most extraordinary experiment and I am still at a loss to say whether this experiment was of any value or not. Adolf harked back to the elementary possibilities of musical expression. Words seemed to him too complicated for this purpose, and he tried to discover how isolated sounds could be linked to notes of music, and with this musical language he combined colours. Sound and colour were to become one and form the foundations of that which would finally appear on the stage as an opera. I myself, convinced of the truth of what I had learned at the Conservatoire, rejected these experiments somewhat disdainfully, which annoyed him very much. He busied himself for some time with these abstract experiments, perhaps because he hoped to strike at the roots of my superior, academic knowledge. I was reminded of my friend's essays in composition when a few years later a Russian composer caused some sensation in Vienna by similar experiments.

In those weeks, Adolf wrote a lot, mainly plays, but also a few stories. He sat at his table and worked until dawn, without telling me very much about what he was doing. Only now and then would he throw on to my bed some closely written sheets of paper or would read out to me a few pages of his work, written in a strangely exalted style.

I knew that almost everything he was writing was set in the world of Richard Wagner, that is to say, Germanic antiquity. One day I remarked, casually, that I had learned during lectures on the history of music that the

189

outline of a musical drama about Wieland the smith had been found amongst Wagner's posthumous writings. It was, in fact, only a short, hastily sketched text, and no drafts for a stage version existed, nor was anything known about the musical treatment of the material.

Adolf immediately looked up the Wieland legend in his book on gods and heroes. Strangely enough he did not object at all to the plot of the Wieland legend, although King Nidur's action is entirely motivated by avarice and greed. The hunger for gold, so important an element in Germanic mythology, produced in him neither a negative nor a positive response. Nor was he at all impressed by the fact that Wieland kills his son out of vengeance, rapes his daughter and drinks from beakers fashioned from the skulls of his sons. He started to write that same night. I was sure that in the morning he would surprise me with the draft of his new drama, *Wieland der Schmied*, yet things turned out differently. In the morning, nothing happened, but when I returned for lunch I found Adolf, to my great surprise, sitting at the piano. The scene that followed has remained in my memory. Without any further explanation, he greeted me with the words, 'Listen, Gustl, I am going to make the Wieland into an opera.' I was so surprised as to become speechless. Adolf enjoyed my reaction to his announcement and went on playing the piano, or what for him passed as playing. Old Prewratzky had taught him something in his day, undoubtedly, but not enough to play the piano as I understood it.

When I had recovered, I asked Adolf how he imagined he would set about it. 'Quite simple – I shall compose the music, and you will write it down.' Adolf's plans and ideas always moved, more or less, on a plane above normal comprehension – I had long since grown used to that – but now, when my own special domain, music, was in question, I really could not keep up with him. With all due respect to his musical gifts, he was no musician; he was not even capable of playing a musical instrument. He had not the slightest idea of musical theory. How could he dream of composing an opera?

I remember only that my pride as a musician was hurt, and I walked out without uttering a word, and went to a small café nearby to do my homework. My friend was not in the least offended by my behaviour, however, and when I returned home that evening he was somewhat calmer. 'Now, the prelude is ready – listen!', and he played from memory what he had thought up as the prelude to his opera. Of course, I cannot recall a single note of this music, but one thing remains in my memory: it was a sort of illustration of the spoken word, by means of natural, musical elements, and he intended to have it performed on old instruments. As this would not have sounded harmonious, my friend decided in favour of a modern symphony orchestra reinforced by Wagner horns. That was at least music which one could follow. Each separate musical theme in itself made sense, and if the whole impressed one as so primitive, it was only because Adolf could not play better; that is to say he was incapable of expressing his ideas more clearly.

The composition was, of course, entirely influenced by Richard Wagner. The whole prelude consisted of a sequence of single themes, but the development of these themes, however well chosen they were, had been beyond Adolf's ability. After all, where should he have acquired the necessary knowledge? He lacked entirely any training for such a task.

Having finished his playing, Adolf wanted to hear my judgment. I knew how highly he valued it and what my praise in musical matters meant to him, but this was no simple problem. The basic themes were good, I said, but he had to realise that with these themes alone it was impossible to write an opera, and I declared my readiness to teach him the necessary theoretical knowledge. This roused his wrath. 'Do you think I'm mad?' he shouted at me, 'What have I got you for? First of all you will put down exactly what I play on the piano.'

I knew only too well my friend's mood when he spoke in this manner, and realised that it was no good arguing. So I wrote down as faithfully as possible what Adolf had played, but it was late, Frau Zakreys was knocking on the door and Adolf had to stop.

Next morning I left early and when I returned for lunch, Adolf reproached me for having run away 'in the middle of working on his opera'. He had already prepared the music paper for me and immediately began to play. As Adolf stuck neither to the same time nor to a uniform key, it was hard to take down what I heard. I tried to make it clear to him that he had to keep to one key. 'Who is the composer, you or I?' he ranted. All I had to do was write down his musical thoughts and ideas.

I asked him to start again. He did, and I wrote. Thus we made some progress, yet for Adolf it was too slow. I told him that to begin with I wanted to play through what I had taken down. He agreed, and I sat down at the piano, and it was his turn to listen. Curiously enough, I liked what I was playing better than he did, perhaps because he had a very precise idea of his composition in his head and neither his own poor playing, nor my notation and playing, corresponded to it. Nevertheless we concentrated for several days, or rather nights, on this prelude. I had to put the whole thing into a suitable metric form, but whatever I did Adolf was not satisfied. There were periods in the course of his composition in which the time changed from one bar to the next. I succeeded in convincing Adolf that this was impossible, but as soon as I tried to render the whole section in one time, he protested again.

Today I can understand what brought him to the edge of despair during those strenuous nights and tested our friendship to the uttermost. He carried this prelude in his head as a finished composition just as he had had ready the plan for a bridge or a concert hall even before he put pencil to paper, but whilst he was complete master of the pencil and could give form to his idea till the drawing was completed, such means were denied him in the musical field. His attempt to make use of me made the whole thing even more complicated, for my theoretical knowledge only hindered his intuition. It reduced him to utter despair that he had an idea in his head, a musical idea which he considered bold and important, without being able to pin it down. There were moments in which he doubted his vocation in spite of his pronounced conceit.

Soon he found a way out of the dilemma between passionate will and insufficient ability as ingenious as it was original: he would compose his opera, he declared determinedly, in the mode of musical expression corresponding to that period in which the action was set, that is to say, in Germanic antiquity. I intended to object that the audience, in order to 'enjoy' the opera properly, should be composed of old *Germanen*, rather than people of the twentieth century, but even before I had raised this objection, he was already working fervently on his new solution. I had no opportunity to dissuade him from this experiment, which I considered quite impossible. Besides, he would probably have succeeded in convincing me that his solution was feasible by insisting that the people of our century would just have to learn to listen properly.

He wanted to know if there was anything preserved of Germanic music. 'Nothing,' I replied briefly, 'except the instruments'.

'And what were they?' I told him that drums and rattles had been found, and in some places in Sweden and Denmark also a kind of flute, made of bones. Experts had succeeded in restoring these strange flutes and in producing with them some not very harmonious sounds, but most important were the luren, wind instruments made of brass, almost two metres long and curved like a horn. They probably served only as bugles between homesteads, and the crude sounds they produced could hardly be called music.

I thought that my explanation, which he had followed with careful attention, would suffice to make him give up his idea, for you could not orchestrate an opera with rattles, drums, bone-flutes and luren, but I was wrong. He started talking about the Skalds, who had sung to the accompaniment of harp-like instruments, something I had really forgotten. It should be possible, he went on, to deduce what their music was like from the kind of instruments the Germanic tribes had. Now my book-learning came into its own. 'That has been done', I reported, 'and it has been shown that the music of the *Germanen* had a vertical structure, and possessed some sort of harmony; they even had, perhaps, some inkling of major and minor keys. To be sure, these are only scientific assumptions, so-called hypotheses . . .'

This was sufficient to induce my friend to start composing for nights on end. He surprised me with ever new conceptions and ideas. It was hardly possible to write down this music, which did not fit into any scheme. As the Wieland legend, which Adolf arbitrarily interpreted and extended, was rich in dramatic moments, a wide scale of sentiments had to be translated into the musical idiom. To make the thing at all tolerable for the human ear, I finally persuaded Adolf to give up the idea of using the original instruments from the Germanic graves and to replace them by modern instruments of a similar type. I was content when, after nights of work, at long last the various leitmotifs of the opera were established.

We then agreed on the characters, of whom only Wieland, the hero of the opera, had any substance so far, wherupon Adolf divided the whole action into acts and scenes. In the meantime he designed the scenery and costumes, and made a charcoal sketch of the winged hero.

As my friend had not made any progress with the libretto which was supposed to be in verse, I suggested that he should finish the prelude first, to which he agreed after several rather heated arguments. I gave him a lot of help with it, and consequently the prelude turned out to be quite presentable, but my suggestion that the composition should be orchestrated and played by an orchestra as soon as an opportunity arose he rejected out of hand. He refused to have the prelude classed as programme music and would not hear of an 'audience' – which was in any case problematical. Yet he worked feverishly on it as though an impatient opera producer had allowed him too little time and was waiting to snatch the manuscript from his hands.

He wrote and wrote and I worked on the music. When I fell asleep, over-whelmed by fatigue, Adolf roused me roughly. I had hardly opened my eyes and there he was in front of me, reading from his manuscript, the words tumbling out over each other in his excitement. It was past midnight and he had to speak softly. This, in its contrast to the scenes of volcanic violence described in his verse, lent to his impassioned voice a sound of strange unreality. I had long since known this behaviour of his when a self-imposed task engrossed him completely and forced him to unceasing activity; it was as though a demon had taken possession of him. Oblivious to his surroundings, he never tired, he never slept. He ate nothing, he hardly drank. At the most he would occasionally grab a milk bottle and take a hasty gulp, certainly without being aware of it, for he was too completely wrapped up in his work. Never before had I been so directly impressed by this ecstatic creativeness. Where was it leading him? He squandered his strength and talents on something that had no practical value. How long would his weakened, delicate body stand this overstrain?

I forced myself to stay awake and to listen, nor did I ask him any of the questions that filled me with anxiety. It would have been easy for me to take as an excuse one of our frequent quarrels to move out. The people at the Conservatoire would have been only too pleased to help me find another room. Why did I not do it? After all, I had often admitted to myself that this strange friendship was no good for my studies. How much time and energy did I lose in these nocturnal activities with my friend? Why then, did I not go? Because I was homesick, certainly, and because Adolf represented for me a bit of home. But, after all, homesickness is something a young man of twenty can overcome. What was it then? What held me?

Frankly it was just hours like those through which I was now living which bound me even more closely to my friend. I knew the normal interests of young people of my age: flirtations, shallow pleasures, idle play and a lot of unimportant, meaningless thoughts. Adolf was the exact opposite. There was an incredible earnestness in him, a thoroughness, a true passionate interest in everything that happened and, most important, an unfailing devotion to the beauty, majesty and grandeur of art. It was this that attracted me especially to him and restored my equilibrium after hours of exhaustion. All this was well worth a few sleepless nights and those more or less heated quarrels to which, in my quiet, sensible way, I had become accustomed.

I remember that some of the opera's more dramatic scenes haunted me for weeks in my dreams. Only some of the pictures which Adolf designed still stand out in my memory. Pen and pencil were too slow for him and he used to draw with charcoal. He would outline the scenery with a few bold, quick strokes. Then we would discuss the action: first Wieland enters from the right, then his brother Egil from the left and then, from the back, the second brother Slaghid.

I have still before my eyes Wolf Lake, where the first scene of the opera was laid. From the *Edda*, a book that was sacred for him, he knew Iceland, the rugged island of the north, where the elements from which the world was created meet now, as they did in the days of creation: the violent storm, the bare dark rock, the pale ice of the glaciers, the flaming fire of the volcanoes. There he laid the setting of his opera, for there nature itself was still in those passionate convulsions which inspired the actions of gods and human beings. There, then, was the Wolf Lake on whose banks Wieland and his brothers were fishing when one morning three light clouds, borne along by the winds, floated towards them, three Valkyries in glittering coats of mail and shining helmets. They wore white fluttering robes, magic garments which enabled them to float through the air. I remember what headaches these flying Valkyries caused us, as Adolf categorically refused to do without them. Altogether there was a lot of 'flying' in our opera. In the last act, Wieland too had to forge himself a pair of wings with which to fly, a flight on wings of metal which had to be accomplished with the utmost ease in order to remove any doubts as to the quality of his workmanship. This was for us, the creators of the opera, one more technical problem which attracted Adolf in particular, perhaps because just in those days the first 'heavier than air machines' were being flown by Lilienthal, the Wright brothers, Farman and Blériot. The flying Valkyries married Wieland, Egil and Slaghild. Mighty horns summoned the neighbours to the wedding feast at the Wolf Lake.

It would take me too long were I to recount the various episodes of the old saga; besides, I can no longer tell whether we followed it word for word in our work, but the impression of dramatic events driven on by wild, unbridled passion, and given expression in verses that inexorably engraved themselves on the heart, carried by just such inexorably severe and elemental music is still vivid in my memory.

I do not know what became of our opera. One day new, pressing problems requiring immediate solution confronted my friend. As even Adolf, in spite of his immense capacity for work, had only one pair of hands, he had to put aside the half-finished opera. He spoke less and less of it, and in the end did not mention it at all. Perhaps the insufficiency of his endeavours had meanwhile dawned on him. To me, it had been obvious from the beginning that we would never succeed in our attempt to write an opera, and I took good care not to raise the subject again. *Wieland der Schmied*, Adolf's opera, remained a fragment.

# Chapter 20

# The Mobile Reichs-Orchestra

My friend's musical interests broke new ground in Vienna. Whereas hitherto he had confined his passion to opera, now he had leanings for the concert hall. Adolf had attended symphony concerts produced by the Music Society at Linz, and probably saw August Göllerich conducting on six or seven of these occasions, but his real purpose was to watch my performance as an instrumentalist. Maybe he considered that my quiet, submissive personality was not up to such a large responsibility before the public and was interested in seeing how I made out. Whatever the reason, I noticed that after each performance he talked about my part in it more than about the concert itself.

In Vienna it was different. Other circumstances interposed themselves. From the Conservatoire I received on a regular basis one to three complimentary tickets to concerts. I would always give one to Adolf, or sometimes all three if I was working late on a score. Since these were good seats, concert-going was not the same struggle as was the opera. From his remarks upon his return from these concerts I noticed to my surprise that Adolf quite liked symphony music, which pleased me, for it broadened our common field of interest in music.

The head of the Conservatoire training school for orchestral leaders, Gustav Gutheil, also conducted the performances of the Vienna Concert Society. We also had a very high opinion of Ferdinand Lowe, Director of the Conservatoire, who occasionally led the Vienna Philharmonic when it played Bruckner. In Vienna there were violent differences between supporters of Brahms and Bruckner even though both masters had been dead for over a century. Even Eduard Hanslick, the hated Viennese music critic whom we nicknamed Benkmesser, was defunct by then, although the wounds he left were still open. Hanslick, our sworn enemy because he had denigrated in brutal fashion our hero Wagner, had come in on the side of Brahms against Bruckner.

Although paying respect to the two masters, Adolf and I sided with Bruckner because we preferred his music; it also helped that he was Austrian. Adolf said that Linz should be home to Bruckner in the same way that Bayreuth was home to Wagner: the Linzer Tonhalle, as he called his nearly complete design for the new edifice, should be dedicated to Bruckner's memory.

Besides the symphonies of the classical masters, Adolf took great delight in hearing the works of the romantic composers Carl Maria von Weber, Schubert, Mendelssohn and Schumann. He was keen on Grieg whose piano concerto in A minor he found enchanting. He regretted very much that Wagner had only worked for the operatic stage so that one only ever got to hear overtures to individual operas in concert halls. In general, Adolf had little enthusiasm for instrumental virtuosos, although he never missed individual solo renditions such as Mozart's and Beethoven's piano and violin concertos, Mendelssohn's violin concerto in A minor and, above all, Schumann's piano concerto in A minor.

These frequent concert visits began to unsettle Adolf, but for some time I could not understand the cause. Any other person would have been satisfied with just hearing the performance. But not Adolf. There he had sat in his free seat in the auditorium letting Beethoven's glorious violin concerto in D minor wash over him and was happy and contented but yet – when he counted the attendance, maybe 500 people – he had to ask himself: 'What about the many thousands of people who have not been able to hear this concert?' Surely there would be not only amongst the music students, but also amongst the artisans and workers very many who would be delighted, as he was, to have free or easily affordable seats to a concert hall and there listen to immortal music. And here he was thinking not only of Vienna, for in the capital it was relatively easy for people to go to concerts if they wanted to, but the small towns in the provinces. From his experience of Linz he knew how poorly it was provided with cultural institutions. That would have to change: concert-going must no longer be the preserve of the privileged few. The free ticket tided him over, and to that extent he profited from it personally, but the system would have to be discontinued in due course.

Such thinking was typical of Adolf. Nothing could happen around him that did not fit into the global view. Even pure artistic experiences such as going to a concert awoke in him the realisation of a problem which affected everybody, something to which the 'ideal state' as he dreamed it could not remain indifferent. The 'storm of the revolution' would tear down the gates of art, closed hitherto to so many – 'social reform', even in the area of enjoying music. Of course, many young people of the time thought as he did, and his protest against the privileged layers of society as regards artistic interests was by no means unusual. Societies and organisations existed for the express purpose of bringing art to the masses, and many fought hard and with visible success, but it was Hitler's approach that was unique. While others were happy to take each day as it came in their pursuit of the goal, Adolf scorned their well-intentioned but inadequate methods and strove for the total solution wherever such a thing could be realised. At the time when he first announced a project, it was for him already reality in the making. Typically, he was not satisfied simply to advocate a policy; he had to work the thing out in all its fastidious detail as if he had received 'orders from above' to do so. When finished the policy was thus pregnant on the mental plane and required only the word of empowerment for its implementation.

During the time I knew him, this word of empowerment was never spoken, and it was for this reason that I considered him a denizen of a fantasy world, even if he had convinced me by argument of the reasonableness of a policy. He was certain that it was he who would in due time issue the single word of empowerment enabling the hundreds and thousands of different plans filed in his mind to be set out and accomplished. He spoke of it rarely, and then only to me, because he knew that I believed in him.

In the past when he had seized upon a particular idea and had worked on it thoroughly and expertly, another listener would interject, 'Yes, but who is going to pay for it all?' In Linz, I had been guilty of raising the point thoughtlessly myself simply because it was obvious. In Vienna I had grown more circumspect and avoided asking where the funding was supposed to come from. Adolf considered the question irrelevant and his response to it varied. In Linz it had been 'the Reich', an answer which I felt was inadequate. In Vienna he was more to the point with 'businessmen will be needed', although it might happen that he would give me shorter shrift with: 'You probably won't be consulted, because you understand nothing of it,' or even shorter, 'I think that is something that is best left to me.'

The first warning that a new policy was in the offing would be a keyword which cropped up during a monologue or debate, a special term which he had never used previously. In the period when he was not yet clear in his own mind where it was leading him, the term might be modified. This happened in the weeks of his frequent concert-going when he began to speak of 'this orchestra that tours the provinces'. I thought that there actually was such an orchestra in Vienna, since he spoke of it as though it actually existed. Then I discovered that the 'mobile orchestra' as he had now become accustomed to call it (the word 'tours' had something of a bad connotation) was a figment of his imagination, and shortly afterwards, since he never did things by halves, we had 'the mobile Reichs-Orchestra'.

I was roped in, of course, and I remember clearly that our joint planning ended with ten touring orchestras so that even citizens living in the remotest inaccessible reaches of the Reich could be treated to Beethoven's violin concerto in D major and other such delights. One evening when he held forth in detail about the orchestra I asked him why he was getting so involved in a musical project when his ambition was to be an architect. The answer was short and to the point: 'Because for the time being I have you.' This meant that for as long as I remained by his side, he would draw on my advice and experience as an orchestral conductor of the future. I was flattered by this, but when I asked whom he had in mind to lead the orchestra he saw through me at once, laughed and replied, 'Definitely not you.' Serious again, he added that at the appropriate time he would certainly consider me for the post, but he had hurt my feelings and I informed him that even if he now offered I would have to decline the honour for I was anxious to be appointed to lead an orchestra that actually existed, and was not merely in his fantasies. This was enough to provoke an outburst of rage, for he would never tolerate people doubting the ultimate fulfillment of his ideas. 'You would still be very happy for me to appoint you to lead it,' he shouted.

After this temperamental overture, the 'planning' could begin. I remember this particular plan very clearly because it involved my speciality and I was on much firmer ground when discussing the matter than I had been during his efforts to tack *Wieland der Schmied* on to Wagner's repertoire. How thoroughly we approached our task can be seen from an altercation next evening over the Pedalharfe – the Louis XVI harp. Adolf wanted to have three of these very costly and extraordinarily heavy instruments. 'Whatever for?' I asked, 'An experienced conductor would make do with just one.'

'Ridiculous,' was the angry reply, 'how will you play the *Feuerzauber* [from *Die Walküre*. Ed.] with only one Pedalharfe?'

'I wouldn't have it in the programme.'

'And if you were forced to have it in the programme?'

I made a final effort to resolve the matter reasonably. 'Look, a Pedalharfe costs 18,000 guilders.' I thought that was bound to shift him off his high horse, from where he was defending his idea with such stubbornness, but I was wrong. 'So what, just money!' he cried, and that settled it, the mobile Reichs-Orchestra would be equipped with three Pedalharfen.

When I reflect with what passion we argued about things which existed only in his imagination I have to smile. It was a wonderful time in which we got more worked up playing vague mind-games than over everyday realities. We ceased to be poor, starving students and became great men of consequence for a while. Although I was surprised at the strength of his imagination for a dream world, an energy which he lacked for the real world surrounding him, naturally I did not suspect that these fantasies meant very much more for him than just a romantic way to idle away the time.

I had myself often reflected on the fact that great orchestras could only be seen in the largest cities: Vienna, Berlin, Munich, Amsterdam, Milan, New York, for it was only there that they could draw on the pool of new talent for the first-class instrumentalists they needed. In consequence, only the populations of these great cities could hear the orchestras perform while those who lived far afield in villages and small provincial towns were denied it. Adolf's Reichs-Orchestra was as brilliant as it was simple. Led by a gifted conductor, it would be of such a size as to be able to perform all symphonies and travel country-wide. When Adolf asked me how large it should be, I was proud that he should have consulted me rather than his books; I felt that he considered me to be a future conductor. I was therefore in my element. I remember how we spread all the plans and papers across the top of the grand piano – the table was too small – for Adolf wished to be informed down to the last minuscule detail about everything. This was the puzzling, noteworthy thing about him, the inexplicable contrast: he created a fantasy in thin air and yet tied down the whole thing to the last detail.

The orchestra was 100 strong, a respectable body able to compete with other great orchestras on equal terms. Adolf was rather taken aback by the logistics. I explained that it required not only first-class instruments, but that the transport question was very important: the care in transit, compre-hensive insurance, the archives of the repertoire for a hundred players, music stands, chairs. Any old chair simply would not do for a first-class cellist. At this he instructed me to obtain from the secretary of the orchestral society better details regarding the overall arrangements, from the Musicians' Union the procedure on hiring musicians and, to cap it all, how one was to cost the project. I did as I was bid, and Adolf was satisfied with my report. The total cost was mammoth, but he dismissed it with a wave of the hand. There was some excitement about the uniform dress to be worn.

I wanted something with a bit of colour in it, but Adolf was firm: it had to be black and elegant, but not striking.

Transport remained a tricky problem, for in 1908 there were areas of the country where the railway had not penetrated. Motor vehicles, noisy and foul-smelling, had begun to roam the streets: we stood and watched them proceeding at their 'murderous' speed of ten miles per hour and wondered if they would be suitable for the mobile Reichs-Orchestra – undoubtedly they would greatly improve its mobility, but personally I was unsympathetic to the idea.

So, the orchestra arrives to schedule in a town, decked out in bunting, to be greeted by the Bürgermeister. Where shall the concert be held? Very few towns had a hall large enough to host a 100-man orchestra and a large audience. 'We should play in the open air,' Adolf decided.

'Concerts under a starry sky are very stimulating,' I replied, 'but you have to guarantee the starry sky for the duration of the performance. And besides that, you lose the acoustics.' The whole endeavour almost collapsed on these facts. Adolf ruminated for a while, then he said, "There are churches everywhere. Why don't we play in the churches?' From a musical standpoint there was nothing against it. Adolf said I should find out from the church authorities if they would be prepared to make churches available for a travelling Reichs-Orchestra. There was absolutely no way I would do any such thing, but I said nothing and luckily Adolf forgot to ask me how my enquiries were progressing in that direction.

We experienced serious difficulties about the repertoire. Adolf wanted to know how long the orchestra would take to be ready to perform a symphony. There was no reliable yardstick, and this annoyed him. Under no circumstances would he accept my opinion that the repertoire, if it had to be limited to German composers only, a matter on which he was adamant, should begin with Bach, Fuchs, Gluck and Händel, and always with individual works by Schütz. 'So what did they do before them, then?' he wanted to know.

'There has never been anything else for an orchestral programme,' I replied. 'Who says so?' he shouted.

I explained to him calmly that he could rely completely on my assurance – unless of course he wished to take up the study of the history of music himself. 'Well, I will,' he answered thornily. This put an end to the discussions about the repertoire. I did not take his retort seriously, for the history of music is not an easy subject to study, and would divert him from his professional interests. Moreover, he knew that I was well up in it since

I had attended lectures on the subject at the university, so I was astonished to find him next day engrossed in a thick volume with some such title as *The Development of Music over the Ages* which at least served to keep him quiet for ages. It did not satisfy him completely, and he sent me out to fetch the historical theses of Dr Guido Adler and Dr Max Grietz, which he read avidly.

'The Chinese composed good music 2,000 years ago,' he declared, 'Why should it be any different with us? They had a definite instrument then – the human voice. Just because these learned men are groping in the dark for the beginnings of music or, better put, they know nothing about it, it does not mean that it didn't exist, not by any stretch of the imagination.'

With what thoroughness did my friend always go about a task. All the same, his predisposition to research a thing to its very depths often brought me to the verge of desperation. There would be no peace until he had exhausted every possible avenue and finally encountered the void, and even then he would put a question mark at its entrance. I can imagine how such an attitude would have made all the professors at the Academy cheerfully imagine strangling him.

Finally he settled for opening the Reichs-Orchestra programme with Bach, progressing through Gluck and Händel to Haydn, Mozart and Beethoven, after which would follow the romantic composers. Everything would be crowned by Bruckner, all of whose symphonies would be included in the repertoire. As for modern, and primarily unknown composers, he would go his own way in the choice. In any case he rejected out of hand the guidelines set by the Vienna music critics, whom he pitched into at every opportunity.

Since the beginning of the Reichs-Orchestra project, Adolf had carried with him a little notebook in which, after every concert he visited, he would enter all details about the work, composer, conductor and so on, and follow it with his own opinion. The highest praise that any concert could receive would be his endorsement 'will be included in the repertoire of our orchestra'.

For a long period I was unable to shake off my attachment to the mobile Reichs-Orchestra. The gramophone had made its debut and, monstrous, scratchy device that it was, it had nevertheless opened the door to 'mechanical' music. Wireless was still in its infancy but it was already clear that gramophone records and wireless ensured that 'performed' music would serve the interests of the 'mechanical' music industry in due course. This was the basic question which concerned all people who truly loved the art, and was what my friend was trying to resolve with the mobile Reichs-Orchestra, bringing high-class symphony music directly to the people wherever they lived, not recorded on machinery.

# Chapter 21

# Unmilitary Interlude

One fine day – it must have been about the beginning of April 1908 – I received a letter. As Adolf never got any letters, I used to be discreet about mine to spare his feelings, but he noticed at once that this letter must have some special significance. 'What's the matter, Gustl?' he asked sympathetically. I replied simply, 'Here, read it.'

I can still see how his face changed colour, how his eyes rook on that extraordinary glitter which used to herald an outburst of rage. Then he started raving.

'You are not to register on any account, Gustl,' he screamed, 'You're a fool if you go there. The best thing to do is tear up this stupid piece of paper!' I jumped up and snatched my calling-up papers away from him before in his fury he tore them to pieces. I was so upset myself that Adolf soon calmed down. Striding angrily between door and piano, he immediately drew up a plan to help me out of my present predicament. 'It's not even certain yet whether you will be passed fit,' he remarked more calmly. 'After all, it's only a year since you nearly went under with that bad attack of pneumonia. If you are unfit, as I hope, all this excitement will have been in vain.'

Adolf suggested that I should go to Linz and present myself before the medical board according to instructions. In case I should be passed fit, I should forthwith cross the border into Germany secretly at Passau. On no account was I to serve in the Austro-Hungarian Army. This moribund Habsburg Empire did not deserve a single soldier, he declared. As my friend was nine months younger than I, he did not expect his call-up until the following year, 1909, but as was now evident, he had already made up his mind in this respect and was determined not to serve in the Austrian Army. Perhaps he was quite pleased to use me as a guinea pig and find out how his suggested solution would really work out in practice.

The next morning I went to the director of the Conservatoire and showed him my conscription papers. He explained to me that, as a member of the Conservatoire, I was obliged to serve only one year, but he advised me that as the son of a businessman I should register with the Reserve. There I should only have to do eight weeks training and later on three further periods of four weeks. I asked him what he thought of the idea of my going to Germany to escape military service altogether. He was shocked by this unusual suggestion and advised me against it forcefully.

For Adolf, even the idea of my serving in the Reserve was too great a concession to the Habsburg Empire and he went on and on, trying to persuade me to fall in with his plan right up to the moment when I finished my packing.

In Linz I told my father what my friend had suggested, for I was more than a little intrigued by the idea. I could not get up any enthusiasm for military service and even the eight weeks in the Reserve seemed to me dreadful. My father was even more horrified than the director had been. 'In heaven's name, what are you thinking of?' he exclaimed, shaking his head. If I went over the border secretly or, to call a spade a spade, deserted, I would be liable to prosecution, he declared. On top of that I could never come home again and my parents, who had already sacrificed so much for me, would lose me altogether.

My father's words, together with my mother's tears, sufficed to bring me to my senses. That very day my father went to see a government official with whom he was friendly about the possibility of getting me put down for the Reserve, and he immediately drafted an application which he advised me to submit should I be passed fit for service.

I wrote to Adolf telling him that I had decided to follow the Conservatoire director's advice and would be attending the medical examination in a few days. After that, I would come to Vienna with my father. Perhaps Adolf too had meanwhile thought better of it and had realised that the way he had devised for himself was not suitable for me, because in his reply he did not even mention it. Or, of course, perhaps he did not like to put down this plan, which after all was fairly risky, in black and white. On the other hand he was obviously very pleased that my father intended coming back with me when I returned to Vienna (the trip never took place).

I had also told Adolf by letter that I would be bringing my viola with me in case I had the chance of an orchestral engagement so that I could make a little extra money. During my studies in Vienna I had contracted conjunctivitis and was treated in Linz by an oculist, and I warned Adolf that he should not be surprised if I arrived at the Westbahnhof wearing spectacles. Fortunately I still have the letter he wrote in reply, addressed to the 'stud. mus. Gustav Kubizek'.

Dear Gustl,

Whilst thanking you for your letter, I must tell you immediately how pleased I am that your dear father is really coming with you to Vienna. Providing that you and he have no objection, I will meet you at the station on Thursday at 11 o'clock. You write that you are having such lovely weather which almost upsets me as, if it were not raining here, we too should be having lovely weather. I am very pleased that you are bringing a viola. On Tuesday I shall buy myself two crowns' worth of cotton wool and twenty kreuzers' worth of paste, for my ears naturally. That – on top of this – you are going blind affects me deeply: you will play more wrong notes than ever. Then you will become blind and I gradually mad. Oh dear! But meanwhile I wish you and your esteemed parents at least a happy Easter and send them my hearty greetings as well as to you.

Your friend,

*Adolf Hitler*

The latter is dated 20 April, so Adolf had written it on his birthday. In view of his circumstances at that time, it is not surprising that he does not mention it. Perhaps he had not even realised that it was his birthday. Everything in the letter that concerns my father is perfectly polite. He even asks if it is in order to come and meet us, but as soon as he refers to the weather his sarcasm breaks though. 'If it were not raining, we too should be having lovely weather.' And then, when he comes to my viola, he gives full play to his grim humour. He even jokes about the trouble with my eyes until he pulls himself up with the 'Oh dear!' and then closes the letter in a very formal manner. That Adolf had still not come to terms with spelling is particularly clear in this letter: his former German-language teacher Professor Huemer would not even have given him a 'fair' for it, and the punctuation is even worse.

On the appointed day I went for my medical examination. I was passed fit and presented my application for acceptance into the Reserve.

When I returned to Vienna – without the dreaded spectacles – Adolf greeted me very warmly because, in spite of everything, he was glad that I would continue to lodge with him. Of course, he made great fun of the

'Reservist'. He could not possibly imagine how they would make a soldier out of me, he said. For that matter, neither could I, but it was something that I could go on with my studies. At home, Adolf sketched my head and drew a cocked hat with a plume on top of it. 'There you are Gustl,' he joked, 'you look like a veteran, even before you're a recruit.'

After the long, dull winter, spring was making its appearance. Since I had seen once again, on my visit to Linz, the familiar meadows, woods and hills, our gloomy back room in the Stumpergasse seemed to me gloomier than ever. Looking back on our countless walks throughout the length and breadth of the countryside around Linz, I tried to persuade Adolf to make some excursions into the country around Vienna. I had more time to spare now as my pupils, having successfully passed their examinations, had returned home, and not without giving me a nice little present, which came as a pleasant surprise, for there was once again a little money in the kitty (so far as I was concerned, at any rate). When, in the gardens along the Ring, the blossom came out and the mild spring sunshine enticed us, I could stand the stifling walls of the city no longer. Adolf, too, was longing to get out into the open.

I knew how fond he was of the open country, the woods and, in particular, in the distance, the blue range of mountains. He found a solution to this problem, in his own way, long before I did, as when it became too close and stuffy for him at Frau Zakreys's, and the stink of the paraffin became unbearable, he went off to the Schönbrunn Park, but this was not enough for me. I wanted to see more of the country around Vienna. So did Adolf but firstly, he explained, he had no money for such 'extra expenses'. That could be got over, as I invited him to be my guest on such excursions and, to make sure of it, I bought provisions for both of us the day before. Secondly – and this was much more difficult – if we really wanted to make a full day's excursion, he had to get up early. He would rather do anything than this, as it was a most difficult thing for him.

To try and shake him awake was a risky undertaking – he was likely to become utterly impossible. 'Why do you wake me so early?' he would shout at me. When I told him that the day was well advanced, he would never believe me. I would lean right out of the window and twist my head upwards so that I could see the small strip of sky. 'Not a cloud in sight: the sun is shining brightly,' I would announce, but even as I turned round, Adolf was fast asleep again.

If I succeeded in getting him out of bed and on the move I had to consider the first few hours lost, because after having been woken up so 'early' he would be silent and sullen for a long time, replying to questions only with reluctant grunts. Only when we got far away into the bright, green countryside did he finally come out of his sulks. Then, to be sure, he was happy and contented and even thanked me for having persisted in my efforts to get him up.

Our first objective was the Hermannskogel in the Vienna woods and we were very lucky with the weather. On the summit we vowed to go out far more frequently. The next Sunday we went to the Vienna woods again. We felt ready for anything, although we certainly did not look very enterprising in our city clothes and light shoes. We made a very long trip that day according to our standards, from the start of the Tullner Feld, and by Ried and Purkersdorf back to the city. Adolf was enchanted by that part of the countryside and said it reminded him of a certain part of the Mühlviertel, of which he was very fond. Undoubtedly he too suffered inwardly from homesickness for the land of his childhood and adolescence, although not a single soul remained there who still cared about him

I took a day off from the Conservatoire for the trip to the Wachau. We had to get to the station very early to catch a train to Melk, and it was not till he saw the marvellous monastery that Adolf became reconciled to this early rising, and then how he enjoyed it – I could hardly tear him away. He would not stick to the conducted tour, but searched everywhere for secret passages and hidden steps, which might take him to the foundations; he wanted to examine how these had been built into the rocks. Indeed, one could almost believe that the mighty pile had grown out of the stone. After that, we spent a long time in the beautiful library and then went on the steamer through the glory of May-bedecked Wachau.

Adolf was a changed person, even if only through being on the Danube, his beloved river, again. Vienna was not so closely built about the Danube as was, for instance, Linz, where one could stand on the bridge and await the approach of a distinguished blonde maiden from Urfahr. He missed the Danube almost as much as he still missed Stefanie. And now the castles, the villages, the hillside vineyards passed us gently by, for it did not seem as though we were moving forwards, but rather as though we were standing still with this wonderful landscape floating by us in a peaceful rhythm. It acted on us like magic. Adolf stood in the bows, engrossed in the landscape. Till long past Krems, sailing along through the broad monotonous woods that line the river on either bank, he did not utter a word. Who knew where his thoughts might be?

As though this magic trip needed a counterbalance, our next trip was down the Danube to Fischamend. I was disappointed. Was this really the same river that had so delighted us, our dear, familiar, Danube? Wharves, warehouses, oil refineries, and in between them fishermen's miserable huts, slums and even real gypsy encampments. Where on earth had we got to? This was the 'other' Danube which no longer belonged to the picture of our homeland, but was part of the strange, eastern world. We went home, Adolf very thoughtful and I disillusioned.

Must vivid in my memory is a mountain excursion we made in early summer. The journey to Semmering was far enough to allow Adolf to recover from his early rising. Immediately after Wiener Neustadt the country became mountainous. The railway had to reach the heights of the Semmering in wide curves. To attain a height of 980 metres, many turns, tunnels and viaducts were necessary. Adolf was thrilled by the bold design of the track; one surprise came on top of another. He would have liked to have got out and walked this stretch of the track so that he could inspect it all. I was already prepared to listen to a comprehensive lecture on the building of mountain railways at the next opportunity, for certainly he would have thought out a bolder design, even higher viaducts and longer tunnels.

Semmering! We got out. A beautiful day. How pure was the air here after all the dust and smoke, how blue the sky! The meadows gleamed green, the dark woods rising above them, and higher still towered the snow-covered peaks of the mountains.

The train back to Vienna did not leave till evening: we had plenty of time, the whole day was ours. Adolf quickly made up his mind what our target should be. Which was the highest of these mountains? We were told, I believe, the Rax. So, let us climb the Rax. Neither Adolf nor I had the faintest idea of mountaineering. The highest 'mountains' we had conquered in our lives were the gentle hills of the Mühlviertel. We had as yet only seen the Alps themselves at a distance, but we were now in the midst of them and very impressed by the thought that this mountain was over 2,000 metres high.

As always with Adolf, his will had to make up for whatever else was lacking. We had no food with us, because we had originally intended just to walk down from the Semmering heights to Gloggnitz. We did not even have a rucksack and our clothes were those we wore for our strolls through the city. Our shoes were much too light, with thin soles and without nails. We had trousers and jackets, but not a scrap of warm clothing – but the sun was shining, and we were young – so forward!

The adventure we had on our way down overshadowed our upward climb so completely that I can longer tell which route we took. I only remember now that we climbed for several hours before we reached the plateau at the summit of the mountain. We now seemed to be on a peak, though it might not have been the Rax. I had never climbed a mountain peak; I had a strange unfettered feeling, as though I no longer belonged to the earth, but was already close to heaven.

Adolf, deeply affected, stood on the plateau and said not a word. We could see far and wide across the land. Here and there in the colourful pattern of meadow and forest a church tower or village would spring up. How puny and unimportant did the works of man look! It was a wonderful moment, perhaps the most beautiful that I ever experienced with my friend. Tiredness was forgotten in our enthusiasm. Somewhere in our pockets we found a bit of dry bread and we made do with that. In the pleasure of the day, we had hardly noticed the weather. Had not the sun just been shining? Now suddenly dark clouds made their appearance and a mist fell; this happened as rapidly as though it were the change of a stage set. The wind sprang up and whipped the mist before us in long, fluttering shrouds. Far off a storm was rumbling, hollow and uncanny, the thunder rolled around the mountains.

We began to freeze in our pitiful Ringstrasse suits. Our thin trousers fluttered around our legs as we hurried down to the valley, but the path was stony, and our shoes not up to the demands the mountain made of them. Moreover, for all our haste, the storm gained on us. Already the first drops were spattering down in the woods, and then the rain really set in. And what rain! Actual streams of water poured down on us from clouds that seemed to hang just above the treetops. We ran and ran, as hard as we could. It was hopeless to try to protect ourselves. Soon there was not a single dry spot on us, and our shoes were full of water; there was no house, no hut, no kind of shelter wherever we turned. Adolf was not at all put out by the thunder and lightning, the storm and the rain. To my surprise he was in a splendid mood and, although soaked to the skin, became more and more genial as the rain grew heavier.

We skipped along the stony path and suddenly, just off it, I spotted a little hut. There was no sense in continuing to run in the rain and, besides, it was getting dark, so I suggested to Adolf that we should stay in this little cabin overnight. He agreed immediately – for him the adventure could not go on long enough.

I searched the little wooden hut. In the lower half lay a pile of hay, dry and sufficient for us both to sleep in. Adolf took off his shoes, jacket and trousers and began to wring out his clothes. 'Are you terribly hungry too?' he asked. He felt somewhat better when I told him that I was. A sorrow shared is a sorrow halved; apparently that applied to hunger too. Meanwhile in the upper part of the hut I had found some large squares of coarse cloth which were used by the peasants to carry the hay down the steep mountain sides. I felt very sorry for Adolf, standing there in the doorway in his soaking underclothes, chattering with cold as he wrung out the sleeves of his jacket. Sensitive as he was to any kind of chill, how easily he could catch pneumonia, and so I took one of the big squares, stretched it out on the hay and told Adolf to take off his wet shirt and pants and to wrap himself in the cloth. This he did.

He laid himself naked on the cloth while I took hold of the ends and wrapped it firmly around him. The I fetched a second square and put that over him. This done, I wrung out all our clothing and hung it up, wrapped myself in a piece of cloth and lay down. So that we should not get icy cold in the night, I threw a bale of hay ovei the bundle that was Adolf, and another over myself.

We did not know the time as neither of us had a watch, but it was enough to know that outside it was pitch dark with rain rattling unceasingly on the roof of the hut. Somewhere in the distance a dog was barking, so we were not too far away from human habitation, a thought that comforted me. When I mentioned it to Adolf, however, if left him quite indifferent. In the present circumstances people were quite superfluous for him. He was enjoying the whole adventure hugely and its romantic ending appealed to him especially. Now we were getting warm, it would have been almost cosy in the little hut if we had not been racked with hunger. I thought once more of my parents, then I fell asleep.

When I awoke in the morning, daylight was already showing through the gaps in the boards. I got up. Our clothes were almost dry. I still remember what a job it was to get Adolf to wake up. When he was finally roused, he worked his feet free of their wrappings and, with the cloth wrapped around him, walked to the door to look at the weather. His slim, straight figure, with the white cloth thrown toga-wise across the shoulders, looked like that of a Hindu ascetic.

This was our last great excursion together. Just as my journey to the medical board had unpleasantly interrupted our stay in Vienna, so were these walks and adventures beautiful and extremely welcome interruptions in our gloomy, sunless existence in the Stumpergasse.

# Chapter 22

# Adolf's Attitude to Sex

As we used to walk up and down the foyer during the intervals at the opera, I was struck by how much attention the girls and women paid to us. Understandably enough, at first I used to wonder which of us was the object of this undisguised interest and thought secretly it must be me. Closer observation, however, soon taught me that the obvious preference was not for me but for my friend. Adolf appealed so much to the passing ladies, in spite of his modest clothing and his cold, reserved manner in public, that occasionally one or the other of them would turn round to look at him which, according to the strict etiquette prevailing at the opera, was considered highly improper.

I was all the more surprised at this as Adolf did nothing to provoke this behaviour: on the contrary, he hardly noticed the ladies' encouraging glances, or at most would make an annoyed comment about them to me. These observations were enough to prove that my friend undoubtedly found favour with the opposite sex although, to my amazement, he never took advantage of it. Did he not understand these unequivocal invitations, or did he not want to understand them? I gathered it was the latter, as Adolf was too sharp and critical an observer not to see what was going on around him, especially if it concerned himself. Then why did he not seize these opportunities?

That comfortless, boring life in the back room in the Mariahilfe suburb, which he himself called 'a dog's life', how much more beautiful it would have been made by a friendship with an attractive, intelligent girl! Was not Vienna known as the city of beautiful women? That this was true we needed no convincing. What was it, then, that held him back from doing what was normal for other young men? That he had never considered this possibility was proved by the very fact that, at his suggestion, we shared a room together. He did not ask me at the time whether that suited me or not. As was his habit, he took it for granted that I should be willing to do what he considered to be the right thing. As far as girls were concerned, he was doubtless quite pleased about my shyness, if only for the reason that it left me with more free time to spare for him.

One small episode has stayed in my memory, One evening at the opera, as we went back to our places in the promenade, a liveried attendant came up to us and, plucking Adolf by the sleeve, handed him a note. Adolf took the note, in no way surprised and acting as if this were an everyday event, thanked him and perused it hastily. Now, I thought, I was on the track of a great secret, or at least the beginning of a romantic one, but all Adolf said, contemptuously, was 'Another one', and passed the note over to me. Then, with a semi-mocking glance, he asked me whether, perhaps, I would like to keep the suggested appointment. 'It's your affair, not mine,' I replied a bit sharply, 'and anyhow I wouldn't like the lady to be disappointed.'

Each time when it had to do with members of the fair sex, it was 'his affair, not mine', no matter to what class the woman in question might belong. Even in the street my friend was shown preference. When at night we came home from the opera or the Burg Theatre. now and again one of the street-walkers would approach us, in spite of our poor appearance, and ask us to come home with her, but here again it was only Adolf who got the invitation.

I remember quite well that in those days I used to ask myself what the girls found so attractive about Adolf. He was certainly a well-set-up young man with regular features, but not at all what is understood by the term 'a handsome man'. I had seen handsome men often enough on the stage to know what women meant by that. Perhaps it was the extraordinarily bright eyes that attracted them, or was it the strangely stern expression of the ascetic countenance? Or perhaps it was just his obvious indifference to the opposite sex that invited them to test his resistance. Whatever it was, women seemed to sense something exceptional about my friend – as opposed to men such as, for instance, his teachers and professors.

The presentiment of decay that existed in those years in the Habsburg Empire had produced in Vienna a shallow, easy-going atmosphere whose empty moral sense was covered by the famous Viennese charm. The slogan then so much in vogue, 'Sell my clothes, I'm going to heaven' drew even the solid bourgeois classes into the superficiality of the morbid 'higher circles'. That sultry eroticism which held sway in Arthur Schnitzler's plays set the tone of society. The then famous saying, 'Austria is going to the bad through her women' certainly seemed to be true as far as Viennese society was concerned. In the midst of this brittle milieu, whose persistent, erotic undertone insinuated itself everywhere, my friend lived in his self-imposed asceticism, regarding girls and women with lively and critical sympathy, while completely excluding anything personal, and handled matters which other young men of his age turned into their personal experiences, as problems for discussion. This he would do in his evening talks as coldy and factually as though he himself were quite remote from such things.

As in all the other chapters of this book, so in this one dealing with Adolf's attitude to women during our friendship I am concerned with keeping entirely to my own personal experience. From the autumn of 1904 to the summer of 1908, that is, for almost four years, I lived side by side with Adolf. In these decisive years when he grew from a boy of fifteen to a young man, Adolf confided to me things that he had told to no one, not even his mother. As far back as the days in Linz, our friendship was so intimate that I should have noticed if he had actually made the acquaintance of a girl. He would have had less time for me, his interests would have taken a different direction, and there would have been many similar signs. Yet, apart from his dream-love for Stefanie, no such thing happened. I cannot give any information about May and June 1906, nor the autumn of 1907, the periods when Adolf was alone in Vienna, but I can only imagine that any really serious love affair would have continued into the period when we were lodging together. I think I can say with certainty: Adolf never met a girl, either in Linz or Vienna, who actually gave herself to him.

My own personal experience from lodging with him, based on small, apparently insignificant details, was confirmed by the profound and penetrating discussions which Adolf used to have with me on all questions concerning the relations between the sexes. I knew from previous experience that between what Adolf preached and what he practised there was indeed no difference. His social and moral conduct was not governed by his own desires and feelings, but by his knowledge and judgment. In this respect, he displayed the utmost self-control. He could not bear the shallow superficiality of certain circles in Vienna, and I cannot remember a single occasion when he let himself go in his attitude to the opposite sex. At the same time, I must assert categorically that Adolf, in physical as well as sexual respects, was absolutely normal. What was extraordinary in him was not to be found in the erotic or sexual spheres, but in quite other realms of his being.

When he used to describe to me in vivid terms the necessity of early marriage, which alone was capable of ensuring the future of the people; when he used to set forth for my benefit measures for increasing the number of children per family, measures which later were actually put into practice; when he expounded to me the connection between healthy

214

housing and a healthy family life and described how, in his 'ideal state' the problems of love, of sexual relations, of marriage, of family, of children, would be solved, I used to think of Stefanie for, after all, what Hitler was laying down here in such a convincing manner, was really only the dreamed-of ideal life with her, transported to a political and social plane. He had wanted Stefanie for his wife; for him she was the ideal of German womanhood personified. From her he hoped for children; for her he had planned that beautiful country house which had become for him a model of the abode for the ideal family life, but all this was illusion, wishful thinking. He had not seen Stefanie for several months, and spoke of her less and less. Even when I left for Linz for my call-up, he did not ask me to find out about Stefanie. Did she still mean anything to him? Had the enforced separation convinced Adolf that the most practical course was to forget Stefanie altogether? Just as I had persuaded myself that this was so, there would be certain to come another tempestuous outburst to prove to me that he still clung to Stefanie with every fibre of his being.

In spite of this, it was clear to me that Stefanie was losing her reality for Adolf more and more, and becoming purely an ideal. He could no longer rush to the Landstrasse to convince himself of the existence of his beloved. He received no further news about her. His feelings for Stefanie were plainly losing real foundation. Was this, then, the end of a love that had begun with such great hopes?

Yes and no. It was the end insofar as Adolf was no longer the sentimental youth who, with the usual extravagance of the adolescent, compensated for the slightness of his hopes by a boundless conceit in himself, and yet, on the other hand, I could not understand how Adolf, now a young man with very concrete ideas and aims, could nevertheless still cling so firmly to this hopeless love, to such an extent, indeed, that it was sufficient to render him immune to the temptations of the big city.

I knew the very strict ideas my friend had about the relations between men and women, and had often wondered how Adolf came to be possessed of this strict moral attitude. His conceptions of love and marriage were definitely not those of his father, and whilst his mother loved him dearly, she certainly had not influenced him much in this respect, nor was such influence needed, as she could see that Adolf was quite correct in his behaviour towards girls. Adolf's background was that of an Austrian civil servant's family and a petit-bourgeois household. Consequently, my only explanation of his strict views – which I shared with him to a certain degree without being dogmatic about them – was his passion for social and political problems. His ideas of morality were based, not upon experience, but on abstract, logical conclusions.

In addition, he still looked upon Stefanie, although she had become unattainable for him, as the ideal model of German womanhood, unrivalled by anything he saw in Vienna. When a woman made a strong impression on him, I often noticed how he began to talk about Stefanie and drew comparisons which were always in her favour.

Incredible as it may sound, the 'distant beloved', who did not even know the name of the young man whose love she was supposed to return, exercised such a strong influence over Adolf that not only did he find his own ideas of morality confirmed in his relations with her, but he regulated his life in accordance with them as seriously and consistently as a monk who had consecrated his life to God. In Vienna, this sink of iniquity, where even prostitution was made the object of the artist's glorification – this was an exception indeed.

Actually, Adolf had written to Stefanie once during that period. It can no longer be established whether this letter was sent before or during our time in Vienna. The letter itself is lost, and I came to hear about it in a curious manner. I told a friend of mine, Dr Jetzinger, an archivist who was working on a biography of Adolf Hitler, about Adolf's love for Stefanie. The scholar ascertained the address of the old lady, the widow of a colonel, living in Vienna, called on her and laid before her his peculiar request – that she should tell him of her youthful acquaintance with a young, pale student from the Humboldtstrasse, who later moved to the Blütengasse in Urfahr. He used to stand and wait for her at the Schmiedtoreck every evening, he added, accompanied by his friend. Upon this, the old lady began telling him about dances and balls, excursions, carriage trips and so on which she had enjoyed with young men, mostly officers, but with the best will in the world she could not recollect this strange young man, even when, to her great astonishment, she learnt his name. Suddenly a memory awoke within her. Did she not once receive a letter, written in a confused manner, which spoke of a solemn vow, begged her to keep faith and only to expect further news of the writer when he had finished his training as an artist and had an assured position? The letter was not signed. From its style, it can almost certainly be concluded that it was Adolf Hitler who sent it, and that was all the old lady could say about it.

When the thought of his beloved became too much for him, he no longer spoke directly of Stefanie, but threw himself headlong, with a great display of feeling, into dissertations about early marriages to be promoted by the state, about the possibility of helping working girls to get their trousseaux by means of a loan, and assisting young families with many children to acquire a house and garden. I remember that here, on one particular point, we had the most violent arguments. Adolf suggested the establishment of state furniture factories in order that young married couples should be able to furnish their homes cheaply. I was strongly against this idea of mass-produced furniture – after all, on this subject I was qualified to speak. I said furniture must be of good, high-quality craftsmanship, not machine-made. We made our calculations and economised in other ways so that the newly-married couple could have fine, good-quality furniture in their home, soft feather beds, cloth-covered chairs and couches, in good taste, so that one could see there still existed master upholsterers who knew their job.

Much that Adolf used to tell me in those long nightly talks is concentrated into one particular phrase in my memory, and in this case, that which connotes these passionate discussions is the strange cliché *Die Flamme des Lebens* – 'the flame of life'. Whenever the questions of love, marriage or sex relations were raised, this magic formula would crop up. To keep the flame of life pure and unsullied would be the most important task of that 'ideal state' with which my friend occupied himself in his lonely hours. With my inherent preference for precision, I was not quite sure what Adolf meant by this flame of life, and occasionally the phrase would change its meaning, but I think that in the end I did understand him aright. The flame of life was the symbol of sacred love which is awakened between man and woman who have kept themselves pure in body and soul and are worthy of a union which would produce healthy children for the nation.

Such phrases, impressively delivered and repeated again and again – and Adolf had a large stock of these expressions – had quite a queer effect on me. When I heard them solemnly proclaimed for the first time they seemed rather pathetic, and I smiled inwardly at these bombastic formulae which were in such contrast to our insignificant existence. Despite that, however, the words stayed in my memory. Just as a thistle clings to one's sleeve with a hundred barbs, so did this phrase cling. I could not get rid of it. Then, if I found myself in a situation which had only the remotest connection with this theme – I would meet a girl as I went along the Mariahilferstrasse, let us say, alone in the evening. A pretty young lady she might seem to me, a little flighty perhaps, for she turned round very openly to look at me. At least this time I was sure it was me that she was interested in. As a matter of fact she must have been very flighty, because she waved to me invitingly, but then suddenly the words flame of life appeared before me – one single, thoughtless hour and this holy flame is extinguished for ever! – and even though I was annoyed by these moralisings, nevertheless in such moments they worked. One phrase was linked to another. It began with the 'storm of the revolution' and went on through countless political and social slogans to the 'holy Reich of all the Germans'. Perhaps Adolf found a certain number of these phrases in books, but others I knew he coined himself.

Gradually these single statement evolved into one compact system. As everything that happened was of interest to Adolf, each new phenomenon of the times was examined to see how it would fit into his political philosophy.

Sometimes my memory indulges in strange juxtapositions, so that immediately following the holy, unapproachable flame of life would come the 'sink of iniquity', although in my friend's world of ideas this expression represented the lowest grade. Of course, in the ideal state there was no longer any sink of iniquity. With these words Adolf described the prostitution which was then rife in Vienna. As a typical phenomenon of those years of general moral decadence, we would come across it in the most varied forms, both in the elegant streets of the centre and in the slums of the suburbs. All this filled Adolf with boundless rage. For this spread of prostitution he blamed not only those actually practising it, but those responsible for the prevailing social and economic conditions. A 'monument to the shame of our times' he called this prostitution. Ever and again he tackled the problem and searched for a solution whereby in the future any kind of 'commercial love' would be rendered impossible.

There was one evening that I have never forgotten. We had been to a performance of Wedekind's *Frühlings Erwachen* and, as an exception, had stayed for the last act. Then we made our way across the Ring homewards and turned down into the Siebensterngasse. Adolf took my arm and said unexpectedly, 'Come, Gustl, we must see the sink of iniquity once.' I do not know what had given him the idea, but he had already turned into the small, ill-lit Spittelberggasse.

So there we were. We walked along past the low, one-storey houses. The windows, which were on street level, were lighted so that passers-by could see directly into the rooms. The girls sat there, some behind a window pane, some at an open window. A few of them were still remarkably young, others prematurely aged and faded. In their scanty and slovenly attire they sat there, making up their faces or combing their hair or looking at themselves in the mirror, without losing sight for one moment of the men strolling by. Here and there a man would stop, lean towards the window to look at the girl of his choice; a hasty whispered interchange would take place. Then, as a sign that the deal was concluded, the light would be turned out. I still remember how this custom in particular struck me, as one could tell by the darkening of the windows how trade was going. Among the men, it was the accepted convention not to stand before the unlighted windows.

For our part we did not even stand in front of the lighted windows, but made our way along to the Burggasse at the other end of the street. Having arrived there, however, Adolf made an about-turn and we walked once more along the sink of iniquity. I was of the opinion that the one experience would have sufficed, but Adolf was already dragging me along to the lighted windows. Perhaps these girls too had noticed the 'something special' about Adolf, perhaps they had realised that here they had to deal with men of moral restraint, such as came sometimes from the countryside to the unholy city. At any rate they thought it necessary to redouble their efforts. I recall how one of these girls seized just the moment when we were passing her window to take off her chemise, presumably to change it, whilst another busied herself with her stockings, showing her naked legs. I was genuinely glad when this exciting running of the gauntlet was over and we finally reached the Westbahnstrasse, but I said nothing, whilst Adolf grew angry at the prostitutes' tricks of seduction.

At home, Adolf started on a lecture on his newly acquired impressions with a cold objectivity, as though it were a question of his attitude towards the fight against tuberculosis, or towards cremation. I was amazed that he could speak about it without any inner emotion. Now he had learnt the customs of the market for commercial love, he declared, and thus the purpose of his visit was fulfilled. The origin lay in the fact that man felt the necessity for sexual satisfaction, whilst the girls in question thought only of their earnings with which, possibly, they kept one man whom they really loved, always assuming that these girls were capable of love. In practice the flame of life in these poor creatures was long since extinct.

There is another incident I should like to recount. One evening, at the corner of Mariahilferstrasse, a well-dressed, prosperous-looking man spoke to us and asked us about ourselves. When we told him that we were students ('My friend studies music,' explained Adolf, 'and I architecture') he invited us to supper at the Hotel Kummer. He allowed us to order anything we pleased and for once Adolf could eat as many tarts and pastries as he could manage. Meanwhile, he told us that he was a manufacturer from Vöcklabruck and did not like anything to do with women, as they were only gold diggers. I was especially interested in what he said about the chamber music which appealed to him. We thanked him, he came out of the restaurant with us, and we went home. There Adolf asked me if I liked the man. 'Very much,' I replied, 'A very cultured man, with pronounced artistic leanings.' 'And what else?' continued Adolf with an enigmatic expression on his face. 'What else should there be?' I asked surprised. 'As apparently you don't understand, Gustl, what it's all about, look at this little card!'

'Which card?' In fact, this man had slipped Adolf a card without my noticing it, on which he had scribbled an invitation to visit him at the Hotel Kummer. 'He's a homosexual,' explained Adolf in a matter-of-fact manner. I was startled. I had never even heard the word, much less had I any conception of what it actually meant. So Adolf explained this phenomenon to me. Naturally this too had long been one of his problems for contemplation and, as an abnormal practice, he wished to see it fought against relentlessly, and he himself scrupulously avoided all contact with such men. The visiting card of the famous manufacturer from Vöcklabruck disappeared into our stove.

It seemed to me quite natural that Adolf should turn with disgust and repugnance from these and other sexual aberrations of the big city, that he refrained from masturbation which was commonly indulged in by youths, and that in all matters of sex he obeyed those strict rules that he had laid down for himself and for the future state. Then why did he not try to escape from his loneliness, to make friends and find fresh stimulus in serious, intelligent and progressive company? Why did he always remain the lone wolf, who avoided any contact with people, although he was passionately interested in all human affairs? How easy it would have been for him, with his obvious talents, to win himself a place in those social circles in Vienna which held themselves aloof from the general decadence, from which he would have gained not only new insight and enlightenment, but which would have wrought a change in his lonely life. There were many more thoroughly decent people in Vienna than the other kind, though they were less in evidence. So he had no reason to avoid people on moral grounds. As a matter of fact it was not arrogance that held him back. It was rather his poverty, and the consequent sensitivity that caused him to live on his own. Moreover, he thought he was lowering himself if he went to a social gathering, or any kind of distraction. He had too high an opinion of himself for a superficial flirtation or for a merely physical relationship with a girl. For that matter, he would never have allowed me to indulge in such affairs. Any step in this direction would have meant the inevitable end of our friendship as, apart from from the distaste with which Adolf viewed such connections, he would never have tolerated my having any interest in other people. As always, our friendship had to be utterly exclusive of all other interests.

One day, although I knew how opposed Adolf was to all social activities, I nevertheless attempted to arrange something for him. The opportunity which occurred seemed to me too good to be missed.

Sometimes music lovers came to the Conservatoire office looking for students to take part in a musical evening at their houses. This meant not only much-needed extra money – we usually received a fee of five crowns, as well as supper – but also brought a little social glamour into my humble student's life. As a good viola player I was much sought after, and it was through this that I came to know the family of a wealthy manufacturer in the Heiligenstädterstrasse, Dr Jahoda. They were people with a deep appreciation of art, of very cultivated tastes, a really intellectual group of the kind that only flourished in Vienna, who traditionally enriched the artistic life of the city. When the opportunity arose at table I mentioned my friend, and was invited to bring him with me next time. This was what I and been aiming at, and now I was content.

Adolf did indeed accompany me, and he enjoyed himself very much. He was particularly impressed with the library, which for Adolf was the real yardstick for judging these people. What pleased him less, however, was that throughout the whole evening he had to remain a silent listener although he himself had chosen this role. On the way home, he said he would have got on quite well with these people, but as he was not a musician he had not been able to join in the conversation. Nevertheless, he also came with me to musical evenings in one or two other houses where it was only his inadequate dress that upset him.

In the midst of this corrupt city, my friend surrounded himself with a wall of unshakeable principles which enabled him to build up an inner freedom in spite of all the dangers around him. He was afraid of infection, as he often said. Now I understand that he meant not only venereal infection but a much more general infection, namely the danger of being caught up in the prevailing conditions and finally being dragged down into the vortex of corruption. It is not surprising that no one understood him, that they took him for an eccentric, and that those few who came in contact with him called him presumptuous and arrogant.

He went his way untouched by what went on around him, but also untouched by a really great, consuming love. He remained a man alone and – an odd contradiction – in strict monk-like asceticism guarded the holy flame of life.

# Chapter 23

# Political Awakening

The picture of my friend as I have drawn it so far would be incomplete without a reference to his immense interest in politics. If I deal with it only at the end of this book and, in spite of all my efforts, inadequately, it is not because of my lack of understanding, but because my interest lay more in art and was hardly concerned with politics at all.

Even more so than in Linz, I felt myself a budding artist at the Vienna Conservatoire and had no wish to be mixed up in politics. My friend's development was just in the opposite direction. Though in Linz his interest in art had far surpassed that in politics, in Vienna, the centre of political life of the Habsburg Empire, politics prevailed to the extent of absorbing all other interests.

I began to understand how almost every problem which he met led him ultimately into the political sphere, however little connection it might have with politics. His original way of looking at the phenomena which surrounded him through the eyes of an artist and aesthete turned increasingly into a habit of regarding them from a politician's standpoint, as he reported in *Mein Kampf*:

> In the time of my bitter struggle between spiritual development and cold reason, the view of life on the streets of Vienna provided me with invaluable insight. The time came eventually when I no longer wandered like a blind man through the city, but with open eyes saw not only the buildings but also the people.

Human beings interested him so much that he began to adjust his professional plans to political considerations. For, if he really wanted to build all that was ready in his mind and even partly laid down in elaborate schemes – a new Linz embellished by impressive edifices such as a bridge over the Danube, a city hall, etc., and a Vienna whose slums were to be replaced by vast residential districts, a revolutionary arm had first to put an end to the existing political conditions which had become unbearable, and to open up the possibility for creative work on an ambitious scale.

Politics came to assume an increasingly important position in his scale of values. The most difficult problems became easy when they were transferred to the political plane. With the same consistency as that with which he explored all phenomena which occupied him until he had reached rock bottom, he discovered amidst the noisy, political life of the metropolis the focal point of all political events: parliament.

'Come with me, Gustl,' he said one day. I asked him where he wanted to go – I had to attend lectures and to practise for my piano examination, but my objections did not impress him at all. He said that none of that was as important as what he intended to do; he had already got a ticket for me. I wondered what this could be – an organ concert perhaps, or a conducted tour through the picture gallery of the Hof Museum? But my lectures and exam? It would be very bad for me if I failed. 'Oh, come on, hurry!' he cried angrily. I was familiar with that look on his face, which would not tolerate any contradiction. Besides it must be something very special, for it was unusual for Adolf to be up and about as early as half-past eight in the morning. So I yielded and went with him to the Ring. At nine o'clock sharp we turned into the Stadiongasse and stopped in front of a small, side entrance where a few nondescript people, idlers apparently, had collected. At long last I saw daylight: 'To parliament?' I said apprehensively: 'What am I supposed to do there?'

I remembered that Adolf had occasionally mentioned his visits to parliament – personally I considered it a sheer waste of time, but before I could say another word, he pressed the ticket into my hand, the door opened and we were directed to the strangers' gallery. Looking down from the gallery, one had a very good view of the imposing semi-circle which the great assembly chamber formed. Its classic beauty would have provided a fitting background for any artistic performance – a concert, a choir singing hymns or even, with some adjustments, an opera.

Adolf tried to explain to me what was really happening:

> The man who sits up there, looking rather helpless, and who rings a bell now and then, is chairman of the house. The worthies on the raised seats are the ministers, in front of them are the stenographers, the only people who do any work in the house. That is why I rather like them, though I can assure you that these hard-working men are of no importance whatsoever. On the opposite benches there should be seated all the deputies of the territories and provinces represented in the Austrian parliament, but most of them are strolling around the lobbies.

My friend went on to describe the procedure. One member had tabled a motion and was now speaking in support of it. Almost all the other deputies, not being interested in the motion, had left the room but soon the chairman called for a debate and things became lively. Adolf was really well versed in parliamentary procedure; he even had an order paper in front of him. Everything happened exactly as he had foretold.

To put it into musical terminology, as soon as the solo performance of the deputy had ended, the orchestra struck up. The deputies flowed back into the chamber and all started shouting together, interrupting each other remorselessly in the process. The chairman rang his bell. The deputies responded by lifting the lids of their desks and banging them down again. Some whistled and words of abuse shouted in German, Czech, Italian and God knows what other languages filled the air.

I looked at Adolf. Was not this the appropriate moment to leave? But what had happened to my friend? He had jumped to his feet, his hands clenched, his face burning with excitement. This being so, I preferred to remain quietly in my seat although I had no idea what the tumult was about.

Parliament attracted my friend more and more whilst I tried to wriggle out of it. Once when Adolf had forced me to go with him – I would have risked the ending of our friendship if I had refused – a Czech member was 'filibustering'. Adolf explained to me that this was a speech only made to fill in time and prevent another member from speaking. It did not matter what the Czech said, he could even go on repeating his words, but on no account must he stop. It really seemed to me as though this man was speaking all the time *da capo al fine*. Of course, I did not understand a word of Czech, nor did Adolf, and I was really upset at wasting my time.

'You don't mind if I go now?' I said to Adolf.

'What, now, in the middle of the thing?' he replied angrily.

'But I don't understand a word the man is saying.'

'You don't have to understand it. This is "filibustering". I've already explained it to you.'

'So I can go then?'

'No!' he cried furiously, and pulled me back on to the seat by my coat-tails.

So I just sat there and let the valiant Czech, who was already nearly exhausted, talk on. I have never been so puzzled by Adolf as I was at that moment. He was so extraordinarily intelligent and certainly had all his senses about him, and I just could not comprehend how he was able to sit there, tense, listening to every word of a speech which, after all, he did not understand. Perhaps the fault is mine, I thought, and presumably I do not realise wherein lies the essence of politics.

In those days I often asked myself why Adolf compelled me to go with him to parliament. I could not solve this riddle until one day I realised that he needed a partner with whom he could discuss his own impressions. On such days he would wait impatiently for my return in the evening, Hardly had I opened the door then he would start, 'Where have you been all this time?' and before I had had time to get myself a bite of supper would come, 'When are you going to bed?'

This question had a particular significance. As our room was so small, Adolf could only walk up and down if either I crouched on the stool behind the piano or went to bed, and so he wanted to clear the decks for what he wanted to say.

No sooner had I crept into bed than he began to stride up and down, holding forth. If only by the excited tone of his voice, I could tell how much his thoughts were pressing on him. He simply had to have an outlet in order to bear the enormous tension.

So there I lay in bed while Adolf, as usual, strode up and down, ranting at me as passionately as though I were a political power who could decide the existence or non-existence of the German people, instead of only a poor little music student. What was it then that moved him so profoundly? Basically always the same thing: his overwhelming attachment to Germanness. With true fervour he clung to the people of his origins, and nothing on earth did he place higher than the love he had for what was German. Within the Danube monarchy this Germanness was engaged in a fierce struggle for its national identity. The argument had been made somewhere, as part of this warring, that Austrian-Germans were not of the best blood. In *Mein Kampf* he wrote on this point:

> It had to be made plain that if the German in Austria was not really of the best blood, he would never have been able to impress his stamp so indelibly on a state of 52 million to the extent that in Germany there was a mistaken impression abroad that Austria was a German-racial state. It was a nonsense but a shining testimony for the 10 million Germans of Austria.

In his book he also alluded to 'enormous, unheard-of burdens' demanding a sacrifice in 'taxation' and 'blood', but what hurt us most' was the fact that the whole Austro-Hungarian system was supported morally by the alliance with Germany so that the inexorable decay of Germanness in the old monarchy was to a certain extent sanctioned by Germany itself. But where would this help come from to destroy it, if not from Germany itself? The old Austro-Hungarian Kaiser was incapable of leading a struggle from within. His heir Franz Ferdinand, on whom many hopes rested, was married to a Czech countess and was planning the setting-up of a strong Catholic–Slav bloc. This meant that the people of German stock in Austria were out on a limb and left to fight for themselves. With overflowing heart, Adolf took part in this passionate struggle. That the political situation for the Germans in Austria seemed so hopeless, lacking any solution, worked him up and made him hate the Austro-Hungarian monarchy.

Another of these nocturnal talks remains in my memory. Hysterically he described the sufferings of this people, the fate that threatened it, and its future full of danger. He was near tears, but after these bitter words, he came back to more optimistic thoughts. Once more he was building the 'Reich of all the Germans' which put the 'guest nations', as he called the other races of the Austro-Hungarian Empire, where they belonged.

Sometimes, when his diatribes became too lengthy, I fell asleep. As soon as he noticed it, he shook me awake and shouted at me to ask whether I was no longer interested in his words – if so, I should go on sleeping, like all those who had no national conscience. So I made an effort and forced myself to keep my eyes open.

Later, Adolf developed more friendly moods on these occasions. Instead of losing himself in utopia, he raised questions which he thought would be of more interest to me. As for instance one day when he inveighed against the savings groups which had been formed in many of the small inns of the working class districts. Each member paid in a weekly sum and received his savings at Christmas. The treasurer was usually the innkeeper. Adolf criticised these groups because the money the worker spent on such 'savings evenings' was greater than the amount laid by, so that in reality the innkeeper was the only one to benefit. Another time he described to me in vivid colours what he imagined the student hostels would be like in his 'ideal state'. Bright, sunny bedrooms, common rooms for study, music and drawing, simple but nourishing food, free tickets for concerts, operas and exhibitions, and free transport to their colleges.

One night he spoke of the aeroplane of the Wright brothers. He quoted from a newspaper that these famous aviators had built a small, comparatively lightweight gun into their aircraft and had made experiments to assess the effect that shooting from the air would be likely to have. Adolf, who was a pronounced pacifist, was outraged. As soon as a new invention is made, he said, it is immediately put to the service of war. Who wants war? he asked. Certainly not the little man – far from it. Wars are arranged by crowned and uncrowned rulers who in turn are guided and driven by their armament industries. While these gentlemen earn gigantic sums and remain far from the firing line, the 'little man' has to risk his life without knowing to what purpose.

Altogether the 'little man', the 'poor betrayed masses', played a dominating role in his thoughts. One day we saw workers demonstrating on the Ring. We were hemmed in among the onlookers near the parliament and got a good view of the exciting scene. Is this the mood, I asked myself anxiously, that Adolf calls the 'storm of the revolution'? Some men walked ahead of the procession carrying a big banner on which was written the one word 'Hunger'. There could not have been any more stirring appeal to my friend because he had so often suffered himself from gnawing hunger. There he stood, next to me, and absorbed the picture eagerly. However strongly he might have felt for these people, he remained aloof and viewed the whole event, in all its detail, as objectively and coolly as though his only interest were to study the technique of such a demonstration. In spite of his solidarity with the 'little man' he would never have dreamed of taking an active part in this manifestation which was, in fact, protesting against the recent increase in the price of beer.

More and more people were arriving. The whole Ring seemed to be crammed with excited humanity. Red flags were carried, but the serious-ness of the situation was shown by the ragged appearance and the hunger-lined faces of the demonstrators far more than by flags and slogans.

The head of the procession had reached parliament and was trying to storm it. Suddenly the mounted police who had accompanied the protesters drew their swords and began to lay about them. The reply was a hail of stones. For a moment the situation was balanced on a razor's edge, but in the end police reinforcements manage to disperse the demonstrators.

The spectacle had shaken Adolf to the core, but not until we arrived home did he voice his feelings. Yes, he was on the side of the hungry, the under-privileged, but he was also against the men who organised such demonstrations. Who are the wire-pullers standing behind these doubly-betrayed masses, guiding them according to their will? None of them appeared on the scene. Why? Because it suited them better to conduct their affairs in obscurity – they did not want to risk their lives. Who are the leaders of the wretched masses? Not men who had themselves experienced the misery of the 'little man', but ambitious politicians, lusting for power, who wanted to exploit the people's poverty for their own benefit. An outburst of rage against these political vultures brought my friend's embittered harangue to an end. That was his demonstration.

One question tormented him after such occurrences, although he never gave expression to it: Where did he himself belong? To judge by his own circumstances and the social environment in which he lived, there was no doubt that he belonged to those who followed the hunger banner. He lived in a miserable, bug-ridden back room; many times his lunch consisted of nothing but a piece of dry bread. Some of the demonstrators were perhaps better off than he. Why, therefore, did he not march with these men? What held him back?

Perhaps he felt that he belonged to a different social class. He was the son of an Austrian state official, whose rank was the equivalent of captain in the Army. He remembered his father as a much-respected customs officer, to whom people raised their hats, and whose word carried much weight amongst his friends. His father had absolutely nothing to do with these people in the street.

Greater even than his fear of being infected by the moral and political decadence of the ruling classes was his fear of becoming a proletarian. Undoubtedly he lived like one, but he did not want to become one. Perhaps what drove him to his intensive studies was his instinctive feeling that only a thorough education could save him from descending to the level of the masses.

In the last resort, the decisive point for Adolf was that he did not feel attracted to any of the existing parties or movements. To be sure, he often told me that he was a convinced follower of Schönerer, but he said so only in the privacy of our room. He, the hungry, penniless student, would have cut a very poor figure in the ranks of Georg Ritter von Schönerer. The Schönerer movement would have needed much stronger socialist tendencies to capture Adolf fully. What had Schönerer to offer to the hungry masses demonstrating in the Ring? Nothing. On the other hand, however, the Social Democrats had no comprehension of German nationalism in Austria. The international Marxist basis on which this movement had developed held at arm's length the broad masses – and that is ultimately the people themselves – from involvement in the decisions which were just as important for the fate of the people as was a solution to the social question. Among the leading political personalities of those days, Adolf had most admiration for the Bürgermeister of Vienna, Karl Lueger, but what put him off his party was the connection with the clergy, which interfered constantly in political questions. Thus, in those days, Adolf found no spiritual home for his political ideals.

In spite of his unwillingness to join a party or organisation – with one exception which I shall mention later – one had only to walk along the street with him to see how intensely interested he was in the fate of others. The city of Vienna offered him excellent object lessons in this respect. For instance, when home-going workers passed us by, Adolf would grip my arm and say, 'Did you hear, Gustl? Czech!' Another time we encountered some brickmakers speaking loudly in Italian, with florid gestures. 'There you have your German Vienna!' he cried indignantly.

This too was one of his oft-repeated phrases: 'German Vienna', but Adolf pronounced it with a bitter undertone. Was this Vienna, into which streamed from all sides Czechs, Magyars, Croats, Poles, Italians, Slovaks, Ruthenians and above all Galician Jews, still indeed a German city? In the state of affairs in Vienna my friend saw a symbol of the struggle of the Germans in the Habsburg Empire. He hated the babel in the streets of Vienna, this 'incest incarnate' as he called it later. He hated this state which ruined Germanism, and the pillars which supported this state: the reigning house, the nobility, the capitalists and the Jews.

This Habsburg state, he felt, must fall, and the sooner the better, for every moment of its continued existence cost the Germans honour, property and their very life. He saw in the fanatical internecine strife of its races the decisive symptoms of its coming downfall. He visited parliament to feel, so to speak, the pulse of the patient, whose early demise was expected by all. He looked forward to that hour full of impatience, for only the collapse of the Habsburg Empire could open the road to those schemes of which he dreamed in his lonely hours.

His accumulated hatred of all forces which threatened Germanness was concentrated mainly on the Jews, who played a leading role in Vienna. I soon came to notice this and a small, seemingly trivial occurrence stands out in my memory.

I had come to the conclusion that my friend could no longer go on in his poverty-stricken circumstances. The easiest way of helping him, I thought, would be to make use of some of his literary work. A fellow student of mine at the Conservatoire worked as a journalist on the *Wiener Tagblatt*, and I mentioned Adolf to him. The young man was full of sympathy for Adolf's precarious situation and suggested that my friend should bring some of his work to him in his office, where the matter could be discussed. During the night, Adolf wrote a short story of which I remember nothing but the title.

It was *The Next Morning* and an ominous one, for the next morning when we went to see my fellow student there was a terrific row. As soon as Adolf had seen the man he turned about even before he had entered the room, and going down the stairs shouted at me, 'You idiot! Didn't you see that he is a Jew?' Actually I had not, but in future I took care not to burn my fingers.

Things got worse. One day, when I was very busy with preparations for my exam, Adolf stormed into our room, full of excitement. He had just come from the police, he said: there had been an incident in the Mariahilferstrasse, connected with a Jew of course. A 'Handelee' had been standing in front of the Gerngross store. The word 'Handelee' was used to designate Eastern Jews who, dressed in caftan and boots, sold shoe-laces, buttons, braces and other haberdashery in the streets. The Handelee was the lowest stage in the career of those quickly assimilated Jews, who often occupied leading positions in Austria's economic life. The Handelees were forbidden to beg, but this man had whiningly approached passers-by, his hand outstretched, and had collected some money. A policeman asked him to produce his papers. He began to wring his hands and said that he was a poor, sick man who had only this little trading to live on, but he had not been begging. The policeman took him to the police station and asked bystanders to act as witnesses. In spite of his dislike of publicity, Adolf had presented himself as a witness, and he saw with his own eyes that the Handelee had 3,000 crowns in his caftan, conclusive evidence, according to Adolf, of the exploitation of Vienna by immigrant Eastern Jews.

In *Mein Kampf* he wrote:

> As I was passing through the inner city one day, I came across a person in a long caftan wearing long dreadlocks. 'Can this be a Jew?' was my first thought. They didn't look like this in Linz. I threw the man a few sidelong glances but the more I stared at his foreign face and examined his features one by one, the more my first question took on another aspect. 'Is this a German?' As always in such cases, I now began to resolve my doubts by books.

I well remember at that time how eagerly Adolf studied the Jewish problem, talking to me of it again and again, although I was not interested. At the Conservatoire there were Jews amongst both teachers and students, and I had never had any trouble with them and indeed had made some friends among them. Was not Adolf himself enthusiastic about Gustav Mahler, and was he not fond of the works of Mendelssohn? One should not judge the Jewish question only on the strength of Handelees. I tried cautiously to deflect Adolf from his point of view. His reaction was very strange.

'Come, Gustl,' he said, and once again to save the fare I had to walk with him to the Brigittenau. I was astounded when Adolf led me to the synagogue there. We entered. 'Keep your hat on,' Adolf whispered, and indeed, all the men had their heads covered. Adolf had discovered that at this time a wedding was taking place in the synagogue. The ceremony impressed me deeply. The congregation started with an alternate chant, which I liked. Then the rabbi gave a sermon in Hebrew and finally laid the phylacteries on the foreheads of the bridal pair. I concluded from our strange visit that Adolf really wanted to study thoroughly the Jewish problem and thereby convince himself that the religious practices of the Jews still survived. This, I hoped, might soften his biased view but I was mistaken, for one day Adolf came home and announced decidedly, 'Today I joined the Anti-Semitic Union and have put down your name as well.'

Although I had got used to his domineering over me in political matters, this was going too far. It was all the more surprising as Adolf usually avoided joining any society or organisation. I kept silent, but resolved to handle my affairs myself in future.

Looking back on those days in Vienna and on our long, nocturnal conversations, I can assert that Adolf then adopted that philosophy of life which was to guide him henceforward. He gathered from it his immediate impressions and experiences in the streets and extended and deepened it by his reading. What I heard was its first version, often still unbalanced and immature, but propounded with all the more passion.

At that time I did not take all these things very seriously because my friend played no part in public life and never met anybody but me, and accordingly all his plans and political projects were floating in mid-air. That later he would bring them to fruition I would never have dared to think.

# Chapter 24

# The Lost Friendship

The competitive examinations at the Conservatoire were over, and I had come out of them very well. Now I had only to conduct the end-of-term concert in the Johannessaal which, in view of the stage fright of the performers – and the conductor – was not an easy task, but everything went well. Much more exciting for me was the second evening when the singer Rossi sang three songs I had composed, and two movements from my sextet for strings were performed for the first time. Both competitions met with great success. Adolf was in the artists' room when Professor Max Jentsch, my composition teacher, congratulated me. The head of the Conducting School, Gustav Gutheil, also added his congratulations and to crown it all the director of the Conservatoire came into the artists' room and shook me warmly by the hand. This was a little too much for me, who only a year ago had been working in a dusty upholsterer's shop. Adolf glowed with enthusiasm and seemed genuinely proud of his friend, but I could well imagine what he was thinking in his heart of hearts. Certainly he had never realised with such bitterness the futility of his time in Vienna as when he saw me in the midst of my resounding triumphs, my feet firmly planted on the road which led to my ultimate goal.

Only a few more days and the term would end. I was looking forward with great pleasure to going home as, in spite of my successful studies, the dire feeling of homesickness had never left me throughout the time I had been in Vienna.

Adolf had no home and did not know where he would go. We discussed how we should pass the coming months. Frau Zakreys joined us in our room and asked us hesitantly what our plans were.

'Whatever happens we shall stay together,' I declared immediately. I did not mean only that I should stay with Adolf – that seemed to me a matter of course – but also that we should both go on lodging with Frau Zakreys, with whom we got on so well. Moreover, my plans were quite decided. Immediately after the end of term I would go to Linz and stay with my parents till the autumn, when I would undergo my eight weeks' training with the Army Reserve. At the latest, I wanted to be back in Vienna by the second half of November. I promised to send my share of the rent regularly to Frau Zakreys so that she should keep the room for us.

Frau Zakreys too wanted to visit relatives in Moravia over the next few days, and she was worried about leaving the flat empty, but Adolf reassured the old dear. He would stay there and wait until she came back, then he could still go for a few days to his mother's family in the Waldviertel. Frau Zakreys was very pleased with this solution and assured us that we had been most satisfactory lodgers: two such nice young gentlemen who paid their rent punctually and never brought girls home you would not find anywhere else in Vienna.

When I was alone with Adolf, I told him that I would try to get an engagement as a viola player with the Vienna Symphony Orchestra during the next school year. This would make me so much better off that I would be able to help him substantially as well. Adolf, who in those days was very irritable, made no response to my suggestion. Neither did he tell me a word of his future plans, but in view of my own success I did not take offence at this. Moreover, to my great astonishment, I was not instructed to keep him informed about Stefanie but nevertheless I made up my mind to write to him with all that I could find out about her. Adolf promised to write often and keep me informed of everything of interest to me that went on in Vienna.

The parting was hard for both of us; its date, the beginning of July 1908, is of particular significance. Although it had not always been easy, in spite of my compliant nature, to get on with Adolf, yet our friendship had always triumphed over personal difficulties. We had known each other now for four years and had got used to each other's ways. The rich treasure of artistic experiences enjoyed together in Linz, as well as the joy of lovely excursions, had been increased and deepened by our time together in Vienna. In that city, Adolf was like a bit of home for me; he had shared the most beautiful impressions of my boyhood, and knew me better than anybody else. It was him that I had to thank for the fact that I was at the Conservatoire.

This feeling of gratitude, strengthened by a friendship springing from shared experiences, bound me firmly to him. I was more than willing, in the future, to put up with any of the peculiarities caused by his impulsive temperament. With growing maturity and discernment, my appreciation of Adolf as my friend increased, as is proved by the fact that in spite of our cramped quarters and the divergence of our interests, we had got on much better together in Vienna than in Linz. I was prepared, for his sake, to go not only to parliament, and to a synagogue but even to the Spittelberggasse, and God knows where, and was already looking forward to spending my next year with him.

Naturally I meant far less to Adolf than he did to me. That I had come with him to Vienna from his home town served to remind him, perhaps unwillingly, of his own difficult family background and the apparent hopelessness of his boyhood though, to be sure, my presence also reminded him of Stefanie. Above all, he had learnt to appreciate me as an eager audience. He could not wish for a better public since, because of his overwhelming gift for persuasion, I agreed with him even when I held a completely different opinion in my heart. For him, and what he had in mind, however, my views were quite unimportant. He needed me just to talk to – after all, he could not sit on the bench in the Schönbrunn and make long speeches to himself. When he was full of an idea and had to unburden himself, then he needed me as a soloist needs an instrument to give expression to his feelings. This, if I may use the expression, 'instrumental character' of our friendship rendered me of more value to him than my own modest nature merited.

So we said goodbye. Adolf assured me for the hundredth time how little he wanted to be left alone. I could imagine, he said, how dull it would be for him alone in the room we shared. Had I not already written the date of my arrival to my parents, perhaps in spite of my attacks of grievous home-sickness I might have stayed in Vienna another couple of weeks.

He accompanied me to the Westbahnhof; I stowed away my luggage and joined him on the platform. Adolf hated sentimentality of any kind. The more anything touched him, the cooler he became. So now he just took both my hands – two hands was most unusual for him – and pressed them firmly. Then he spun on his heel and made for the exit, perhaps a little over-hastily, without once turning round. I felt wretched. I got on to the train and was glad that it started right away and prevented me from changing my mind.

My parents were delighted to have their only son home again. In the evening, I had to tell them all about the end-of-term concert. My mother's eyes, shining with happiness, were my greatest reward. When next morning I appeared in the workshop in my blue apron with my shirt sleeves rolled up and set to work, my father too was satisfied. Without more ado, he asked me to carry out an important order commissioned by the government.

In my free time I missed Adolf sadly. I would have liked to write to him about Stefanie, although he had not asked me to do so, but I never managed to see her. Probably she had gone on holiday with her mother.

As there were still some things to be settled in Vienna, I wrote to Adolf asking him to deal with them. There were my dues to be paid to Riedl, treasurer of the Musicians' Union, and I also wanted him to collect my member's book and send on to me all the union's publications. Adolf attended to all this most conscientiously, and on a picture postcard dated 15 July 1908 depicting the so-called 'Graben' he confirms this. The card reads:

> Dear Gustl,
>
> I called on Riedl three times and never found him in, and it was not until Thursday evening that I could pay him. My heartiest thanks for your letter and particularly your postcard. It looks very prosaic, I mean the fountain. I've been working very hard since you left, sometimes till two or three in the morning. I'll write you when I'm leaving. I'm not very keen on it if my sister is coming too. It is not warm here now, and it even rains occasionally. I am sending you your newspapers and also the little book. Kindest regards to you and your esteemed parents.
>
> *Adolf Hitler*

The fountain which Adolf describes as 'very prosaic' had been erected in the public park. The sculpture that was supposed to adorn it was by Hanak and called 'The Joy of Beauty', a description which Adolf, in view of the dullness of the work, considered ironical.

The remark concerning his sister is interesting: he means Angela Raubal. Adolf was not at all pleased with the idea that she might also go to the Waldviertel since, after his violent quarrel with her husband, he did not wish to meet her again.

A few days later another card arrived from Adolf, dated 19 July 1908 and showing a picture of a Zeppelin airship. It read:

> Dear Friend,
>
> My best thanks for your kindness. You don't need to send me butter and cheese now. But I thank you most gratefully for the kind thought. Tonight I am going to see *Lohengrin*. Kindest regards to you and your esteemed parents.
>
> *Adolf Hitler*

Around the edge is written. 'Frau Zakreys thanks you for the money and sends regards to you and your parents.' I had told my mother how hard up my friend was and that he sometimes went hungry. That was enough for my dear mother. Without saying a word to me she had sent Adolf a number of food parcels during that summer of 1908. The reason he asked her not to send any more was because of his forthcoming trip to the Waldviertel, but more important than all this was the fact that he could see *Lohengrin*. I was with him in this.

I wondered what he would be doing alone in our room, and I often thought of him. Perhaps he took advantage of the fact that he now had the room to himself to start, once again, on his big building plans. He had long ago decided to rebuild the Vienna Hofburg. On our strolls through the centre of the city he was always coming back to this project, the ideas for which were already formulated, and needed only to be put on paper. It annoyed him that the old Hofburg and the court stables were built of brick. Bricks, according to him, were not a solid enough material for monumental buildings. So these buildings must come down and be rebuilt, in a similar style, in stone. In addition, Adolf wanted to match the wonderful semi-circle of columns of the new Burg with a corresponding one on the opposite side, and thus magnificently enclose the Heldenplatz. The Burgtor should remain. Across the Ring, two mighty triumphal arches – the question which 'triumphs' they should commemorate Adolf very wisely left unanswered – should bring the wonderful Platz and the Hof Museum into one design. The old Hof stables should be demolished and replaced by a monumental building equal to the Hofburg and linked by two triumphal arches to the whole complex. Thus, according to my friend, Vienna would have a Heldenplatz worthy of a metropolis.

In my belief about him I was mistaken. Adolf was not concerned about Vienna, but about Linz. Perhaps this was for him the best way to still that bitter feeling which the loss of his parental home and the estrangement from his home town had roused in him. Linz, where he had suffered such cruel blows from fate, should now learn how much he loved her.

A letter arrived, a rarity for Adolf, for, if only to save the postage, his custom was to write only postcards. Although he has no idea 'what he can dish up for me', he feels the urge to chat with me about his hermit life. The letter is dated 21 July 1908 and reads:

> Dear Friend.
>
> Perhaps you will have wondered why I haven't written for so long. The answer is simple. I didn't know what I could dish up for you and what would be of particular interest to you. Firstly, I am

still in Vienna and will stay here. I am alone because Frau Zakreys is at her brother's. Nevertheless, I am getting on quite well in my hermit's life. There is only one thing I miss. Until now, Frau Zakreys always banged on my door early in the morning and I got up and started work, whereas now I have to depend on myself. Has anything fresh happened in Linz? One doesn't hear any more of the society for rebuilding the theatre. When the bank is finished please send me a picture postcard. And now I have two favours to ask of you. First, would you be so good as to buy for me the *Guide to the Danube City of Linz*, not the Wohrl but the actual Linz one published by Krakowitzer. On the cover there is a picture of a Linz girl, and the background shows Linz from the Danube, with the bridge and castle. It costs sixty hellers which I enclose in postage stamps. Please send it to me immediately, either postage paid, or collect. I will repay you the expenses. But be sure that the timetable of the steamship company, as well as the map of the town, are both there. I need a few figures which I have forgotten and which I can't find in the Wohrl. And secondly, I would ask you, when you go on the boat again, to get me a copy of the guide you had this year. This 'pay-what-you-wish' cost I will refund to you. So, you will do this for me, won't you? There is no other news except that this morning I caught an army of bugs which were soon swimming in my blood, and now my teeth are chattering with the 'heat'.

I think there have been very few summers with such cold days as this. It's the same with you, isn't it? Now with kindest regards to you and your esteemed parents, and once more repeating my requests, I remain your friend,

*Adolf Hitler*

Adolf was so keenly interested in his new plans for rebuilding Linz that he spared from his scanty means sixty hellers for me to buy the Krakowitzer edition of the town guide. The bank he refers to is the building for the Bank of Upper Austria & Salzburg. Adolf was very worried lest this building should detract from the compact appearance of the Linz main square. I could understand that he waited impatiently for definite news of the Theatre Rebuilding Society because the theatre, together with the Danube bridge, were his favourite building projects.

How conscientious Adolf was, in spite of his desperate poverty, is shown not only by the enclosure to pay for the guide, but by the remark that he would repay me the small sum I might spend for the 'pay-what-you-wish' guide obtainable on board the steamers.

And, oh the bugs! That spiteful trick of fate. I was practically immune, whilst Adolf was terribly afflicted by them. When I used to sleep through his nightly bug-hunt, how often the next morning would he show me, carefully spiked on a pin, the result of his night's activity. At that time many houses in Vienna suffered from bugs. Well, another army of them had paid the extreme penalty.

For some time I did not hear from him, but then there came a lovely letter, dated 17 August 1908, probably the most revealing letter he ever sent me. It reads:

> Good Friend,
>
> First I must ask you to forgive me for not having written for so long. This has its own good – or rather bad – reasons: I didn't know what I could find to tell you. That I am writing you now only shows how long I had to search before I could collect together a little news. Firstly, our landlady Zakreys thanks you for the money. And secondly, I want to thank you heartily for your letter. Probably Frau Zakreys finds writing letters difficult (her German is so bad) but she has asked me to thank you and your esteemed parents for the money. I have just got over a sharp attack of bronchial catarrh. It seems that your Musicians' Union is facing a crisis. Who actually published the newspaper that I sent you last time? I had already paid the money long since. Do you know anything more about it? We're having nice fine weather now: it's pouring with rain. And this year, with the baking heat we've had, that's really a blessing from heaven. But I shall only be able to enjoy it for a little while now. Probably Saturday or Sunday I shall have to leave. Shall let you know exactly. Am writing quite a lot lately, mostly afternoons and evenings. Have you read the latest decision of the council with regard to the new theatre? It seems to me they intend to patch up the old junk-heap once more. It can't go on like this any longer because they won't get permission from the authorities. In any case, the whole clap-trap of these highly respected and all-powerful people shows that they understand about as much about building a theatre as a hippopotamus does of playing the violin. If my architect's manual didn't look so shabby,

I would like to pack it up and send it to them with the following address: 'Theatre-Rebuilding-Society-Committee-for-the-Execution-of-the-Project-for-the-Rebuilding-of-the-Theatre' [written as one word in the original German]. To the local, highly well-born, most strict and arch-laudable committee for the eventual construction and required decoration!

And with this I close. With kindest regards to you and your esteemed parents. I remain, your friend,

*Adolf Hitler*

This is absolutely typical of Adolf. Even the unusual opening, 'Good Friend', shows that he is in an emotional state. Then follows the long-winded introduction corresponding to that characteristic 'take-off' of his which he always used for his nocturnal orations in order to get going.

The joke about 'pleasant rainy weather', which already appears in another guise in his letter of 20 April of the same year, is warmed up to loosen the hesitant pen. To begin with, our good old landlady, with her melodious accent, is pulled to pieces. Then Adolf has a go at the Musicians' Union. But these are only preliminary skirmishes, just to sharpen up the sword, for now he slashes out with all his own special vehemence against the Linz Theatre Society, which is not putting up a new building, but which proposes to renovate the 'old junk-heap'. Bitterly he denounces these retrograde petit-bourgeois who are destroying his favourite project, one that has occupied him for years. Reading this letter I could, so to speak, see Adolf pacing up and down between door and piano, going bald-headed for these bureaucratic city councillors. He did actually go on the journey that he mentions in this letter, as on 20 August, that is three days later, he sent me a picture postcard of Weitra castle from the Waldviertel. He does not seem to have liked it much at his relatives', as very soon there comes a card from Vienna congratulating me on my saint's day.

So everything went according to plan: Frau Zakreys went to Moravia and Adolf to the Waldviertel. While life in the Stumpergasse was once again running on its accustomed lines, I – greatly to my distress – had to report at the barracks of Infantry Regiment No. 2. What I had to do in those eight weeks – or to be more precise, what was done with me in this period of training – I prefer to leave unrecorded. These eight weeks are a complete void in my life, but at last they came to an end and finally, on 20 November 1908, I was able to inform Adolf of my arrival in Vienna.

I had, as I had written to him, taken the early train to save time, and arrived at the Westbahnhof at three o'clock in the afternoon. He would be waiting, I thought, at the usual spot, the ticket barrier. Then he could help me carry the heavy case which also contained something for him from my mother. Had I missed him? I went back again, but he was certainly not at the barrier. I went into the waiting room. In vain I looked around me: Adolf was not there. Perhaps he was ill. He had indeed written me in his last letter that he was still being plagued by his old trouble, bronchial catarrh. I put my case in the left-luggage office and, very worried, hastened to the Stumpergasse. Frau Zakreys was delighted to see me, but told me immediately that the room was taken. 'But Adolf, my friend?' I asked her astonished.

From her lined, withered face Frau Zakreys stared at me with wide open eyes. 'But don't you know that Herr Hitler has moved out?'

No, I did not know.

'Where has he moved to?' I asked.

'Herr Hitler didn't tell me that.'

'But he must have left a message for me – a letter perhaps, or a note. How else shall I get hold of him?'

The landlady shook her head. 'No, Herr Hitler didn't leave anything.'

'Not even a greeting?'

'He didn't say anything.'

I asked Frau Zakreys if the rent had been paid. Yes, Adolf had duly paid his share. Frau Zakreys refunded the money that was due to me, as I had already paid my rent until November. She was very sorry to lose us both but nothing could be done about it, and she gave me a makeshift bed for the night. Next morning I went to look for other lodgings, found a pleasant, light little room in the Glasauerhof, and hired an upright piano.

Nevertheless I missed Adolf very much, although I was convinced that one day he would turn up again at my lodgings. To make it easier for him I left my new address with Frau Zakreys. Now Adolf had three ways of getting in touch with me – through Frau Zakreys, through the Conservatoire office or through my parents. He would certainly adopt one of these ways if he wanted to contact me again. That I could have found him through the central registration office at police headquarters naturally did not occur to me. Days went by, a week, another week – Adolf still did not come. What had happened to him? Had something come between us which made him leave me?

In my thoughts I went over again the last weeks we had spent together. Of course there had been differences of opinion and rows, but with Adolf this was quite normal. It had always been the same with him. However much I pondered, I could not discover the slightest reason for his silence. After all, he himself had said many times that when I came back to Vienna in the autumn we should lodge together again. He had never so much as hinted at our parting, even in moments of anger. In these four years, our friendship had become so close that it was taken for granted, and so was our resolve to stay together in the future.

When I thought back over the last weeks we had spent together I could only establish, on the contrary, that our relationship had been better than ever before, closer and more full of meaning. Yes, those last few weeks in Vienna, when we had so many marvellous experiences at the opera, at the Burg Theatre and on the adventurous trip to the Rax, had indeed been the climax of our friendship. What could have made Adolf leave me without a word or a sign?

The more I racked my brain about it, the more I realised how much Adolf meant to me. I felt deserted and alone, and with the constant memory of our friendship in my mind I just could not decide to turn elsewhere for companionship. Although I appreciated that my studies would gain by it, yet my whole life now seemed to me so ordinary, almost boring. It certainly was some consolation to hear beautiful performances at concerts and the opera, but it was depressing to have no one to share them with. At every concert and every opera I went to, I hoped to see Adolf. Perhaps he would be standing at the exit at the end of the performance, waiting for me, and I should hear again his familiar, impatient voice saying, 'Oh, come on, Gustl', but all my hopes of seeing him again proved vain, and meanwhile, something became clear: he did not want to come back to me. It was not by chance that he had left me, neither was it the outcome of a passing mood or a series of mishaps. Had he wanted to find me, he certainly would have done so.

It distressed me that he should want to break off this friendship that had meant so much to me, without a sign of thanks, a token of future meetings, so the next time I was in Linz, I went to see Frau Raubal in the Bürgerstrasse to get his address from her. She was alone, and received me with perceptible coolness. I asked her where Adolf was now living in Vienna. She did not know, she answered crossly, Adolf had never written to her again. So here, once more, I met with failure, and when Frau Raubal began to reproach me, saying that it was partly through my artistic ambitions that Adolf, now twenty years of age, still had no profession and no position. I told her plainly what I thought and defended Adolf vigorously for, after all, Angela was only repeating her husband's opinion, and my opinion of him was no better than Adolf's. As the conversation was growing more and more unpleasant, I rose and took my leave abruptly.

The year came to an end, without my having heard or seen anything of Adolf. It was from a Linz archivist's research into Adolf Hitler's life that I was to learn, forty years later, that my friend had moved out of the Stumpergasse because the rent was too much for him and had found much cheaper accommodation at a so-called 'men's hostel' in the Meldemann-strasse. Adolf had disappeared into the shadowy depths of the metropolis. Then began for him those years of misery of which he himself says little, and concerning which there is no reliable witness, for one thing is certain, that in this most difficult phase of his life, he no longer had a friend. I can now understand his behaviour at that time. He did not wish to have a friend, because he was ashamed of his own poverty. He wanted to go his way alone, and bear alone whatever destiny brought him. It was the road into the wilderness. I experienced personally, after that parting, that one is never so lonely as in the midst of crowds of people in a big city.

Thus our fine, adolescent friendship came to an end that was anything but beautiful, but with the passing of time I became reconciled. Indeed, I came to feel that this sudden termination of our friendship by Adolf was of much more significance than if it had finished through our growing indifferent towards each other, or if it had ceased to mean anything to him. Certainly such an end would have been harder for me to bear than that forced farewell, which was really not a farewell at all.

Chapter 25

# My Subsequent Life and Reunion with My Friend

After an intensive four-year course of study at the Vienna Conservatoire, in October 1912 I was engaged as deputy conductor at the Marburg an der Drau city music theatre and made my debut conducting Lortzing's *Der Waffenschmied*. When my contract there ended in the spring of 1914, I was contracted to Klagenfurt, which had a good forty-man orchestra, a fine opera house and modern stage. Thus all my dreams were becoming reality.

It was quite another kind of music I was to experience that summer, however, facing the Russian guns in Galicia as a mobilised reservist of the Landwehr Infantry Regiment No. 2. During the fearful Carpathian winter campaign of 1915 I was wounded at Eperjes in Hungary, and endured an horrific seven-day ride in an ambulance train to Budapest. The train made regular stops to unload the dead. I survived, but my strength was gone for ever.

After months of convalescence I returned home to find everything changed. My father, exhausted by work and robbed of his ambition to hand over to me, his only son, the business he had built up, had retired in 1916 and bought a small-holding at Fraham near Eferding in the hope of recovering his health and spirits. I returned to the front and during my absence he died in September 1918, surrounded by the grief and misery of the time. How I wish I could have granted him a better evening of his life!

I was attached to a mechanised corps in Vienna when discharged from military service on 8 November 1918. What to do now? My prospects were non-existent. The provincial theatres were closed. I scoured Vienna for work but nothing was available except in the dance orchestras of the larger coffee houses, which was not for me. For a while I conducted a six-man orchestra in the pit at one of the new cinemas. In vain I sought a position as viola player or even as a relief, and nobody wanted private tuition.

I was at my wits' end when a letter arrived from my mother. She stated that the post of district secretary was being advertised at Eferding near Linz. She had already spoken to the Bürgermeister about my musical virtuosity, the latter having expressed the hope that the successful applicant would set about reorganising the music society, which had been disbanded, and take over as its director. I went home and considered it. The salary was poor, the artistic possibilities very modest, but I had meanwhile abandoned the idea of being a career conductor and so, more for my mother's sake than anything else, I applied for the position and then returned to Vienna to look for work.

In January 1920 I received notification from the Bürgermeister that the district committee had selected me for the position of secretary from amongst thirty-eight other applicants, and so I became a civil servant. Gradually I found my feet in the post and a few years later I passed the provincial government's examination for a district officer. So modest an existence was it, however, that I had plenty of time to indulge my musical inclinations. I built up a respectable orchestra, and soon the musical life of the small town was looking up – from the house recitals of a string quartet to the brass band in the town square and the festival performances of the local choir, I had a wonderful, successful occupation.

I had had no further news of the friend of my youth who had left me in such a strange manner, and finally I gave up the search. I had no means of tracing him. His brother-in-law Raubal was long dead, and Angela, his half-sister, no longer lived in Linz. What might have become of him? He would certainly have been a better soldier than I, but perhaps he lay amongst the ranks of the dead as did so many young men.

Now and again I heard talk of a German politician by the name of Adolf Hitler, but I thought this must certainly be another man who happened to have the same name; the surname was not rare, and in any case I expected that he would be an important architect by now, or an artist, not an unimportant politician, and especially not in Munich. One evening in the bookshop at Eferding I glanced at a copy of the *Münchner Illustrierte*. On the front page was the photograph of a man in his mid-thirties with narrow, pale features whom I recognised at once. It was Adolf, scarcely changed. I worked out how long it had been – fifteen years! His face seemed stronger, more manly, more mature, but not really much older. The caption below the photograph read: 'The well-known orator of the National Socialists, Adolf Hitler'. So my friend was one and the same as that notorious politician.

I regretted very much that he had not been able to pursue an artistic career any more than I had. I knew only too well what it meant to bury all one's hopes and dreams. Now he earned his living addressing the mob – a bitter bread, even though he was a good, convincing speaker. His interest in politics I could understand, but politics was a dangerous and thankless business.

I was glad that my professional position as civil servant kept me out of local politics, for as head of the municipal office I had to treat everybody the same. My friend, on the other hand, steamed full ahead into politics, and it came as no surprise to me when his impetuous behaviour, about which I had read in the newspapers, landed him in Landsberg prison.

Yet he rose again. The press began to take notice of him, more than ever. That his political ideas were gradually taking hold in Austria did not surprise me either, for they were basically the same ideas, if then somewhat confused and high flown, as he had preached to me in Vienna. When I read the text of his speeches, I could visualise him holding forth as he strode up and down between door and piano in our room at 29 Stumpergasse. At that time I was his only audience, now millions listened. His name was on everybody's lips, and everybody was asking: 'Where does this Hitler come from?'

I had, perhaps, more to tell on that score than many others. In my attic at Fraham – my mother had sold the small-holding and moved in with my family – I kept in a large wooden chest the old correspondence with my friend and his sketches. After some reflection, I decided to leave them where they were. Through the newspapers I followed his career – he amassed millions of supporters, and without having trodden Austrian soil for the purpose, his radical ideas and opinions had brought speculation and unrest to what was now a small country. It may seem strange that I did not contact my erstwhile friend now that he had made a name for himself, but really our common interest had been music and not politics. I had nothing to offer him in respect of the latter.

Adolf Hitler became Reich Chancellor of Germany on 30 January 1933, and at once I remembered that midnight experience on the Freinberg in 1905 when he had prophesied to me that like Rienzi of Wagner's opera he would rise to be *Volkstribun* – the leader of the people. What the sixteen-year-old had seen in a visionary trance had become reality. I took pen and paper and wrote a few lines to 'Reichkanzler Adolf Hitler in Berlin' but I expected no reply, for German chancellors had better things to do than write letters to old friends from twenty-five years back. Nevertheless it seemed to me right and proper, as a family friend of his youth, to pay my respects by offering him my congratulations. One day, to my great surprise, I received

245

the following letter dated 4 August 1933 from Nazi Party headquarters, The Brown House, Munich:

> My Dear Kubizek,
>
> Only today was your letter of 2 February placed before me. From the hundred of thousands of letters I have received since January it is not surprising. All the greater was my joy, for the first time in so many years, tò to hear news of your life and to receive your address. I would very much like – when the time of my hardest struggles is over – to revive personally the memory of those most wonderful years of my life. Perhaps it would be possible for you to visit me. Wishing yourself and your mother all the best, I remain in the memory of our old friendship.
>
> Your,
>
> *Adolf Hitler*

He had not forgotten me, and that he remembered despite the burden of his office gave me great pleasure. To visit him as he had suggested was not so easy. I could hardly just turn up at Obersalzberg and say 'here I am', and in any case my own life, compared to his, was dull and uninteresting. News about Eferding would bore him. So I put the matter to one side, deciding that his kind invitation was merely an act of formal courtesy just as, twenty-five years earlier, he had never forgotten to sign off in his letters with a respectful greeting to my parents.

On 12 March 1938, Adolf Hitler crossed the frontier into Austria at the spot in Braunau am Inn where his father had been a customs official. The German Wehrmacht had moved into Austria. That same evening, he spoke to the townspeople of Linz from the balcony of the city hall. I would have loved to have gone to Linz to hear this address but had my hands full arranging accommodation for the German troops and so was unable to leave Eferding. On 8 April 1933, when he visited Linz for the second time, after a political rally at the Kraus locomotive factory workshop, he retired to the Hotel Weinzinger, and I decided to call on him there. I found a huge crowd gathered in the square facing the hotel. After working my way through to the line of SA security people, I told them I wanted to speak to the Reich Chancellor. At first I got a strange reception – they obviously considered me to be a madman – but once I had shown them Hitler's letter an officer was summoned. After reading it he led me at once into the foyer of the hotel where the activity was like a beehive. Generals stood around in groups discussing events, ministers of state whom I recognised from the news-papers, Nazi Party bosses and other uniformed officials came and went. Adjutants, identifiable by their shining aiguillettes, flitted here and there busily. And all this exciting industry revolved around the very man with whom I wished to speak. My head spun and I saw that my enterprise was senseless. I had to realise, I told myself, that the erstwhile friend of my youth was now Reich Chancellor, and that this highest of all offices of state put a gap between us which could not be bridged. The years in which I had been the only person to whom he had dedicated his friendship, and entrusted his personal affairs of the heart, were over. Therefore the best thing to do would be to withdraw quietly and no longer bother these highly-placed gentlemen, who doubtless had very important matters to attend to.

One of the senior adjutants to whom I had given my letters, Albert Bormann, returned after a while and told me that the Reich Chancellor was a little unwell and was not receiving guests today, but I should come again tomorrow at noon. Bormann then invited me to have a seat for a moment, since he wanted to ask me something. Had the Reich Chancellor always slept in so late in his youth, he asked with a whine, for he never went to bed until after midnight and then slept in very late next morning while his entourage, who had to keep the same hours he did at night, were obliged to be up bright and early next morning. He went on to complain at Hitler's outbursts of temper, which nobody could quieten, and about his strange diet which was vegetarian with a flour basis and lots of fruit juices. Had he always been like that? I said that he had, except that he used to like meat. With that I took my leave. Albert Bormann was the brother of Reichsleiter Martin Bormann.

Next day I returned to Linz. The whole city was in the streets, and the closer I got to the Hotel Weinzinger, the greater was the crush. Finally I fought my way through to the hotel foyer, where the excitement and activity were even more hectic than the night before. Today was the eve of the Austrian plebiscite. That all great decisions revolved around Hitler's person made one think. I could not have found a more unfavourable time for the reunion than this. I calculated back. It had been at the beginning of July 1908 that we had parted in the station hall of the Westbahnhof. Today was 9 April 1938. There were therefore almost thirty years between that unexpected last parting in Vienna and today's meeting, should it take place, of course. Thirty years. A generation! And what revolutionary changes had those thirty years brought about. I had no illusions about this meeting with Hitler. A brief handshake, perhaps a friendly clap on the shoulder, a few warm words spoken quickly as I was shown the door – I should have to satisfy myself with that.

I had already prepared a few words, but the form of address worried me. I could hardly call the Reichskanzler 'Adolf', and I knew how upset he could get at any breach of protocol. As Hitler emerged suddenly from a room at the Hotel Weinzinger, he recognised me at once, and with the joyful cry, 'It's you, Gustl!' he gestured for his following to remain behind and took my arm. He grasped my right hand with both of his and looked into my eyes. His gaze was as bright and penetrating as ever. That he was as moved as I was I could hear in his voice. The worthy gentlemen in the foyer looked at each other in astonishment. Nobody knew this strange civilian whom the Führer und Reichskanzler greeted with a heartiness that many envied.

I regained my composure and made my little prepared speech. He listened carefully and gave a small smile. When I finished, he nodded, and I left it at that – any further sign of intimacy on my part seemed to me improper. After a brief pause he said, 'Kommen Sie!' Although he had addressed me with the familiar 'Du' in his letter of August 1933, the formal 'Sie' in reply to my use of it in the little speech came as a relief to me. The Reich Chancellor led me to the lift and we went up to his suite on the second floor. The personal adjutant opened the door; we entered and the adjutant left. We were alone. Again, Hitler took my hand, gave me a long look and said, 'You haven't changed, Kubizek. I would have recognised you anywhere. The only thing different is that you've got older.' Then he led me to a table and offered me a chair. He assured me how much pleasure it gave him to see me again after so many years. My good wishes had pleased him especially, for I knew better than anybody else how difficult his path had been. The present time was unfavourable for a long talk, but he hoped that there would be an opportunity in the future. He would contact me. To write to him directly was not advisable, for all his mail was dealt with by his aides.

'I no longer have a private life and cannot do what I like as others can.' With these words he rose and went to the window, which overlooked the Danube. The old bridge with its steel bars, which had so annoyed him in his youth, remained in use. As I expected, he mentioned it at once. 'That ugly footbridge!' he cried, 'It's still there. But not for much longer, I assure you, Kubizek.' With that he turned and smiled. 'All the same, I would love to take a stroll with you over the old bridge. But I can't, for wherever I go, everybody follows me. But believe me, Kubizek, for Linz I have many plans.' Nobody knew that better than I. As expected, he drew forth from his memory all the plans which had occupied him in his youth just as though not thirty, but no more than three years, had passed since then. Shortly before receiving me he had driven through the city to see the architectural changes. Now he revised the individual schemes. The new bridge over the Danube, to be called Niebelungenbrücke, must be a masterpiece. In detail he described how he wanted the two bridgeheads. Then he turned – I knew exactly the order he had in his head -- to the Landestheater, which as a first step would receive a new stage. When the new Opera House, which would replace the ugly railway station, was completed, the theatre would be used only for plays and operettas. Besides that, Linz needed, to merit being called a 'Bruckner-city', a modern auditorium. 'In the cultural respect I want Linz to have a leading role, and will make the necessary preparations.'

I thought that this brought the discussion to an end, but Hitler now came to speak about a new symphony orchestra for Linz, and the conversation turned to personal matters. 'What have you actually become, Kubizek?' he asked. I told him that since 1920 I was a municipal official, more recently in the post of Stadtamtsleiter.

'Stadtamtsleiter. What's that then?' Now I was in difficulties. How could I explain, in a few words, what this title meant. I fumbled in my mental dictionary for suitable terms. He interrupted me. 'So, you are a civil servant, a clerk. That doesn't suit you. What did you make of your musical talents?' I answered truthfully that the lost war had thrown me off course. If I didn't want to starve, I had to change horses. He nodded gravely and repeated, 'Yes, the lost war.' With a look he added, 'You won't be ending your career as a municipal clerk, Kubizek.' Moreover he wanted to see this Eferding for himself. I asked him if he meant it.

'Naturally I will visit you, Kubizek,' he declared, 'but only you. Then we will have a walk along the Danube. I can't do it from here, they never leave me in peace.'

He asked if I was as keen on music as I had always been. This was my pet subject, and I related in detail the musical life of our small town. I was worried that my account would bore him, seeing how many international problems of great moment he had to decide upon, but I was wrong. When I summarised something to save time, he would take me up on it. 'What, Kubizek, you even perform symphonies in your little town? That's amazing! Which ones?' I counted them off: Schubert's Unfinished, Beethoven's Third, Mozart's Jupiter, Beethoven's Fifth.

He wanted to know the strength and composition of my orchestra, was amazed at what I told him and congratulated me on my success. 'I really must help you, Kubizek,' he said, 'make out a report and tell me what you're short of. And how are things with you personally? You're not in need?' I told him that my job provided me with a satisfying, if modest, existence and that I had no wish for anything more. He looked at me in surprise. He was not used to somebody having no wishes to be fulfilled. 'Have you any children, Kubizek?' 'Yes, three sons.'

'Three sons!' he cried emotionally. He repeated the words several times and with an earnest expression. 'You have three sons, Kubizek. I have no family. I am alone. But I would like to help with your sons.' He made me tell him everything about them. He was delighted that all three were talented musically and two of them were skilled sketch-artists.

'I will sponsor the education of your three sons, Kubizek,' he told me, 'I don't like it when young, gifted people are forced to go along the same track that we did. You know how it was for us in Vienna. After that, for me, came the worst times of all, after our paths had separated. That young talent goes under because of need must not be allowed to happen. If I can help personally, I will, even if it's for your children, Kubizek!'

I have to mention here that the Reich Chancellor actually did have his office foot the bill for the musical education of my three sons at the Linz Bruckner-Conservatoire and on his orders the sketches of my son Rudolf were assessed by a professor at the Munich Academy. I had reckoned on nothing more than a brief handshake and now we had sat talking together for over an hour. The Reich Chancellor rose. I thought that the conversation was now at an end and also stood, but he merely called for his adjutant and passed to him his instructions for my sons.

Next he referred to the documents in my possession dating from our youth. I had to spread out on the table all the letters, postcards and sketches I had brought with me. He was astonished at the wealth of material I had. He asked how the documents had been preserved, and I explained about the wooden chest in my attic. He examined his Pöstlingberg water-colour very closely. There were a few skilful painters around who could make such good copies of his water-colours that it was impossible to tell the original, he said. They had a profitable business for it was always possible to find people to dupe. The best thing was never to let the original out of one's hand.

As an 'official' attempt had already been made to relieve me of the documentation I asked his opinion on the matter. 'These documents are your personal property, Kubizek,' he replied, 'nobody can argue you out of them.'

He now spoke about the book by Rabitsch. This person had attended

Linz Realschule a few years after Hitler did and with the best intentions had written a book about the latter's schooldays.* Hitler was very annoyed, however, because Rabitsch had not known him personally. 'See here, I was not in agreement with this book from the very beginning. There is only one person who can write about my youth, who really knew me, and that person is yourself, Kubizek.' Summoning his adjutant he said, 'Make a note of what I said.' At that he took my hand once more. 'You see, Kubizek, how necessary it is that we speak regularly. As and when it becomes possible, I will call you again.' The meeting was ended, and in a daze I left the hotel.

From then the waters of my placid, withdrawn existence were flurried and I was to discover that it was not necessarily a good thing to have been the friend of a national leader in his youth. Although I had scarcely mentioned it to anybody previously, and only rarely spoke of it subsequently, I soon got to see the shadowy side of this youthful friendship. I had had a foretaste of what awaited me in March 1938. Austria had only just been annexed to the German Reich. A car drew up outside my Eferding home and three SS men got out. They had come all the way from Berlin to see me. On the orders of the Führer they were confiscating all the documents in my possession dating from the time of the Führer's youth so that they could be stored safely in a vault at the Reich Chancellery. Luckily I was not fooled. Hitler was not involved, since at the time of the proposed seizure he had no knowledge of the existence of this material. It was probably the independent decision of some Party office or other which had come across my name. I denied all knowledge of any such memorabilia to the three SS men. I suppose they thought Austrians were quite gullible people, and their police-like appearance should have settled the matter, but they failed to make the desired impression on me. The amazing thing was that this intractable civilian was not even a Party member. They must have thought to themselves as they drove away empty-handed: what an old fogey for the Führer to have had for a friend when he was young.

I had done well to stand my ground and resist this first attack. All future efforts would be easy to ward off, for I had Hitler's personal guarantee that the material was my personal property. The next attempt by the Party involved pulling rank on me. Often when with his close entourage, Hitler would talk of his childhood, and my name would crop up regularly. 'Ask Gustl!' was his stock answer to all questions about this period. Thus,

---

* Rabitsch, Hugo: *Jugend-Erinnerungen eines zeitgenössischen Linzer Realschüler*: also *Aus Adolf Hitlers Jugendzeit*: Deutsche Volksverlag, Munich 1938.

without a big thing being made of it, the people in his close circle became aware of a man living in Austria who knew all about Hitler's youth. Fortunately for them as they saw it, this 'Gustl', who had been more or less out of reach until March 1938, had become a German citizen when Austria was annexed, and was thus now very much in reach.

Reich Minister Goebbels sent a very nice young man to see me, Karl Cerff, whose rank and official position I no longer remember. Cerff stated that a biography of the Führer was being planned for which they wanted me to write the 1904–8 chapters. When the time was ripe, I would be summoned to Berlin where, supported by recognised experts in the field, I would be able to carry out the task. Meanwhile, perhaps I might like to prepare just a detailed synopsis of my recollections. I informed the caller that I had no time available for such an editorial mission because, since the annexation, we civil servants were simply inundated with work. He probably saw that I was wriggling out of giving any undertaking for the future and was clearly amused by my verbal antics. In conclusion he cautioned me against underestimating 'my unique responsibility to history' as he put it. If I was interested, there would be no problem in his arranging leave of absence for me, but I turned this down decisively. He took his leave hoping to see me again at 'a better time', but as the future only brought 'a worse time', Karl Cerff never returned. All the same, I have to say that he had carried out his awkward mission on behalf of the Propaganda Ministry with understanding and grace.

Much less charming was the contact from Martin Bormann, who apparently felt himself solely competent with regard to my knowledge and watched anxiously to ensure that nobody else got in first. It was intended to be inferred from his memoranda and letters that he had the licence for Hitler's biography and nobody could say or write anything about it without his previous perusal of the script and approval. After the failure of his attempt in March 1938 to grab the material in my possession for the Party Chancellery – 'the place where it belongs' – I had received the strictest orders never to allow these papers out of my hand, not even to allow another to see them without previous authorisation. On the latter point he needed to have no worries, for such was my intention. Next came an order from Bormann to set down at once in writing my reminiscences of my youthful friendship with Adolf Hitler and supply him with the synopsis. I replied that I would need to discuss the matter with Hitler beforehand. This method was strikingly successful, and whenever I was pressurised by any powerful gentlemen afterwards, I would say, 'Forgive me, please, but I would like to discuss your suggestion first with the Reich Chancellor personally. What was your esteemed name again?' The mood would then ameliorate amazingly, and I would be treated with kid gloves.

On the other hand I remember with great pleasure my meeting with Rudolf Hess. He was visiting Linz and asked me to call on him. A car was sent to bring me to the Bergbahnhotel on the Pöstlingberg. Reich Minister Hess greeted me effusively. 'So you are Kubizek!' he cried, beaming with joy, 'the Führer has told me so much about you!' I sensed at once that this friendliness was honest and came from the heart, and it was through Hess that I had a certain suspicion confirmed: the closer a person stood in his relationship to Hitler, the more that person knew about me. Rudolf Hess and Frau Winifred Wagner were the best informed about Hitler's early years, and therefore about myself.

The minister invited me to dine on the wonderful hotel terrace. Afterwards he made me relate in detail all my experiences, throwing in many questions and observations to help me along. I had the impression that Rudolf Hess, from the human point of view, was closer to Hitler than most of the others, and that pleased me very much. Even the other gentlemen at table joined in the lively, open conversation, the attitude being quite different from that of the usual Party Chancellery officials.

I had to point out to the Reich minister all the significant spots on the Linz city skyline from this wonderful high point. There behind the green hill on which the Pulverturm stood was the Leonding suburb with the path that Hitler took daily on his way to Realschule: there was the Humboldt-strasse, where Frau Hitler lived after her husband's death, much nearer and below us was Urfahr with the Blütengasse and other important locations for my friend.

Hess's simplicity, which differed so markedly from the conduct of other, less significant political personalities, left a great impression on me. My only regret was that he must have been ill, for he looked it.

Meanwhile I had become known in Austria. Previously nothing had been known of a friend of Adolf Hitler's youth from Upper Austria, a circumstance which had been my good fortune for many years. Now I had been discovered. I was not a Party member, something which many could not understand for, as they reasoned it, Hitler's friend ought to have Party card No. 2. I had been a very doubtful adherent of my friend in political matters not only because I rejected his political outlook but also because I had no interest in politics and did not understand it.

It was only natural that I was soon roped in as an intermediary to present pleas in high places. I helped willingly although I had no illusions about the weight I carried. 'A friend of Adolf Hitler in his youth' had no brief to intervene in grand affairs and when I failed to get through to Hitler personally with a plea I would be informed, pleasantly but firmly, that this or that affair was not within my competence. As I expected, the planned visit of Hitler to Eferding was never made.

Suddenly, completely unexpectedly, my rather resigned mood was shattered by the arrival of a registered letter written on the finest vellum from the Reich Chancellery. It was to lead to the greatest joy in my life. I received the invitation of the Reich Chancellor to participate in the Wagner Festival at Bayreuth: I should present myself on Tuesday 25 July 1939 at Haus Wahnfried, where Hitler's housekeeper, Herr Kannenberg, would attend to me.

What I had scarcely dared dream in my lifetime was now to become a reality. I cannot describe my happiness in words. Ever since I could remember it had been my ambition to make the pilgrimage to Bayreuth and experience there the performance of the master's musical dramas, but I was not wealthy and my modest income did not extend to such an adventure.

The train passed through Passau, Regensburg and Nuremberg. As I stepped from the carriage at Bayreuth and glimpsed for the first time the opera house on the hill, I thought I would die of joy. Herr Kannenberg received me in an exceedingly friendly manner and introduced me to the Moschenbach family at Linzstrasse 10, in a beautiful quarter of town, where I would lodge. I reported for the performance punctually. The 1939 festival opened with *Die fliegende Holländer* and closed on 2 August 1939 with *Götterdämmerung*. I sat through every performance. After packing my bags I went to see Herr Kannenberg to thank him for his kindness. 'Must you go home straight away?' he enquired with a smile, 'it might be good if you stayed over one more day.' I understood what he was suggesting and remained in Bayreuth until 3 August.

At two o'clock that afternoon an SS officer came to my room to fetch me to Haus Wahnfried. From the entrance, Obergruppenführer Julius Schaub led me into a large hall where many people were gathered, most of whom I had either met in Linz or recognised from newspaper photos. Frau Winifred Wagner was in animated conversation with Reich Minister Hess; Obergruppenführer Bruckner stood talking with Herr von Neurath and a number of generals. It struck me suddenly how many military men were present. I could sense the tension in the air. The talk was about Poland and I got the drift about an armed conflict in the offing.

In this highly charged atmosphere, similar to Hotel Weinzinger, I felt a stranger, out of my element. I experienced a kind of stage-fright. Probably the Reich Chancellor would say just a few kind words before he returned to Berlin, I thought. At the far end of the hall was a pair of large double doors. The adjutant opened them both and stood aside. Schaub escorted me inside and reported, 'Mein Führer! Herr Kubizek is here!' At that he retired and shut the doors behind him. I was alone with the Reich Chancellor.

It was a joyful reunion of two old friends. Nothing about him spoke of the dreadful responsibility he carried on his shoulders. Here he was simply a guest of Frau Wagner, and one could feel that wonderful atmosphere which Bayreuth generates. He took my right hand in both of his and welcomed me. His greeting in such a hallowed location moved me so deeply that words failed me, and I was glad when he said, 'Let's sit, shall we?'

After discussing my impressions of Bayreuth I had regained my composure somewhat and we talked about old times. This brought us to the Wagner performances at Vienna and Linz, and he told me of his plans to make the works of Richard Wagner available to as many sections of the German people as possible. I knew these plans from long ago; in principle they had occupied his thoughts for almost thirty-five years but were now no longer dreams. Some 6,000 people who had never been in a position to visit the Bayreuth Festival had done so this year thanks to an excellent organisation for guests, he said. I remarked that I was numbered amongst them. With a laugh he replied – and I remember his words exactly – 'Now I have you as a witness here in Bayreuth, Kubizek, for you were the only one there when I, a poor unknown, unveiled these plans for the first time. I remember you asked me how these plans could be realised. Now you see how it was done.' Then he went on to explain what he had achieved so far for Bayreuth and what he proposed for the future, just as though he had a responsibility to account for it to me.

In my pocket I had a pack of postcards bearing his image. In Eferding and Linz many people would give anything to own such a postcard autographed by Hitler personally. I hesitated a while before making the banal request. Hitler sat at the table, took the postcards and, while he searched for his reading glasses I passed him my fountain pen. He began signing, and I dried the ink with the blotting-weight. Halfway through the task he looked up suddenly and said with a smile, 'It's obvious you are a clerk, Kubizek. What I can't understand is how you can put up with it. In your shoes I would have bolted long ago. Why didn't you come to me earlier?'

After you wrote to me on 4 August 1933 saying that you wanted to revive our common memories only after the time of your hardest struggle was done with, I decided to wait until then. In any case, before 1938, as an Austrian civil servant, I would have required a passport to come to Germany. They would certainly not have granted it once they knew the purpose of my visit.

Hitler laughed heartily. 'Yes, politically you were always a child.' I had expected him to use another word and grinned upon seeing that the 'turkey' of the Stumpergasse had become 'a child'. The Reich Chancellor made the postcards into a pack, handed them to me and rose. I thought the visit was at an end, but he said, 'Kommen Sie', and, opening the door which led into the garden, bid me follow him down the stone steps. Neat pathways brought us to a tall, hand-wrought iron gate which he opened. Beyond lay a flower garden. Deciduous trees formed a great arch below which everything was in semi-darkness. A few steps over the gravel path and we stood before the grave of Richard Wagner.

Hitler took my hand in both of his. I felt how moved he was. Ivy climbed around the granite slabs covering the remains of the master and his spouse. There was a stillness about the place; nobody disturbed the sacred peace. Then Hitler said: 'I am happy that we meet again at this place, which was always the holiest for us both.'

We returned to Haus Wahnfried. Wieland, Frau Wagner's son, and the grandson of the master, was waiting for us at the garden entrance with a ring of keys. He unlocked the individual rooms and Hitler gave me a guided tour. I was introduced to Frau Wagner and, as the conversation turned to our youthful enthusiasm for Wagner's music, I reminded Hitler of that memorable *Rienzi* performance at Linz in 1905. He related the events including the strange nocturnal experience and concluded with the unforgettable words, 'In that hour it began!'

As Obersalzberg was not a favourable venue for our reunions, Hitler gave instructions that I should always be invited to attend Bayreuth when he did. 'I would like to have you always around me,' he said, then waved to me from the garden gate as I left.

When the tickets for the first cycle of the 1940 Wagner season arrived on 8 July that year, I felt rather guilty about going because of the pressure of work I had. I justified the trip by telling myself that the Führer had ordered it. In contrast to 1939 only *Die fliegende Holländer* and the *Ring* were performed. Frau Wagner invited me to share her box where she informed me that Hitler might come for *Götterdämmerung*. Later she confirmed that he would be flying down from his field headquarters and would return as soon as it concluded. 'He asked me at once if you were here, Herr Kubizek. He would like to see you in the interval,' she said.

During the second act on 23 July 1940, Wolfgang Wagner, her second son, hurried up and asked me to follow him. We went to the lounge where about twenty people were gathered, speaking in excited tones. Hitler's personal adjutant had reported my arrival, and Hitler appeared wearing uniform – a field-grey jacket as opposed to the civilian clothes he wore in 1939 – and greeted me as usual by extending both hands. He was tanned and looked healthy. He seemed even more pleased to see me than before. Guiding me to the long wall of the room, we stood alone, the guests continuing their private conversations. 'This performance is nowadays the only one I can attend,' he said. 'There is nothing else for it; it is the war.' With a growling undertone he added, 'This war will set us back many years in our building programme. It is a tragedy. I did not become Chancellor of the Greater German Reich to fight wars.' I was surprised that he spoke in that vein after his great military successes in Poland and France. Perhaps he saw in my countenance the unmistakable signs of age and realised that time was not leaving him untouched.

'This war is robbing me of my best years,' he went on, 'You know, Kubizek, how many things I have planned, what I still want to build. But I would like to be around to see it, understand me? You know better than anyone how many plans I have carried with me from my youth. So far I have only been able to realise a few. I still have an enormous amount to do, but who will do it? Time will not stand still. We are getting older, Kubizek. A few more years and it is too late to do what remains to be done.'

That strangely excited voice which I knew from my youth, trembling with impatience, now began to describe the great projects for the future: the spread of the autobahns, the modernisation of the commercial waterways and railway network, and much else. I was scarcely able to keep up with it all. Again I received the impression that he wanted to justify his intentions to the witness of his youthful ideas. I might be only an insignificant civil servant, but for him I was the only person who remained from his teenage days. Possibly it was more satisfying for him to lay bare his ideas to a simple compatriot who was not even a Party member than to the military and political decision-makers who surrounded him.

When I attempted to return the conversation to our common erstwhile reminiscences, he seized at once on a loose remark I made and continued:

'Poor students, that is what we were. And we starved, by God. With nothing more than a chunk of bread in our pockets we would set off for the mountains. But things have changed now. A couple of years ago, young people sailed aboard our ships to Madeira. See, over there is Dr Ley together with his young wife. He built up the organisation.' Now he broached his cultural plans. The crowds before the Festival Hall might be calling for him to appear, but he had the bit between his teeth now and would not break off. Just as in his monologues in the dark room at old Frau Zakreys's house, he knew that as soon as he started on the problems affecting art I would be with him whole-heartedly.

'The war is tying me down but not for much longer, I hope,' he said, 'then I can get back to building and creating what is still to be created. Then I will send for you, Kubizek, and you will always be at my side.'

Outside, the Wehrmacht band struck up, indicating that the performance was about to resume. I thanked the Reich Chancellor for his kindness and wished him good luck and success in the future. He accompanied me to the door, then stood and watched me leave.

After *Götterdämmerung* concluded, I walked down the drive and saw that the Adolf-Hitler-Strasse was cordoned off. I stood at the entrance to watch the Reich Chancellor pass. A few minutes later his cavalcade came in sight. Hitler was standing up in his car receiving the ovation of the crowd. On either flank drove the vehicles of his military escort. What happened next I have never forgotten. The general music director, Elmendorf and three ladies who had been at Haus Wahnfried came up and congratulated me. I had no idea why. The convoy of vehicles was almost abreast, moving at slow speed. I stood by the cordon and gave a salute. At that moment Hitler recognised me and gave his driver a signal. The cavalcade stopped, and Hitler's car sheered over to my side of the street. He smiled, reached out his hand to me and said, 'Auf wiedersehen'. As his car rejoined the convoy, he turned and waved. Suddenly I was the centre of all the hubbub and attention. Hardly anybody knew who I was or what had merited me such attention from the German leader.

23 July 1940 was the last time I saw Adolf Hitler. The war developed in extent and intensity. There was no longer an end in sight for it. My employment took up all my time; my sons were conscripted. In 1942 I joined the National Socialist Party. It was not that my basic attitudes to political questions had changed; my superiors in office considered it right and proper, now that the struggle was one of national survival, that municipal leaders should show their colours. Naturally I was outwardly a

supporter of Adolf Hitler, but not politically. But this was war, and I had to do what was expected of me.

'Has the Führer never asked you about your Party membership?' the Bürgermeister enquired one day. I told him that the question had never arisen. There had been just one sly dig once in 1939 when I was presented to Frau Wagner. Hitler pointed out that I wore no Party badge nor medals and, knowing that I was secretary of the Linz branch of the Richard-Wagner-Bund deutscher Frauen, remarked, 'That is Herr Kubizek for you. He is a member of your League of German Women. Very nice!' What he implied was: 'The only society to which my friend belongs is – a women's organisation. That is enough to show the man he is.'

The war cast a long shadow. To the general misery and woe came personal disappointment and bitterness – I am thinking here especially of Dr Bloch. The good 'poor people's physician' as they called in him Linz was by now a very old man. He wrote to me through the intermediary of Professor Huemer, Hitler's former form-master, asking that I intercede with the Reich Chancellor on his behalf and let an old Jew be, since it was he who had attended to Frau Hitler in her last illness. To be an advocate for him seemed to me the right thing to do. I did not know Dr Bloch personally, but I wrote at once to the Reich Chancellery enclosing the old doctor's letter. After a few weeks Bormann replied, expressly forbidding me to intercede in future on behalf of third parties. As for Dr Bloch, he could tell me that the matter had been assigned to 'the general category', whatever that was. This was a Führer instruction. Whether Hitler had seen my plea I had no idea. The fact that Dr Bloch, so far as I could determine, continued to be left in peace was not really reassuring. All I saw from this was that I could not approach Hitler without getting to him face-to-face, and that was impossible so long as the war lasted.

In time the end came. The war was lost. I listened to the radio transfixed in those fearful days of May 1945 as the Reich Chancellery fell and the European conflagration terminated. The closing scene of *Rienzi* came to mind in which the *Volkstribun* dies in the flames of the Capitol.

> ... the Volk abandon me also,
> whom I elevated to be worthy of the name:
> Every friend abandons me,
> who created for me my luck.

Though basically an unpolitical being who had not identified himself with the political events of that epoch which ended in 1945, I was resolute

259

that no power on earth could force me to deny my friendship with Adolf Hitler. My first and immediate concern in this respect was the memorabilia. Come what may these items had to be preserved for posterity. I had wrapped the letters, postcards and sketches in cellophane years previously; now I placed them in a leather case and slipped them behind the brickwork in the cellar of my Eferding house. After the mortar was carefully reapplied, there was no trace of the hiding place. It was none too soon, for the next day the Americans came. I spent the next sixteen months in the notorious Glasenbach internment camp. The Americans searched my house for the memorabilia but left empty handed. They also interrogated me on two occasions, at Eferding and Gmunden, where I made no secret of my friendship for Adolf Hitler. Eventually I was released from custody on 8 April 1947.

# Index

# Index

# Index

Raubal, Angela (Geli; niece of AH) 142
Raubal, Leo 31, 45, 51, *100*, 125, 133, 138–40, 142, 235, 241, 244
Rax (mountain) 209–11, 241
Rechberger, Franz 58
*Rienzi* 12, 81, 116–18, 256, 259
Rilke 164
*Ring der Niebelungen, Der* 185, 256
Ringstrasse (Vienna) 29, 120, 127, 165–7, 178, 207, 218
Rodel, River 39, 41
Rosegger, Peter 181
Rossini, Gioacchino Antonio 187
Rothenburg 109

Saalfelden 54
St Andrä 65
St Florian 41
St Georgen 41
Schicklgruber, Alois, *see* Hitler, Alois
Schicklgruber, Anna Maria 53
Schiller, Johann von 181, 185
Schmeidtoreck (Linz) 67, 71, 72, 75, 186, 216
Schnitzler, Arthur 213
Schönbrunn 157, 160, 162, 177, 207, 234
Schonerer, Georg Ritter von 93–4, 228
Schopenhauer, Artur 181
Schubert, Franz 197, 249
Schumann, Robert 197
Schütz, Heinrich 201
Schwab, Gustav 82
Schwarz, Franz 95
Semmering 209
Sixtl, Prof. 58
Smetana, Bedřich 187
Spital 46, 133
Stefanie (Isak) 13, 34, 36, 62, 66–75, 76, 85–6, 89, 92, *101*, 106, 121–4, 126, 128, 132, 134–5, 138–9, 143, 147, 151, 156, 159, 160, 178, 186, 208, 214–6, 233–4
Stefansdom (Vienna) 108, 109, 151, 178
Steyr 58, 60
Stifter 181
Stockbauerstrasse (No. 7) 105
Strones 53
Stumpergasse (No. 29) 129, 150–61, 167, 207, 240, 242, 245, 256

Sturmlechner 36

*Tannhauser* 184
Tchaikovsky, Pyotyr 187
Teutoburger Wald, Battle of the 110
Trevor-Roper, H. R. 9
*Tristan und Isolde* 121, 126, 184–5, 187
Trummelschlager, Johann 53
Turmleitenweg (Linz) 40

Urban, Dr 132
Urfahr (Linz) 66, 67, 74, 88, 112–13, 122, 137

Valhalla 83, 110
Verdi, Guiseppe 184–5, 187
Vienna (generally, *see also* various streets, districts, etc.) 9, 14, 113, 120–3, 126–7, 150–2, 162–70
Vienna Burgkapelle 157
Vienna Boys' Choir 157
Vienna Philharmonic Orchestra 126, 196
Viertelmeister 78
Volksoper, Vienna 185

Wachau 208
Wagner, Richard 12, 25, 68, 76–86, 110, 116–18, 176, 184–8, 189–91, 196–7, 199, 245, 254, 255–6
Wagner, Wieland 256
Wagner, Winifred 12, 119, 253–9
Wagner, Wolfgang 257
Walding 41
Waldviertel 46, 52, 126, 233, 236, 239
*Walküre, Die* 199
Weber, Carl Maria von 187
Wedekind, Frank 181, 218
Weidt, Lucie 68
Weitra 46, 54, 239
Wilbrandt 181
Wildberg Castle 109, 110
Wildgans 164
*Wilhelm Tell* 80, 181

Zakreys, Maria 129, 144, 147, 151–3, 155–6, 159, 164, 168, 173, 191, 207, 232–3, 235, 237, 238, 239, 240, 258